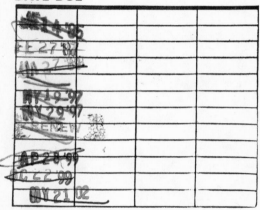

In the Beginning

IN THE BEGINNING

A New English Rendition
of the Book of Genesis

TRANSLATED WITH
COMMENTARY AND NOTES BY
Everett Fox

SCHOCKEN BOOKS / NEW YORK

First published by SCHOCKEN BOOKS 1983

10 9 8 7 6 5 4 3 2 1   83 84 85 86

Copyright © 1983 by Schocken Books Inc.

Library of Congress Cataloging in Publication Data

Bible. O.T. Genesis. English. Fox. 1983.
  In the beginning.
  The first edition of this translation appeared as a
complete issue of *Response* 14 (Summer 1972) "—T.p. verso.
  Bibliography: p.
  1. Bible. O.T. Genesis—Commentaries. I. Fox,
Everett. II. Response (New York, N.Y.) III. Title.
BS1233.F68 1983   222'.1107'7   83-42724

Designed by Peter Oldenburg
Manufactured in the United States of America
ISBN 0-8052-3870-0

Dedicated to
NAHUM N. GLATZER
on the occasion of
his eightieth birthday

בן שמונים לגבורה

CONTENTS

TRANSLATOR'S PREFACE

> . . . read the Hebrew Bible as though it were something entirely
> unfamiliar, as though it had not been set before you ready-made. . . .
> Face the Book with a new attitude as something new. . . . Let whatever
> may happen occur between yourself and it. You do not know which of
> its sayings and images will overwhelm you and mold you. . . . But hold
> yourself open. Do not believe anything a priori; do not disbelieve any-
> thing a priori. Read aloud the words written in the book in front of you;
> hear the word you utter and let it reach you.
>
> —*adapted from a lecture of Martin Buber, 1926*

I

THIS TRANSLATION is guided by the principle that the Hebrew Bible
originated largely as a spoken literature, and that consequently it must be
translated with careful attention to rhythm and sound. The translation
tries to reflect the particular rhetoric of the Hebrew wherever possible,
preserving such devices as repetition, allusion, alliteration, and word-
play. It is therefore intended to echo the Hebrew, and when read aloud,
to lead the reader back to the sound structure and form of the original.

Such an approach was first espoused by Martin Buber and Franz
Rosenzweig in their monumental German translation of the Bible (1925–
1961) and in subsequent interpretive essays. *In the Beginning* is in many
respects an offshoot of the Buber-Rosenzweig work (hereafter abbrevi-
ated as B-R), and can trace its basic principles, its general layout of the
text, and many specific readings to its influence. If at the same time I
have made numerous departures from B-R, it has been with an eye
toward greater faithfulness to the Hebrew, as it is understood by contemporary scholarship.

The idea that the Bible has oral roots has long been acknowledged by
scholars. On the other hand there has been little agreement on exactly
how those roots manifest themselves in the text. One cannot suggest that
the Bible is a classic work of oral literature in the same sense as the *Iliad*
or *Beowulf*. It does not employ regular meter or rhyme, even in sections

that are clearly formal poetry. The text of the Bible that we possess is most likely a mixture of oral and written material from a variety of sources and periods, and recovering anything resembling original oral forms would seem to be impossible. This is particularly true given the considerable chronological and cultural distance at which we stand from the text, which does not allow us to know how it was performed in its own time.

Nevertheless the nature of the Bible's style points unmistakably to spoken origins, and this fact is crucial for interpretation and translation. The rhetoric of the text is such that many passages and sections are fully understandable only when they are analyzed in their "oral" form—*as they are heard*. Using echoes, allusions, and powerful inner structures of sound, the text is often able to convey ideas in a manner that mere vocabulary cannot do. A few illustrations may suffice to introduce this phenomenon to the reader; he will encounter it constantly throughout this volume.

A noteworthy example of the importance of the oral quality of the biblical text occurs in one of the climactic sequences in Genesis, Chapters 32–33. Jacob, the central figure of the narrative, has not seen his brother Esau in twenty years. Now a successful and prosperous adult, on his way back to Canaan, he sends messengers to his brother to forestall Esau's vengeance for Jacob's misdeeds of twenty years earlier—namely, the theft of the birthright and blessing which Esau felt were rightly his. When Jacob finds out that Esau "is already coming . . . and four hundred men are with him" (v.7), he goes even further, preparing an elaborate gift for his brother in the hopes of appeasing his anger. The text in verses 21–22 presents Jacob's thoughts and actions (as translated in the *New English Bible*):

> for he thought, "I will appease him with the present that I have sent on ahead, and afterwards, when I come into his presence, he will perhaps receive me kindly." So Jacob's present went on ahead of him. . . .

This is an accurate though highly idiomatic translation of the Hebrew, and the reader will notice nothing unusual about the passage. The sound of the Hebrew here, on the other hand, gives one pause. It is built on variations of the word *panim*, whose basic meaning is "face," although the Hebrew uses it idiomatically to encompass various ideas. (Note: In Hebrew, *p* is pronounced *ph* under certain conditions.) If the text is translated on the basis of sound, its oral character, and something quite remarkable, emerge (italics mine):

> For he said to himself:
> I will wipe (the anger from) his *face* (*phanav*)
> with the gift that goes ahead of my *face;* (*le-phanai*)
> afterward, when I see his *face,* (*phanav*)
> perhaps he will lift up my *face!* (*phanai*)
> The gift crossed over ahead of his *face.* . . . (*al panav*)

Comparison of these two English versions is instructive. In the *New English Bible,* as in most other contemporary versions, the translators are apparently concerned with presenting the text in clear, modern, idiomatic English. For example, they render the Hebrew *yissa phanai* as "receive me kindly." The N.E.B. translates the *idea* of the text; at the same time it translates *out* the sound by not picking up on the repetition of *panim* words.

What does the reader gain by hearing the literalness of the Hebrew? And what is lost by the use of its idiomatic meaning? As mirrored in the second translation, it is clear that our text is signaling something of significance. The motif of "face" (which might be interpreted as "facing" or "confrontation") occurs at crucial points in the story. The night before his fateful meeting with Esau, as he is left to ponder the next day's events, Jacob wrestles with a mysterious stranger—a divine being. After Jacob's victory, the text reports (32:31):

> Yaakov called the name of the place: Peniel/*Face of God,*
> for: I have seen God,
> *face to face,*
> and my life has been saved.

The repetition suggests a thematic link with what has gone before. One could interpret that once the hero has met and actually bested this divine being, his coming human confrontation is assured of success. Thus upon meeting Esau at last, Jacob says to him (33:10):

> For I have, after all, seen your *face,* as one sees the *face* of God,
> and you have been gracious to me.

It could be said that in a psychological sense the meetings with divine and human adversaries are a unity, the representation of one human process in two narrative episodes. This is accomplished by the repetition of the word *panim* in the text.

The above interpretation depends entirely on sound. Once that focus is dropped, either through the silent reading of the text or a standard translation, the inner connections are simply lost and the reader is robbed of the opportunity to make these connections for himself. Clearly there is a difference between translating what the text means and translating what it says.

While the Jacob passages use the sound of a specific word to indicate an important motif in the narrative, there are other cases where sound brings out structure, and the structure itself conveys the principal idea of the passage. A striking example of this is found at the beginning of Genesis. God's first acts of creation in 1:3–5 are portrayed in a highly ordered fashion, suggesting that creation itself is orderly, and this idea is the thematic backbone of the whole chapter. We are meant to experience the orderliness of God's activity through the sensuality of the language and through the particular way in which the text speaks:

> God said: Let there be light! And there was light.
> God saw the light: that it was good.
> God separated the light from the darkness.
> God called the light: Day! and the darkness he called: Night!

The four occurrences of "God" plus verb accomplish the narrator's goal, and give a tone to the creation account that makes it akin to poetry. In contrast, virtually all modern translations treat the passage as prose, rendering it into clear written English but simultaneously removing its inner structure. What remains is a statement of what is taking place in the narrative, but without its underlying thrust. Again the *New English Bible:*

> God said, "Let there be light," and there was
> light; and God saw that the light was good, and
> he separated light from darkness. He called the
> light day, and the darkness night.

This translation is cast in good English style. For just that reason two occurrences of "God" have been omitted, and the passage consequently reads smoothly—so smoothly that one glides past it as if creation were the same as any other narrated action. But what has been lost is the characteristic oral ring of the text, and with it, its intent to say something beyond the content of words.

Once the spokenness of the Bible is understood as a critical factor in the translation process, a number of practical steps become necessary which constitute radical changes from past translation practices. Buber and Rosenzweig introduced three such major innovations: the form in which the text is printed, the reproduction of biblical names and their meanings, and the utilization of the "leading-word" technique, by means of which important repetitions in the Hebrew are retained in translation. These innovations have largely been followed in *In the Beginning*. Some further explanations will facilitate the reader's encounter with this text.

First, the translated text is printed in lines rather than in paragraphs. These lines, known as "cola," are based on natural spoken phrasing, with each representing a unit of breathing. Each one similarly represents a unit of meaning, thus illustrating the principle that form and content are inseparable in the Bible. Division of the text into cola facilitates its reading aloud and makes it possible for the listener to feel its inner rhythm. Only at that point can the text begin to deliver its message with full clarity and force. A case in point is the concluding passage of the creation story, Gen. 2:1–3. Rendered in cola, the text emerges as a tightly constructed poem, whose rhythm and repetitions provide a fitting summary for the majestic account of creation:

> Thus were finished the heavens and the earth, with all of their array.
> God had finished, on the seventh day, his work that he had made,
> and then he ceased, on the seventh day, from all his work that he had made.
> God gave the seventh day his blessing, and he hallowed it,
> for on it he ceased from all his work, which by creating, God had made.

Cola do not correspond to the traditional verse divisions in Jewish and Christian Bibles. Those divisions are of late origin (perhaps from the ninth century in written form), and were adopted for the sake of reference. Instead, cola arise from the experience of reading the Hebrew text aloud and of feeling its spoken rhythms. The specific divisions are somewhat arbitrary, in that each reader will hear the text differently. What is important, however, is that this practice in general points away from the concept of the Bible as a written book and restores the sense of it as a spoken performance.

Second, personal and place names generally appear in Hebrew forms throughout this translation. Thus, for example, the Hebrew *Moshe* is retained instead of Moses, *Kayin* instead of Cain, and *Rivka* instead of Rebecca. This practice stems from the central role that names play in biblical stories. In biblical Israel as throughout the ancient world, names are often meant to give clues about the bearer's personality or fate. The meaning of a name is often explained outright in the text itself. In *In the*

Beginning this is represented by a slash in the text, as in the following example (Gen. 30:23–24):

> She said:
> God has removed/*asaf*
> my reproach.
> And she called his name: Yosef,
> saying:
> May YHWH add/*yosef*
> another son to me.

The name here is a play on words, hinting at Joseph's eventual fate (he will be a son "removed" and "added," that is, lost and found by his family). By retaining the Hebrew sounds in translation, a meaningful portion of the narrative is thus moved from footnotes, where it appears in most modern translations, back to the body of the text. That this is important is demonstrated by the fact that virtually every major (in this case, usually male) character in Genesis has his name explained in this manner.

It should be noted that such interpretations of names in the Bible are not based on philological derivations, that is, on scientific etymology. The name Jacob/Yaakov, for instance, which is understood in Gen. 25 as "Heel-Holder" and in Chapter 27 as "Heel-Sneak," probably held the original meaning of "may (God) protect." But the biblical writers were not so much concerned with what a name originally meant as they were with its sound, and with the associations inherent in that sound. Therefore what is important in our example is that "Yaakov" recalls *ekev*, "heel." This kind of interpretation is known as "folk etymology" or "popular etymology."

A third important technique through which biblical literature often conveys its message is what Buber called the "leading-word" principle. It holds that key ("leading") words are repeated within a text to signal major themes and concerns, rather like recurring themes in a piece of music. A leading-word operates primarily on the basis of sound: its repetition encourages the listener to make connections between diverse parts of a story and to trace a particular theme throughout. This is not, however, a static process. Such a word may appear in different contexts within a story, with changed meaning, thus lending a sense of movement and development to the text. One example may be cited here, to indicate the possibilities opened up by this technique (for others, the reader should consult "On the Book of Genesis and Its Structure," below, and the Commentary that accompanies the text of this book).

Buber's essay, "Abraham the Seer," traces the biblical tradition's portrayal of Abraham through the use of key words and phrases in the text. Chief among these is the verb "to see" (Hebrew *ra'o*), which appears constantly in the Abraham narratives and which tells us something significant about both the man himself and how he is meant to be remembered. At the outset of Abraham's journey to Canaan, which signals his entry into biblical tradition as an independent personality, God sends him off to a land that he will "let him see" (12:1). Arriving in the land, Abraham is granted a communication from God, expressed by the phrase "YHWH was seen by Avram . . ." (12:7). God subsequently promises the land to him and his descendants ("see from the place that you are . . . for all the land that you see, to you I give it and to your seed, for the ages"; 13:15). "Seeing" comes to the fore in the story of Abraham's concubine Hagar; her encounter with God's messenger ends with her addressing a "God of Seeing" (16:13). Further meetings between Abraham and God (17:1, 18:1) likewise express themselves visually, with the latter scene, where God announces Isaac's impending birth at Abraham's tent, almost unique in the Bible for its bold picture of God appearing directly to human beings. Finally, with the great test of Abraham in Chapter 22, the "Binding of Isaac," the theme of seeing is brought to a climax. Buber describes the use of the leading-word in that passage, summarizing how it rounds out the entire Abraham cycle.

> It appears here more often than in any previous passage. Abraham *sees* the place where the act must be accomplished, at a distance. To the question of his son, he replies that God will provide ("see to") the lamb for the burnt offering. In the saving moment he lifts up his eyes and *sees* the ram. And now he proclaims over the altar the name that makes known the imperishable essence of this place, Mount Moriah: YHWH Will See. . . . God sees man, and man sees God. God sees Abraham, and tests him by seeing him as the righteous and "whole" man who walks before his God (17:1), and now, at the end of his road, he conquers even this final place, the holy temple mountain, by acting on God's behalf. Abraham sees God with the eye of his action and so recognizes Him, just as Moses, seeing God's glory "from behind," will recognize Him as Gracious and Merciful.*

Buber goes one step further in his analysis of the leading-word *see:* he views it as a clue to the biblical concept of Abraham's role in history.

---

*Martin Buber, *On the Bible: Eighteen Studies*, edited by Nahum N. Glatzer (New York: Schocken Books, 1982), p. 42.

Taking the hint from I Sam. 9:9 ("the prophet of our day was formerly called a seer"), he posits that the Bible wants us to understand Abraham as the spiritual father of the later prophets. Abraham is preeminent as the first man in the Bible of whom it is told that God "was seen by him."

Such an understanding of the role of leading-words as crucial to biblical style rarely makes itself felt in translation. Bible translators are reluctant to reproduce repetitions of Hebrew words in the text because they are generally fearful of creating a tedious English style. However, once one abandons the idea of the Bible as primarily a written work, the repetitiveness of leading-words becomes a signal rather than a stumbling block, freeing the reader to experience the dynamic manner in which the Bible expresses itself. That this sometimes entails a loss of nuance in the translation (where "see" in Hebrew may signify "perceive" or "understand" in a particular passage, for instance) is a price that must be paid; yet such a translation may in fact retain more of the breadth of the Hebrew than is immediately apparent.

A final word needs to be said about the leading-word technique. It may serve a purpose in the text beyond conveying meaning: it may play a structural role, unifying sections that have been culled from different sources within biblical Israel to form a composite account. The ancient redactors of the Bible apparently crafted the material they received into an organic whole. Using such means as leading-word repetition, they in effect created a new literature in which deep relationships exist between the parts of the whole.

Such a view is outside, though not incompatible with, biblical scholarship's century-old concern with finding "original sources." It takes as its starting point the text as we now have it, and with some exceptions does not try to reconstruct an earlier version or extensively emend what we have. In that sense *In the Beginning* is a translation not of the Genesis of Moses' or Solomon's time, but of the Genesis that was included in the biblical canon in the formative, postbiblical period of Judaism and early Christianity.

The above three translation techniques—setting out the text in cola, transliterating and explaining Hebrew names, and reproducing leading-words—form the crux of an approach to the Bible's spokenness, but there are other methods used by the text to the same end. Three are particularly worthy of mention: word-play, allusion, and what I have termed small-scale repetition.

The Bible uses word-play to make a point forcefully, especially in prophetic passages or those with a prophetic flavor. In Gen. 40:13 and 19, for instance, Joseph predicts that the king of Egypt will end the imprisonment of two of his courtiers. When the cupbearer is to be restored to his former position, Joseph says,

> in another three days
> Pharaoh will lift up your head. . . .

In contrast, when Joseph predicts that the chief baker will be executed, the text reads:

> in another three days Pharaoh will lift up your head
> from off you. . . .

By beginning both statements with the same phrasing, the narrator is able to heighten the impact of "from off you" on both audience and victim.

Allusion is utilized in Gen. 39:6, where Joseph is described as "fair of form and fair to look at." Only one other character in the Bible is described with exactly the same expression—his mother, Rachel. By suggesting that Joseph is the image of his mother, the text reinforces the reason for Jacob's earlier obsessive love for him. Rachel's early death was a source of pain for Jacob until the end of his life (cf. 48:7), and Joseph's strong resemblance to her may have played a large role in shaping the relationship between father and son.

Small-scale repetition, unlike the leading-word technique, is limited to a brief report and is used to express one specific idea. In Gen. 6:11–13, for instance, it illustrates an important biblical concept: just punishment. Three times in the passage we hear the word "ruin," indicating what human evil has done to the world; the fourth time (v.13) it appears in a causative form, to show that God retaliates in exactly the same terms, measure for measure.

> Now the earth had gone to *ruin* before God; the earth was filled with
>   wrongdoing.
> God saw the earth, and here: it had gone to *ruin,*
> for all flesh had *ruined* its way upon the earth.
>
> God said to Noah:
> An end of all flesh has come before me,
> for the earth is filled with wrongdoing through them;
> here, I will bring *ruin* upon them, along with the earth.

The Bible is fond of this technique, which it uses in a number of narratives that deal with human misbehavior (e.g., the Tower of Babel story
in Gen. 11). It is another example of how the form in which the text is
cast goes a long way toward expressing its intent.

I have taken pains to illustrate some of the rhetorical devices that
emerge from an oral reading of Genesis in order to indicate the direction
taken in *In the Beginning*. A concluding observation must be made.
Every critic knows, or should know, that art defies categorization and
exact description. We try to understand what makes a masterpiece tick,
whether it be a painting, a piece of music, or a work of literature, yet in
the end our analyses fall silent before the greatness and subtlety of the
work itself. The techniques that I have described above must remain
suggestive rather than definitive; they point in a direction rather than
speaking directly. Biblical narratives do not end with the phrase "The
moral of the story is . . . ," any more than biblical laws overtly spell out
their assumptions. Translating with attention to sound therefore may
help to preserve not only the message of the text but also its ambiguity
and open-endedness. In that persona the Bible has been familiar to Jewish and Christian interpreters, who for centuries have sought to fill in the
gaps and resolve the difficulties in the text by means of their own ingenu-
ity. This volume is aimed at helping present-day readers to share in that
experience.

2

SOME READERS may wonder whether *In the Beginning* is merely an
English translation of B-R. It is not. Although B-R served as the theoretical basis for my work, I have found it necessary to modify their
approach in the present setting. There are a number of reasons for this.

For one, Bible scholarship has made notable advances since Buber's
heyday (Rosenzweig had already died in 1929). Although he completed
the German translation in 1961, and kept abreast of work in the field, it
must be said that Buber did not greatly modify the text of the Pentateuch
translation, philologically speaking, between 1930 when the second edition appeared and the revised printings of the mid-1950s. It seemed
imperative to me to bring the work of postwar biblical philology to bear
on the English translation, rather than relying solely on Buber's etymolo-
gies. Some of the changes in this area have been cited in the Notes to the
text (as "B-R uses . . .").

Second, in the attempt to make the German translation mirror the Hebrew original Rosenzweig did not hesitate to either create new German words or reach back into the German literature of past ages to find forms suitable for rendering certain Hebrew expressions. To perform a corresponding feat in English would simply not work; the language is not flexible, and usages change so quickly that an artful appeal to the past seems futile except for the benefit of linguistic historians. While I have endeavored to produce an English text that reflects the style of biblical Hebrew, I have in the main shied away from pushing the language beyond reasonable and comprehensible limits.

There are other significant deviations from B-R here. I have used a different rendering of the name of God, which had been a distinctive B-R trademark (for an explanation, see "On the Name of God and Its Translation"). I have sometimes opted for different line divisions, based on my own hearing of the Hebrew; indented purely poetic passages, a practice not followed by B-R in narrative texts; read a large number of clauses differently from a grammatical or syntactical point of view; and loosened the practice, sometimes overdone in B-R, of reproducing a Hebrew root by a single English one wherever it occurs.

Finally, I have included here the one element that many readers of B-R felt was sorely lacking: notes and commentary. Every translation of the Bible implies a commentary but few have supplied one with the text. *In the Beginning* especially requires such an apparatus, both to explain its translation technique and to show how it may be used in interpreting the text. Along with the text, the explanatory material presents a methodology for studying the Bible.

All this said, *In the Beginning* is still very much in the B-R tradition. It retains the general approach adopted by its predecessor, exclusive of those principles that are dependent on the form and character of the German language. In addition it has continued to draw nourishment from its source, extending beyond the translation itself to Buber's and Rosenzweig's working papers. So I should like to think that this book continues a tradition, across a barrier of time and language, and that the last great contribution of German-Jewish culture has not been entirely lost.

3

IN THE BEGINNING is most heavily indebted to B-R, but there is also a contemporary context in which it may be viewed. In recent years interest has been increasing in so-called literary interpretation of the Bible. A number of scholars have turned their attention to the forms and rhetoric of the biblical text, and the list of pertinent articles and books has begun to grow. While it is difficult to speak of these developments in terms of a "movement," there seems to be a strong trend emerging.

A "literary" approach, whose focus diverges from traditional (i.e., nineteenth- and twentieth-century) biblical scholarship's concern with historical and comparative study, is hardly new. Already in late antiquity Jewish explication of the Bible frequently centered around the text's style and exact wording, especially as heard aloud. Similarly, medieval Jewish commentators in Western Europe showed great sensitivity to the Bible's linguistic aspects. In both cases, however, a systematic approach was not developed, but rather literary interpretation remained interwoven with very different concerns such as homiletics, mysticism, and philosophy. It has remained for modern scholars, reacting partly against what they perceived to be the excessive historicizing of German Bible scholarship, to press for a literary reading of the Bible. Early pioneers in this regard include Umberto Cassuto, Buber and Meir Weiss in Israel, and Benno Jacob (who was consulted frequently during the writing of B-R) in Germany. More recently we might mention James Muilenburg (who labeled his approach "Rhetorical Criticism"), Edwin Good, James Ackerman, Robert Culley, and Robert Alter in North America, and to cite an oft-quoted European example, J. P. Fokkelman in Holland. A full list would be much longer. *In the Beginning* is related to the work of such scholars, not always directly, but as a kindred work. It has benefited greatly from exchanges with people in the field.

In that vein it should be noted that translations parallel to the present one have recently appeared in several languages. André Chouraqui in France and the Amsterdam Society for Old Testament Study have produced colometric (i.e., in cola) versions of various biblical books, with a full awareness of the contribution of B-R and a willingness to adapt their approach to new linguistic and philological requirements. It would appear that the groundwork is being laid for a new appreciation of the biblical text's artistry, above and beyond historical questions.

Can Bible scholarship ever get "beyond historical questions," and should that be the desired goal? Literary study of the Bible, like any relatively new discipline, occasionally suffers from either shallowness or interpretive overkill. As a field it is still struggling to achieve full legitimacy with historical study. But it would be a mistake to set up the two disciplines in an adversarial relationship, as is often done. The Hebrew Bible is by nature a complex and multi-faceted piece of literature, in terms of both its origins and the history of its use and interpretation. No one "school" can hope to illuminate more than part of the whole picture, and even then one's efforts are bound to be fragmentary. It is probably only a synthesis of all the fruitful approaches available, into a fully interdisciplinary methodology, that will provide a truly balanced approach to the biblical text. Perhaps analogous to the relationship between concert performers and musicologists, literary and historical scholars need each other's skills and perceptiveness to do full justice to their subject. It is to be hoped that *In the Beginning* will make a contribution to that goal, by providing an English text and an underlying reading of the Hebrew that complement the existing translations.

4

MY ULTIMATE GOAL in this volume has been to show that reading the Hebrew Bible is a process, in the same sense that performing a piece of music is a process. Rather than carrying across ("translating") the content of the text from one linguistic realm to another, I have tried to involve the reader in the experience of giving it back ("rendering"), of returning to the source and recreating some of its richness. My task has been to present the raw material of the text as best as I can in English, and to point out some of the methods that may be fruitfully employed in wrestling with it.

Translators, said Goethe, should "arouse an irresistible desire for the original." They should also be able to communicate that the greatness of a work of art is not always something immediately accessible, but rather to be acquired through strenuous and loving effort. If *In the Beginning* helps to provide a medium for that kind of encounter to take place, then my own strenuous and loving efforts will have been more than amply rewarded.

EVERETT FOX

Brookline, Massachusetts
February 1983
Adar 5743

ACKNOWLEDGMENTS

IT IS CUSTOMARY for scholars to thank researchers for their help, colleagues for their critical reading and advice, publishers for their technical expertise, and family for their understanding. My task goes well beyond those limits. This translation project, often a lonely procedure, has profited chiefly from moral support; to readers and well-wishers I owe a great debt of gratitude.

Thanks go first of all to William Novak, who as editor of *Response* magazine was responsible for publishing the first edition of *In the Beginning*, as a complete issue of the magazine, in 1972. The appearance of the translation in print has enabled me to reap the benefits of the many reactions of both scholarly and general readers over the years, as well as to test its workability in a variety of educational, artistic, and liturgical settings.

I am deeply indebted to Arthur Waskow, who gave continued encouragement, spurred me on to continue the work past Genesis, and was instrumental in finding a publisher for it. Arthur Samuelson, at the time Judaica editor at Schocken, my present editor Bonny Fetterman, and the entire staff at Schocken have my heartfelt thanks for having expended so much energy and skill toward presenting the volume in an attractive and usable form. Above all, my wife, Cherie Koller-Fox, has been unflagging in her belief in the translation's artistic and pedagogical value, and has supported its place in my life through difficult times.

Among colleagues, Professor James Ackerman of Indiana University and Dr. Isaac Kikawada have been particularly supportive, and have given me a sense of commonality with those doing work in literary criticism of the Bible. I have profited greatly from years of discussion and sharing of work with Professors Herbert Mason and Dennis Tedlock of Boston University, in oral literature and in related religious literature. Of special meaning to me has been contact with the Amsterdam Society for Old Testament study, which thus far has produced notable Dutch "translations to be read aloud" of Jonah, Ruth, and Judges. I am grateful for the kindness of Dr. F. J. Hoogewoud of the Society, who is also librarian at the Bibliotheca Rosenthaliana in Amsterdam, for sharing work on biblical texts and as it were inviting me into that circle of colleagues. Last, and most important, is Professor Edward Greenstein of the Jewish Theological Seminary of America, who has been both constructive critic and vocal advocate over the past few years, and who made numerous helpful suggestions regarding the text and the Notes.

General readers have of course been crucial. Members of various *havurot* in Boston, New York, Washington, D.C., and elsewhere have for the past decade and more given the translation a home, coddling it in its infancy and providing a welcome sounding board. I am also grateful to the participants in the many study groups I have conducted on biblical narrative at various conferences, and in general to readers around the country (with special thanks to Mr. Clifford Anderson and Rabbi Baruch Frydman-Kohl).

Recent and hearty thanks go to Professor Theodor Gaster, special editor for *In the Beginning,* for his many specific textual suggestions and stimulating insights on biblical matters. While not in full agreement with the principles of this translation, he nonetheless served as a gentle critic and, not infrequently, an appreciative one. In the area of specifics I must also mention Franz Rosenzweig's widow, the late Mrs. Edith Rosenzweig-Scheinmann, who gave both encouragement and textual suggestions. Her comments were deeply meaningful to me.

I have, as is traditional, saved the most heartfelt thanks for the end. Professor Nahum N. Glatzer of Boston University has followed this work since its inception in 1968. As teacher and helpful reader, and equally as living link to the B-R translation and its creators, he has made a contribution to this volume that goes beyond the printed page.

TO AID THE READER

THE PRESENT Commentary to the text has deliberately been kept brief and suggestive. It is keyed to this particular English text as a reflection of the Hebrew, and is therefore designed to point out some of the structurally significant aspects of Genesis, tying together major themes and concerns. In that sense it may be termed a literary commentary, to distinguish it from historical treatments. It should be noted that the titled sections into which the Commentary is divided are not ironclad, but have been chosen for convenience of discussion.

The Notes to the text deal basically with textual matters. These include alternative translations (marked, "others use . . ."), sound-play in the Hebrew which is sometimes not reflected in the translation ("Heb. . . ."), allusions to other passages, clarifications of phrases, concepts, and institutions, and occasionally other readings or vocalizations of the Hebrew text ("some read . . ."). They also indicate places where the syntax or meaning of the Hebrew is in doubt ("Hebrew difficult"). Finally, the Notes include literary comments not found in the Commentary; these have been keyed to specific passages in the text.

I have mentioned in the Commentary and Notes only such material about the text's ancient Near Eastern background as I felt was absolutely necessary. A fuller treatment of this issue can be found in the standard commentaries such as Cassuto, Plaut, and Speiser. I have also chosen not to deal with matters of the origins or textual history of Genesis; these are complex and somewhat theoretical. The interested reader should again consult the standard works.

Names cited in parentheses in the Commentary and Notes refer to authors whose appropriate works are listed in "Suggestions for Further Reading," at the end of the book.

ON THE NAME OF GOD
AND ITS TRANSLATION

THE NAME of God, which has been translated here by the letters YHWH, has undergone numerous changes in the history of both its transcription and its translation. At an early period the correct pronunciation of the name was either lost or deliberately avoided out of a sense of religious awe. Jewish tradition came to vocalize and pronounce the name as "Adonai," that is, "the/my Lord," a usage that has remained in practice since late antiquity. In the Orthodox Jewish community one also hears "Ha-Shem," "The Name," used regularly.

Historically, Christian and Jewish translations in English have tended to use "Lord," with some exceptions (such as Moffatt's "The Eternal"). Both old and new attempts to recover the "correct" pronunciation of the Hebrew name have not succeeded; neither the sometimes-heard "Jehovah" nor the current scholarly "Yahweh" can be conclusively proven.

For their part, Buber and Rosenzweig sought to restore some of the name's ancient power; early drafts of their translation reveal a good deal of experimentation to this end. They finally settled on a rather radical solution: representing the name by means of capitalized personal pronouns. The use of YOU, HE, HIM, etc., stemmed from their conviction that God's name is not a proper name in the conventional sense, but rather one which evokes his immediate presence as such. Buber and Rosenzweig based this on their reading of Exodus 3:14, a text in which another verbal form of YHWH appears, and which they translated as "I will be-there as I will be-there") (i.e., God explaining his name as a sign of presence).

The B-R rendering has its attraction in reading aloud, but it is on doubtful etymological ground. In addition it introduces an overly male emphasis through the constant use of "HE," something which is not found in the text. I have therefore decided to follow the practice of printed Hebrew Bibles, which leave the name YHWH unvocalized. As one reads the translation aloud, one should pronounce the name according to one's custom or based on one of the traditional options above.

GUIDE TO THE PRONUNCIATION
OF HEBREW NAMES

THE PRECISE pronunciation of biblical Hebrew cannot be determined with certainty. The following guide uses a standard of pronunciation which is close to that of modern Hebrew, and which will serve for the purpose of reading the text aloud.

a (e.g., Adam, Avraham) as in f*a*ther
e (e.g., Lea, Levi, Rahel) as the *a* in c*a*pe
o (e.g., Edom, Lot) as in h*o*rn
u (e.g., Luz, Zevulun) as in B*u*ber

When *e* occurs in both syllables of a name (e.g., Hevel, Lemekh), it is generally pronounced as the *e* in ten. In such cases the first syllable is the accented one; generally speaking, Hebrew accents the last syllable.

When *e* is the second letter of a name (e.g., Devora, Yehuda), it is often pronounced as the *a* in *a*go.

kh (e.g., Hanokh, Yissakhar) is to be sounded like the *ch* in Johann Sebastian Ba*ch*.

h (e.g., Havva, Het) most often indicates Hebrew *het,* pronounced less heavily than *kh* but not as English *h*.

Some names in the English text have kept their traditional English spelling; they refer to well-known terms. These include Canaan (Hebrew *Kena'an*), Egypt (*Mitzrayim*), Israel (*Yisrael*), Jordan (*Yarden*), and Pharaoh (*Par'o*). Otherwise, I have indicated the familiar forms of biblical names in the Notes, under the rubric "Trad. English . . .".

ON THE BOOK OF GENESIS AND ITS STRUCTURE

THE TEXT of Genesis seems to speak with many voices. For a book whose basic arrangement is chronological, tracing the history of a single family, it exhibits a good deal of discontinuity on the surface. Here time flows uniformly, there taking startling jumps; fragments are followed by more or less full-blown tales; genres alternate, from mythic to genealogical to folkloristic. In addition, scholars often portray Genesis as a collection of historically diverse materials that were compiled by scribes for whom deviating from received tradition was anathema. Hence the repetitions, the inconsistencies, and the irregular pacing.

Is Genesis then at best a collection of stories related to the origins of Israel, with most of its seams showing? That hardly seems likely. If one approaches the book with an open mind, alert to its structure, without making assumptions beforehand, there is a scheme that begins to emerge. Whatever the compositional history of Genesis may have been— and it certainly appears to have been a complex one—we have before us the product of a rather single-minded consciousness. Using the Buber-Rosenzweig method of focusing on repeating words and key themes as the text presents them, it is possible to make some careful generalizations about the book's organization and to speculate on its overall intent.

On its most obvious level Genesis is a book about origins. It seeks to link the origin of the people of Israel with that of the world, relating in the process how various human characteristics and institutions arose.

On the surface this parallels much of ancient literature and folklore. All peoples are interested in their own beginnings, picturing them in a way which validates their present existence. Genesis, however, is different in that like the rest of the Torah, it downplays the heroic element of the people's origins and in its place stresses God's role in them. Moreover the one great omission—the origin of God—establishes from the beginning a unique basis for a tribal chronicle. From Genesis and subsequent books we learn primarily about God's relationship to the people and what he expects of them; almost everything else is subordinated to this purpose.

Preliminarily one can speak of at least seven major themes whose recurrence establishes their importance in the book:

1. *Origins:* Of the world, of humanity, and of the people of Israel.
2. *Order/Meaning in History:* By means of stylized or patterned chronology—reliance on certain round numbers such as 3,7, and 40—it is suggested that human events are not random but somehow planned.
3. *Blessing:* From creation onward God bestows blessings on his creatures in general and on the fathers and mothers of Israel in particular.
4. *Covenant:* God concludes agreements with human beings.
5. *God Punishes Evildoing:* God is provoked to anger not by his capriciousness but by human failure to uphold justice and morality.
6. *Sibling Conflict, with the Younger Usually Emerging the Victor:* The order of nature (primacy of the firstborn) is overturned, demonstrating that God, not nature, is the ruling principle in human affairs.
7. *Testing:* God tests those who are to carry forth his mission; the result is the development of moral character.

Superseding these important themes, which occur throughout the Bible in various forms, is the dominant one of *continuity*, represented by the unifying word in Genesis *toledot* ("begettings"). The word appears eleven times, often accompanied by long genealogical lists. The names may deflect attention from what is central to Genesis. The major thrust of the book would seem to be toward human fecundity, following the early divine command to "bear fruit and be many" (1:28), and pointing toward the eventual fecundity of the people of Israel (which will only be realized in the book of Exodus). Such an emphasis seems appropriate in a book about origins.

Ironically, however, the undercurrent in Genesis points not to life and its continuation, but rather to its threatened extinction. In story after story the protagonist, his people, and occasionally the entire world are threatened. In at least one case (Avraham) a perfectly legal and natural solution is found—the birth of Yishmael as his heir—only to be rejected by God in favor of a more difficult one: a son born to an elderly woman.

It is clear that the stress on continuity and discontinuity has one purpose: to make clear that God is in control of history. Human fertility and continuity in history come not from magical rites or from the arbitrary decisions of the gods, but from a God who bases his rule on justice.

Nature disappears as a ruling factor in human affairs, replaced by a principle of morality which is unshakable precisely because it comes from a God who is beyond the rules of nature.

But the result is a book which abounds in tension. From the beginnings of human history (Chapter 4) we encounter contradictions and opposites, whether on a small scale (fertility and barrenness) or a large one (promise and delayed fulfillment). Nowhere is this so clear as in the dramatic high point of the book, Genesis 22. As Avraham stands with knife upraised, the entire enterprise of Genesis hangs in the balance. But the entire book is replete with such tensions and continuity-threatening situations. There are barren wives, brothers vowing to kill brothers, cities and even a world being destroyed by an angry God. The main characters of Genesis thus emerge as survivors, above all else. Noah sets the pattern, but he is merely the first, and too passive an example. The Patriarchs must brave hostile foreigners, bitter intrafamily struggles, and long wanderings before they can find peace.

While by the end of the book many of the tensions have been resolved, one conspicuously has not: God's promise of the land of Canaan. As the book ends, "in Egypt," we are left to ponder how this God, who keeps his promises to "those who love him" (Ex. 20:6), will bring the people back to their land—a land inhabited by someone else and in which the Children of Israel own only a burial site. Yet despite the tension, we may assume from the experiences of the Patriarchs that God will indeed "take account of" the Israelites (50:24), that he will take whatever ill has been planned against them and "plan-it-over for good" (50:20).

A word should also be said here about hero traditions. In the great epics of the ancient world the hero often stands as a lonely figure. He must overcome obstacles, fight monsters, acquire helpers (whether women, "sidekicks," or magic objects); and his triumph in the end signals man's triumph over his archenemy, Death. Every battle won, every obstacle hurdled, is psychologically a victory for us, the audience, a cathartic release from our own frustrating battle against death.

The Bible sees things rather differently. Death is also overcome, but not only by the individual's struggle. It is rather through the covenant community, bound together by God's laws and his promises, that the heroic vision is lived out. Despite the triumphs of the characters in Genesis, it is really in the book of Exodus that the great battle scenes (the plagues in Egypt, the Red Sea) and meetings with the divine (Mount Sinai) take place. And it is therefore God himself who is most properly the "hero" of these stories. No major character in Genesis achieves success without depending fully on God, and the standards that are held up to them are ultimately seen as God's own, to be imitated by imperfect humankind.

The book of Genesis falls naturally into four large sections. The first, usually termed the "Primeval History" (Chapters 1–11), begins with creation and progresses through the early generations of humanity, ending in Mesopotamia. The second (Chapters 12 through 25:18) is the cycle of stories concerning Avraham, the father of the people of Israel. Part III (Gen. 25:19 through Chapter 36) deals in the main with stories about his grandson Yaakov. The final section (Chapters 37–50) is the tale of Yosef and of how the Children of Israel came to live in Egypt (thus paving the way for the book of Exodus).

The following skeletal outline will lay out some of the interesting structural features of the book. There is an elemental symmetry that emerges from the four sections; further comments, especially about how the sections cohere, will be found in the explanatory material accompanying the text in this volume.

I. Chosen Figure (Noah)
    Sibling Hatred (Kayin–Hevel), with sympathy for youngest
    Family Continuity Threatened (Hevel murdered)
    Ends with Death (Haran, Terah; Sarai barren)
        Humanity Threatened (Flood)
        Ends Away from Land of Israel ("In Harran")

II. Chosen Figure (Avraham)
    Sibling Hatred (Yishmael–Yitzhak) Implied, with sympathy for youngest
    Family Continuity Threatened (Sarai barren, Yitzhak almost sacrificed)
    Ends with Death (Sara, Avraham)
        Rivalry Between Wives (Hagar–Sarai)
        Barren Wife (Sarai)
        Wife–Sister Story (Chaps. 12 and 20)
        Ends with Genealogy of Non-Covenant Line (Yishmael)

III. Chosen Figure (Yaakov)
    Sibling Hatred (Esav–Yaakov), with sympathy for youngest
    Family Continuity Threatened (Yaakov almost killed)
    Ends with Death (Devora, Rahel, Yitzhak)

Rivalry Between Wives (Lea–Rahel)
Barren Wife (Rahel)
Wife–Sister Story (Chap. 26)
Ends with Genealogy of Non-Covenant Line (Esav)

IV. Chosen Figure (Yosef)
Sibling Hatred (Brothers–Yosef), with sympathy for youngest
Family Continuity Threatened (Yehuda's sons die; Yosef almost
killed; family almost dies in famine)
Ends with Death (Yaakov, Yosef)
Humanity Threatened (Famine)
Ends Away from Land of Israel ("In Egypt")

There is of course great variety within this bare structure; each version of a motif has its own special characteristics and emphases. Yet the patterning observed above gives the book a general coherence, above and beyond differences. It also demonstrates a conscious hand at work, one concerned about the texture of the book as a whole and able, despite the possible rigidity of what had been handed down, to shape the received material into a plastic and breathing unity.

Two general observations about Genesis will round out the picture here. First, as the book progresses there is a tendency for the style of the literature to become smoother. The abrupt changes and sometimes fragmentary nature of the material in Part I, and the vignettes built around Avraham's life in Part II, give way to a greater coherence and concentration in Part III, and finally to a relatively flowing and psychologically complete narrative in Part IV. Along with this, the characters in the latter half of the book seem to be more changeable and human, in contrast to Noah and Avraham, who often appear almost perfect models of piety.

Second, contact with God becomes less and less direct as Genesis moves on. Avraham's dreams and visions seem a far cry from Adam's conversations with God in the garden (although see Chapter 18); Yaakov's encounters with God are less frequent than Avraham's; and finally, Yosef never has a conversation with God, although he receives dream interpretations from him. This process of distancing may reflect an often-observed tendency in religions to think of primeval times as a "golden age" of closeness between gods and men, as contrasted to today (whenever one is writing), when humankind finds itself tragically distant from the divine and in need of communication.

In the Beginning

PART I The Primeval History
(1–11)

THE COLLECTION of stories which forms Part I of Genesis has been assembled for a number of purposes:

1. History is traced from the creation of the world, in a direct line, down to Avraham, father of the People of Israel. Through use of the leading-word *toledot*, "begettings," we are meant to view him as the logical end point in God's preliminary plan in history.

2. The nature of God, as he will appear throughout the Hebrew Bible, is firmly established. He is seen as a Creator who is beyond fate, nature, and sexuality; as an all-powerful orderer and giver of meaning to history; as a bestower of blessing to living creatures; as a giver of choice to human beings; as a just punisher of evil and, simultaneously, a merciful ruler; and as a maker of covenants. The one quality of God which does not unfold until the Patriarchal stories (Parts II–IV) is his shaping of human destiny through focusing on the People of Israel. It is portrayed as the logical outcome of the characteristics just mentioned.

3. It appears that the Mesopotamian origins of Israel are reflected in such narratives as the Creation, the Flood, and the Tower of Babel, and are transformed or repudiated in the biblical versions. What in the older culture appears arbitrary and chaotic has been changed in the Bible into stories that stress morality and order. Further, human beings in Genesis Chapters 1–11, despite their failure to live up to God's expectations, are nevertheless considered capable of doing so, in contrast to the Mesopotamian view that humankind was created merely to be slaves to the gods.

4. Like virtually all other creation stories, Part I is concerned with the origin of the world and its institutions. Chapter 1 expounds on the origins of earth, sky, vegetation, animals, and human beings (as well as the Sabbath); Chapter 2, of sexuality, death, pain in childbirth, and work; Chapter 4, of sin, hatred, and murder, as well as of cities and

crafts; Chapter 6, of giants; and Chapter 10, of nations (including the low status of the Canaanites) and languages.

In sum, Part I serves as a fitting Prologue, not only to Genesis but to the entire Bible. The reader's chief task in interpreting it is to be able to determine the reason for the inclusion of any one section into the whole.

1:1 In the beginning God created the heavens and the earth.

2 —Now the earth had been wild and waste,
darkness over the face of Ocean,
breath of God hovering over the face of the waters—

3 God said: Let there be light! And there was light.
4 God saw the light: that it was good.
God separated the light from the darkness.
5 God called the light: Day! and the darkness he called: Night!
There was evening, there was morning: one day.

6 God said:
Let there be a dome amid the waters,
and let it separate waters from waters!
7 God made the dome
and separated the waters that were below the dome from the waters that were above the dome.
It was so.
8 God called the dome: Heaven!
There was evening, there was morning: second day.

9 God said:
Let the waters under the heavens be gathered to one place,
and let the dry land be seen!
It was so.
10 God called the dry land: Earth! and the gathering of the waters he called: Seas!
God saw that it was good.

11 God said:

Let the earth sprout forth with sprouting-growth,
plants that seed forth seeds, fruit trees that yield fruit, after
their kind, (and) in which is their seed, upon the earth!
It was so.

God as Creator (1:1–2:4a): Three principal themes emerge from the great
creation account with which Genesis opens. The first is the total and
uncompromised power of God as creator; the second, the intrinsic order
and balance of the created world; and the third, humankind's key position in the scheme of creation. These themes are brought home as much

I:I **In the beginning . . .** : This phrase, which has long been the focus of
debate among grammarians, can also be read: "At the beginning of God's
creating of the heavens and the earth,/ when the earth was. . . ." The
translation here, which is traditional in English, has been retained for stylistic reasons. **God created:** Indicative of God's power and not used in
reference to humans, although later in the chapter such words as "make"
and "form" do appear.

2 **Now the earth . . .** : Genesis I describes God's bringing order out of
chaos, not creation from nothingness. **wild and waste:** Heb. *tohu va-vohu*,
indicating "emptiness." **Ocean:** The primeval waters, a common (and
usually divine) image in ancient Near Eastern mythology. **breath of God:**
Others use "wind," "spirit"; the word (Heb. *ru'ah*) is open to both possibilities. See Ps. 33:6. **hovering:** Or "flitting." The image suggested by the
word (see Deut. 32:11) is that of an eagle protecting its young.

3–5 **God said . . . God saw . . . God separated . . . God called:** Here, from
the outset of the story the principle of order is stressed, through the rhythmic structure of "God" plus four verbs.

4 **God saw . . . that it was good:** The syntax is emphatic here; others use
"God saw how good it was." The phrase is reminiscent of ancient Near
Eastern descriptions of a craftsman being pleased with his work.

4 **separated:** The verb occurs four more times early in the chapter (vv.6, 7,
14, 18), and further points to the concept of order.

6 **dome:** Heb. *raki'a*, literally a beaten sheet of metal.

8 **Heaven:** The sky.

11 **sprout forth with sprouting-growth . . . seed forth seeds . . . fruit
trees . . . fruit:** The three sound doublets create a poetic effect in God's
pronouncement. Note that they are not repeated by the narrator in verse
12. See also verse 20, ". . . swarm with a swarm. . . ." **after their kind:**
Here as in a number of passages in the translation I have shifted some
words that occur in the singular (especially collectives) for the sake of
clarity. See, for example, 6:3, 5.

12 The earth brought forth sprouting-growth,
   plants that seed forth seeds, after their kind,
   trees that yield fruit, in which is their seed, after their kind.
   God saw that it was good.
13 There was evening, there was morning: third day.

14 God said:
   Let there be lights in the dome of the heavens, to separate
      the day from the night,
   that they may be for signs—for set-times, for days and
      years,
15 and let them be for lights in the dome of the heavens, to
      provide light upon the earth!
   It was so.
16 God made the two great lights,
   the greater light for ruling the day and the smaller light for
      ruling the night,
   and the stars.
17 God placed them in the dome of the heavens
18 to provide light upon the earth, to rule the day and the
      night, to separate the light from the darkness.
   God saw that it was good.
19 There was evening, there was morning: fourth day.

20 God said:
   Let the waters swarm with a swarm of living beings, and let
      fowl fly above the earth, across the dome of the heavens!
21 God created the great sea-serpents
   and all living beings that crawl about, with which the waters
      swarmed, after their kind,
   and all winged fowl after their kind.
   God saw that it was good.
22 And God blessed them, saying:
   Bear fruit and be many and fill the waters in the seas,
   and let the fowl be many on earth!
23 There was evening, there was morning: fifth day.

24 God said:
   Let the earth bring forth living beings after their kind,

by the form in which they are presented as by their actual mention.

God (Heb. *elohim,* a generic term) is introduced into the narrative without any description of origins, sex, or limitations of power. As the only functioning character of the chapter, he occupies center stage. There is no opposition, no resistance to his acts of creation, which occur in perfect harmony with his express word.

As a sign of both God's total control and his intent, the world unfolds in symmetrical order. The division of God's labor into six days, plus a seventh for rest, itself indicates a powerful meaningfulness at work, as well as providing the external structure for the narrative. Interpreters have tended to divide these into either three groups of two days or two groups of three, with always the same results: a balanced and harmonious whole. In addition, the number seven is significant (as it will be elsewhere in the Bible) as a symbol of perfection, not only in Israel but in the ancient world in general.

The narrative uses several repeating words and phrases to both unify the story and underscore the theme of order. These include "God said," "Let there be . . . ," "God saw that it was good," "It was so," and "There was evening, there was morning . . ."

The text is so formed as to highlight the creation of humankind. Although in each previous day "God said" is the keynote, suggesting forethought as well as action, here (v.26) God fully spells out his intentions, as it were thinking out loud. Humanity, created in the divine "image," is to hold sway over the rest of creation. Only with the addition of humankind is God able to survey his newly formed world and to pronounce it "exceedingly good" (v.31).

At least two motifs appear in this chapter which will become important later in Genesis. The three occurrences of "blessing" (1:22, 1:28, 2:3) point to a central idea in the Patriarchal stories. In addition the concept of order and its logical conclusion—that history makes sense—figures prominently in the familial histories of the book. This is accomplished largely by the meaningful use of numbers, as above.

14 **lights:** In the sense of "lamps." **for signs—for set-times** . . . : Hebrew difficult.

21 **great sea-serpents:** The rebellious primeval monster of Ps. 74:13 (and common in ancient Near Eastern myth) is here depicted as merely another one of God's many creations.

22 **And God blessed them:** The first occurrence in Genesis of the key motif of blessing, which recurs especially throughout the Patriarchal stories. **Bear fruit and be many and fill:** Heb. *peru u-revu u-mil'u.*

herd-animals, crawling things, and the wildlife of the earth
after their kind!
It was so.

25 God made the wildlife of the earth after their kind, and the
herd-animals after their kind, and all crawling things of
the soil after their kind.
God saw that it was good.

26 God said:
Let us make humankind, in our image, according to our
likeness!
Let them have dominion over the fish of the sea, the fowl of
the heavens, animals, all the earth, and all crawling things
that crawl upon the earth!

27   God created humankind in his image,
             in the image of God did he create it,
             male and female did he create them.

28 God blessed them,
God said to them:
Bear fruit and be many and fill the earth
and subdue it!
Have dominion over the fish of the sea, the fowl of the
heavens, and all living things that crawl about upon the
earth!

29 God said:
Here, I give you
all plants that bear seeds that are upon the face of all the
earth,
and all trees in which there is tree fruit that bears seeds,
for you shall they be, for eating;

30 and also for all the living things of the earth, for all the fowl
of the heavens, for all that crawls about upon the earth in
which there is living being—
all green plants for eating.
It was so.

31 Now God saw all that he had made,
and here: it was exceedingly good!
There was evening, there was morning: the sixth day.

2:1 Thus were finished the heavens and the earth, with all of
their array.

2 God had finished, on the seventh day, his work that he had
made,
and then he ceased, on the seventh day, from all his work
that he had made.
3 God gave the seventh day his blessing, and he hallowed it,
for on it he ceased from all his work, that by creating, God
had made.

The entire account concludes (2:1–3) with a tightly structured poem.
"God," "the seventh day," "work," and "made" are mentioned three
times, "finished," "ceased," and "all" twice; and "created" returns,
echoing 1:1, to round out the whole creation narrative.

The postscript (2:4a; some scholars align it with what follows in
Chapter 2 instead) introduces the key structural phrase of Genesis,
"These are the begettings. . . ." It may also indicate the polemical intent
of the creation story. Rosenzweig understood the verse to contrast "be-
getting," i.e., sexual creation as it occurs in non-Israelite myths, with the
"true" creation.

In that vein, a final word needs to be said about extrabiblical evidence.
As has often been pointed out, Genesis 1 is unmistakably reacting against
prevailing Near Eastern cosmogonies of the time. Most of the cultures
surrounding ancient Israel had elaborate creation stories, highlighting the
birth, sexuality, and violent uprisings of the gods. As we indicated at the
outset, the concept of God presented here militates against such ideas,
arguing chiefly out of omission and silence. (It should also be noted that
in poetic books such as Isaiah, Job, and Psalms, a tradition about violent

26 **in our image:** The "our" is an old problem. Some take it to refer to the
heavenly court (although, not surprisingly, no angels are mentioned here).
27 **God created humankind:** The narrative breaks into verse, stressing the
importance of human beings. "Humankind" (Heb. *adam*) does not specify
sex, as is clear from the last line of the poem.
29 **I give you:** "You" in the plural.
30 **all green plants for eating:** Human beings in their original state were not
meat-eaters. For the change, see 9:3ff.
31 **exceedingly good. . . . the sixth day:** The two qualifiers "exceedingly"
and "the" are deviations from the previous expressions in the story, and
underscore the sixth day (when humankind was created) as the crowning
achievement of creation (or else serve as a summary to the whole).
2:3 **gave . . . his blessing:** Or "blessed," here expanded in English for rhythmical reasons. **by creating, God had made:** Hebrew difficult. Buber's
working papers show numerous attempts at a solution.

4 These are the begettings of the heavens and the earth: their
being created.

On the day that YHWH, God, made earth and heaven,
5 no bush of the field was yet on earth,
no plant of the field had yet sprung up,
for YHWH, God, had not made it rain upon earth,
and there was no human/*adam* to till the soil/*adama*—
6 but a surge would well up from the ground and water all
the face of the soil;
7 and YHWH, God, formed the human, of dust from the
soil,
he blew into his nostrils the rush of life
and the human became a living being.

8 YHWH, God, planted a garden in Eden/Land-of-Pleasure,
in the east,
and there he placed the human whom he had formed.
9 YHWH, God, caused to spring up from the soil
every type of tree, desirable to look at and good to eat,
and the Tree of Life in the midst of the garden
and the Tree of the Knowing of Good and Evil.

10 Now a river goes out from Eden, to water the garden,
and from there it divides and becomes four stream-heads.
11 The name of the first one is Pishon/Spreader—that is the
one that circles through all the land of Havila, where gold
is;
12 the gold of that land is good, there too are bdellium and the
precious-stone carnelian.
13 The name of the second river is Gihon/Gusher—that is the
one that circles through all the land of Cush.
14 The name of the third river is Hiddekel/Tigris—that is the
one that goes to the east of Assyria.
And the fourth river—that is Perat/Euphrates.

15 YHWH, God, took the human and set him in the garden of
Eden,
to work it and to watch it.

16 YHWH, God, commanded concerning the human, saying:
From every other tree of the garden you may eat, yes, eat,
17 but from the Tree of the Knowing of Good and Evil—
you are not to eat from it,
for on the day that you eat from it, you must die, yes, die.

---

conflict at creation has been preserved.) The Genesis narrative has taken
such old mythological motifs as battles with the primeval (female) waters
or with sea monsters and eliminated or neutralized them. What remains
is both utterly simple and radical in its time.

Garden and Expulsion (2:4b–3:24): From the perspective of God in
Chapter 1, we now switch to that of humankind (note how the opening
phrase in 2:4b, "earth and heaven," reverses the order found in 1:1).
This most famous of all Genesis stories contains an assortment of mythic

4b **On the day:** At the time.   **YHWH:** For a discussion of the name of God
and its translation and pronunciation, see p. xxix.
5 **human/*adam* . . . soil/*adama:*** The sound connection, the first folk etymology in the Bible, establishes the intimacy of mankind with the ground
(note the curses in 3:17 and 4:11). Human beings are created from the soil,
just as animals are (v.19).
6 **surge:** Or "flow."
7 **rush:** Or "breath."
8 **Eden/Land-of-Pleasure:** For another use of the Hebrew root, see 18:12.
The usage here may be a folk etymology; Speiser translates it as "steppe."
9 **Tree of Life:** Conferring immortality on the eater of its fruit.   **Knowing
of Good and Evil:** Interpreters disagree on the meaning of this phrase. It
could be a merism (as in "knowledge from A to Z"—that is, of everything),
or an expression of moral choice.
10 **stream-heads:** Branches or tributaries.
12 **bdellium . . . carnelian:** Identification uncertain; others suggest, for instance, "lapis" and "onyx."
15 **work:** A different Hebrew word (here, *avod*) from the one used in 2:2–3
(*melakha*).
16 **eat, yes, eat:** Heb. *akhol tokhel,* literally, "eating you may eat." Others use
"you may freely eat"; I have followed B-R's practice of doubling the verb
throughout, which retains the sound as well as the meaning. In this passage, as in many instances, I have inserted the word "yes" for rhythmical
reasons.
17 **die, yes, die:** Others use "surely die."

18 Now YHWH, God, said:
     It is not good for the human to be alone,
     I will make him a helper corresponding to him.
19 So YHWH, God, formed from the soil every living-thing of
     the field and every fowl of the heavens
     and brought each to the human, to see what he would call
     it;
     and whatever the human called it as a living being, that
     became its name.
20 The human called out names for every herd-animal and for
     the fowl of the heavens and for every living-thing of the
     field,
     but for the human, there could be found no helper
     corresponding to him.
21 So YHWH, God, caused a deep slumber to fall upon the
     human, so that he slept,
     he took one of his ribs and closed up the flesh in its place.
22 YHWH, God, built the rib that he had taken from the
     human into a woman
     and brought her to the human.
23 The human said:
          This-time, she-is-it!
          Bone from my bones,
          flesh from my flesh!
          She shall be called Woman/*Isha*,
          for from Man/*Ish* she was taken!
24 Therefore a man leaves his father and his mother and clings
     to his wife,
     and they become one flesh.

25 Now the two of them, the human and his wife, were nude,
     yet they were not ashamed.

3:1 Now the snake was more shrewd than all the living-things
     of the field that YHWH, God, had made.
     It said to the woman:
     Even though God said: You are not to eat from any of the
     trees in the garden . . . !
  2 The woman said to the snake:

elements and images which are common to human views of prehistory: the lush garden, four central rivers located (at least partially) in fabled lands, the mysterious trees anchoring the garden (and the world?), a primeval man and woman living in unashamed nakedness, an animal that talks, and a God who converses regularly and intimately with his creatures. The narrative presents itself, at least on the surface, as a story of origins. We are to learn the roots of human sexual feelings, of pain in childbirth, and how the anomalous snake (a land creature with no legs) came to assume its present form. Most strikingly, of course, the story seeks to explain the origin of the event most central to human consciousness: death.

The narrative unfolds through a series of contrasts: good and evil, life and death, heaven and earth, give and take, knowledge and ignorance, mankind and animals, hiding and revealing. Some of these concepts appear literally as key words in the text. The characters also appear through contrasts: man as God's image and as dust, woman as helper and hinderer, the snake as shrewd and (after the curse) lowly.

A further focus is provided by the echoing of the word "eat," whose connotation changes from sustenance/bounty (2:9, 16) to prohibition (2:17) to misunderstanding (3:1–5) and disobedience (3:6, 11–13), and finally to curse (3:14, 17, 19). Such a flexible use of words sets up a rhythmic drama which, as much of Genesis, bears resemblance to poetry rather than to prose.

Part I of the story (Chapter 2) sets the stage in the garden, focusing on *Adam,* "Everyman" (see *Cambridge Bible Commentary,* Gen. 1–11). God is here regularly called "YHWH, God," a rare designation which may suggest a preexpulsion view of the wholeness of God as well as of mankind. Man continues his status as "God's image" (1:26–27), imitating

18 **It is not good:** In contrast to the refrain of Genesis 1, "God saw that it was good." **corresponding to:** Lit. "opposite." The whole phrase (Heb. *ezer kenegdo*) could be rendered "a helping counterpart." At any rate, the Hebrew does not suggest a subordinate position for women.

20 **called out:** Or "gave." **for the human:** Others use "for Adam" or "for a man."

21 **ribs:** Or possibly "sides," paralleling other ancient peoples' concept of an original being that was androgynous.

23 **She:** Lit. "this-one."

3:1 **Even though God said:** Others use "Did God really say . . . ?" **in the garden . . . !:** Such an uncompleted phrase, known as aposeopesis, leaves it to the reader to complete the speaker's thought, which in the Bible is usually an oath or a threat (see also, for instance, 14:23, 21:23, 26:29, 31:50).

From the fruit of the other trees in the garden we may eat,
3 but from the fruit of the tree that is in the midst of the
garden, God has said:
You are not to eat from it and you are not to touch it,
lest you die.
4 The snake said to the woman:
Die, you will not die!
5 Rather, God knows
that on the day that you eat from it, your eyes will be
opened
and you will become like gods, knowing good and evil.
6 The woman saw
that the tree was good for eating
and that it was a delight to the eyes,
and the tree was desirable to contemplate.
She took from its fruit and ate
and gave also to her husband beside her,
and he ate.
7 The eyes of the two of them were opened
and they knew then
that they were nude.
They sewed fig leaves together and made themselves
loincloths.

8 Now they heard the sound of YHWH, God, who was
walking about in the garden at the breezy-time of the day.
And the human and his wife hid themselves from the face
of YHWH, God, amid the trees of the garden.
9 YHWH, God, called to the human and said to him:
Where are you?
10 He said:
I heard the sound of you in the garden and I was afraid,
because I am nude,
so I hid myself.
11 He said:
Who told you that you are nude?
From the tree about which I command you not to eat,
have you eaten?
12 The human said:

The woman whom you gave to be beside me, she gave me
from the tree,
and so I ate.
13 YHWH, God, said to the woman:
What is this that you have done?
The woman said:
The snake enticed me,
and so I ate.

---

the divine act of giving names (1:5, 8, 10). He is also nevertheless a
creature of the dust, both at the beginning (2:7) and end (3:19) of the
story.

The bridge to Part II (Chapter 3) is deftly accomplished by linking two
identical-sounding words in the Hebrew, *arum* (here, "nude" and
"shrewd"). The choice of the snake as the third character is typically
ancient Near Eastern (it is so used in other stories about death and
immortality, such as the *Gilgamesh Epic* from Mesopotamia). Some interpreters have seen sexual overtones in this choice as well. Yet a plain
reading of the text need not overemphasize the snake, who disappears as
a personality once the fatal fruit has been eaten.

The ending of the story has also raised questions of interpretation.
Buber was among those who see in the act of expulsion from the garden a
deed of mercy rather than one of fear or jealousy. Certainly a creature
whose first act upon acquiring new "knowledge" is to cover himself up
poses no threat to the Creator. The text, like its late successor, the book
of Job, may be suggesting that in the human sphere, unlike the divine,
knowledge and mortality are inextricably linked. This is a tragic realization, but it is also the world as human beings know it.

Although the specifics of this story are never again referred to in the
Hebrew Bible, and are certainly not crucial for the rest of Genesis, one
general theme *is* central to the Bible's world view. This is that rebellion

5 **you:** Plural. **like gods:** Or "like God."
8 **breezy-time:** Evening. **face of God:** The "face" or presence of God is a
   dominating theme in many biblical stories and in the book of Psalms. Man
   seeks God's face or hides from it; God reveals it to him or hides it from
   him.
12 **gave to be:** Put. "Give" has been retained here, despite its awkwardness,
   as a repeating word in the narrative.

14 YHWH, God, said to the snake:
   Because you have done this,
   cursed be you from all the animals and from all the
      living-things of the field;
   upon your belly shall you walk and dust shall you eat, all
      the days of your life.
15 I put enmity between you and the woman, between your
      seed and her seed:
   they will bruise you on the head, you will bruise them in
      the heel.
16 To the woman he said:
   I will multiply, multiply your pain (from) your pregnancy,
   with pains shall you bear children.
   Toward your husband will be your lust, yet he will rule
      over you.
17 To Adam he said:
   Because you have hearkened to the voice of your wife
   and have eaten from the tree about which I commanded
      you, saying:
   You are not to eat from it!
   Cursed be the soil on your account,
   with painstaking labor shall you eat from it, all the days of
      your life.
18 Thorn and sting-shrub let it spring up for you,
   when you seek to eat the plants of the field!
19 By the sweat of your brow shall you eat bread,
   until you return to the soil,
   for from it you were taken.
   For you are dust, and to dust shall you return.

20 The human called his wife's name: Havva/Life-giver!
   For she became the mother of all the living.

21 Now YHWH, God, made Adam and his wife coats of skins
      and clothed them.

22 YHWH, God, said:
   Here, the human has become like one of us, in knowing
      good and evil.

So now, lest he send forth his hand
and take also from the Tree of Life
and eat
and live throughout the ages . . . !
23 So YHWH, God, sent him away from the garden of Eden,
to work the soil from which he had been taken.
24 He drove the human out
and caused to dwell, eastward of the garden of Eden,
the winged-sphinxes and the flashing, ever-turning sword
to watch over the way to the Tree of Life.

---

against or disobedience toward God and his laws results in banishment/
estrangement and, literally or figuratively, death. Thus from the beginning the element of *choice*, so much stressed by the Prophets later on, is
seen as the major element in human existence.

All this said, it should be recognized that the garden story, like many
biblical texts, has been the subject of endless interpretation. One line of
thought takes the psychological point of view. The story resembles a
vision of childhood and of the transition to the contradictions and pain of
adolescence and adulthood. In every way—moral, sexual, and intellec-
tual—Adam and Havva are like children, and their actions after partak-
ing of the fruit seem like the actions of those who are unable to cope with
newfound powers. The resolution of the story, banishment from the
garden, suggests the tragic realization that human beings must make
their way through the world with the knowledge of death and with great

15 **seed:** Offspring, descendants.
17 **painstaking labor:** Heb. *itzavon.* Man and woman receive equal curses (see
verse 16, "pain . . . pains").
18 **sting-shrub:** Heb. *dardar;* thistle ("thorns and thistles" suggests an alliteration not found in the Hebrew).
20 **Havva:** Trad. English "Eve."
21 **God . . . clothed them:** Once punishment has been pronounced, God cares
for the man and the woman. Both aspects of God comprise the biblical
understanding of his nature, and they are not exclusive of each other.
22 **one of us:** See note on 1:26. **throughout the ages:** Or "for the eons";
others use "forever."
24 **winged-sphinxes:** Mythical ancient creatures, also represented on the Ark
of the Covenant (Ex. 25:18). "Cherubim," the traditional English rendering, has come to denote chubby, red-cheeked baby angels in Western art,
an image utterly foreign to the ancient Near East.

4:1 The human knew Havva his wife,
     she became pregnant and bore Kayin.
     She said:
     Kaniti/I-have-gotten
     a man, as has YHWH!
  2 She continued bearing—his brother, Hevel.
     Now Hevel became a shepherd of flocks, and Kayin became a
       worker of the soil.

  3 It was, after the passing of days
     that Kayin brought, from the fruit of the soil, a gift to
       YHWH,
  4 and as for Hevel, he too brought—from the firstborn of his
       flock, from their fat-parts.
     YHWH had regard for Hevel and his gift,
  5 for Kayin and his gift he had no regard.
     Kayin became exceedingly enraged and his face fell.
  6 YHWH said to Kayin:
     Why are you so enraged? Why has your face fallen?
  7 Is it not thus:
     If you intend good, bear-it-aloft,
     but if you do not intend good,
     at the entrance is sin, a crouching-demon,
     toward you his lust—
     but you can rule over him.

  8 Kayin said to Hevel his brother . . .
     But then it was, when they were out in the field
     that Kayin rose up against Hevel his brother
     and he killed him.
  9 YHWH said to Kayin:
     Where is Hevel your brother?
     He said:
     I do not know. Am I the watcher of my brother?
 10 Now he said:
     What have you done!
     A sound—your brother's blood cries out to me from the
       soil!

physical difficulty. At the same time the archetypal man and woman do not make the journey alone. They are provided with protection (clothing), given to them by the same God who punished them for their disobedience. We thus symbolically enter adulthood with the realization that being turned out of Paradise does not mean eternal rejection or hopelessness.

The First Brothers (4:1–16): With the story of Kayin and Hevel the narrative points both forward and backward. For the first time the major Genesis themes of struggle and sibling hatred, and discontinuity between the generations, make their appearance. In addition the concept of *sin* is introduced (Rosenzweig), having not appeared by name previously.

One may observe significant links to the garden story. Once again human beings are given a choice; once again disregarding the warning leads to death and estrangement from God; and once again the primal bond between mankind and the soil is ruptured. Chapter 3 is directly recalled by the use of specific wording: God echoes the curse he had put on the woman (3:16) in his warning to Kayin (4:7), and "Where is Hevel your brother?" (4:9) brings to mind "Where are you?" (3:9), which had been addressed to Kayin's father.

The text is punctuated by the use of "brother," a meaningful seven times, as well as by changing connotations of the word "face" (Kayin, unable to bring about a "lifting" of his own face, becomes estranged from God's). Repetition also helps to convey the harshness of Kayin's punishment: he is exiled to the "land of Nod/Wandering" (v.16), for which we have been prepared by the "wavering and wandering" of verses 12 and 14.

4:1 **knew:** Intimately; a term for sexual intercourse. **Kayin:** Trad. English "Cain." The name means "smith" (see also v.22, below). **I-have-gotten:** Others use "I have created." **as has YHWH:** Hebrew difficult.

2 **Hevel:** The name suggests "something transitory" (see the opening of the book of Ecclesiastes: *havel havalim*).

3 **gift:** Heb. *minha*, usually referring to sacrifices.

4 **fat-parts:** I.e., the choicest.

5 **enraged:** Lit. "his (anger) was kindled."

7 **Is it not thus . . . :** Hebrew obscure. **bear-it-aloft:** Others use "there is forgiveness," "there is uplift." **toward you his lust—/ but you can rule over him:** Recalling God's words to Havva in 3:16.

8 **Kayin said . . . :** The verse appears incomplete. Ancient versions add "Come, let us go out into the field."

10 **A sound:** Or "Hark!"

11 And now,
   cursed be you from the soil,
   which opened up its mouth to receive your brother's blood
      from your hand.
12 When you wish to work the soil
   it will not henceforth give its strength to you;
   wavering and wandering must you be on earth!
13 Kayin said to YHWH:
   My punishment is too great to be borne!
14 Here, you drive me away today from the face of the soil,
   and from your face must I conceal myself,
   I must be wavering and wandering on earth—
   now it will be
   that whoever comes upon me will kill me!
15 YHWH said to him:
   No, therefore,
   whoever kills Kayin, sevenfold will it be avenged!
   So YHWH set a sign for Kayin,
   so that whoever came upon him would not strike him down.
16 Kayin went out from the face of YHWH
   and settled in the land of Nod/Wandering, east of Eden.

17 Kayin knew his wife;
   she became pregnant and bore Hanokh.
   Now he became the builder of a city
   and called the city's name according to his son's name,
      Hanokh.
18 To Hanokh was born Irad,
   Irad begot Mehuyael,
   Mehuyael begot Metushael,
   Metushael begot Lemekh.

19 Lemekh took himself two wives,
   the name of the first one was Ada, the name of the second
      was Tzilla.
20 Ada bore Yaval,
   he was the father of those who sit amidst tent and herd.
21 His brother's name was Yuval,
   he was the father of all those who play the lyre and the
      pipe.

22 And Tzilla bore as well—Tuval-Kayin,
   burnisher of every blade of bronze and iron.
   Tuval-Kayin's sister was Naama.

23 Lemekh said to his wives:
       Ada and Tzilla, hearken to my voice,
       wives of Lemekh, give ear to my saying:
       Aye—a man I kill for wounding me,
       a lad for only bruising me!
24   Aye—if sevenfold vengeance be for Kayin,
       then for Lemekh, seventy-sevenfold!
25 Adam knew his wife again, and she bore a son.
   She called his name: Shet/Granted-One!
   meaning: God has granted me another seed in place of
      Hevel,
   for Kayin killed him.

Although this story may well have originated as a tale of enmity between two ways of life (farmer and shepherd), or in another context, it has obviously been transformed into something far more disturbing and universal.

The Line of Kayin (4:17–26): From whole stories the text turns to several brief accounts, some of which are clearly fragments. The first of these deals with origins: of cities, of certain crafts, and of worship. The former two are associated (perhaps negatively) with Kayin's line. The only personality in these texts about whom we learn anything is Lemekh—and his "saying" (vv.23–24) seems hopelessly obscure. Some interpreters have understood it as a challenge to God, and thus believe that it has been included here as an example of the wickedness typical of the generations that preceded the Flood.

The names of Adam and Havva's son and grandson (vv.25–26) are sad reminders of Hevel's death—a personal touch in an otherwise prosaic section of narrative.

15 **a sign:** The exact appearance of the sign is not specified. It is a warning and
    a protection, not the punishment itself (which is exile).
17 **Now he:** "He" refers to Kayin.
18 **Mehuyael begot:** Heb. *Mehiyael.*
19 **Ada . . . Tzilla:** The names suggest "dawn" and "dusk" (Gaster).
20 **father:** Ancestor or founder.
22 **burnisher . . . :** Or "craftsman of every cutting-edge of copper and iron."

26 To Shet as well a son was born,
   he called his name: Enosh/Mortal.

   At that time they first called out the name of YHWH.

5:1 This is the record of the begettings of Adam/Humankind.
       On the day of God's creating humankind,
       in the likeness of God did he then make it,
2   male and female he created them
       and gave blessing to them
       and called their name: Humankind!
       on the day of their being created.
3 When Adam had lived thirty and a hundred years,
   he begot one in his likeness, according to his image,
   and called his name Shet.
4 Adam's days after he begot Shet were eight hundred years,
   and he begot other sons and daughters.
5 And all the days that Adam lived were nine hundred years
   and thirty years,
   then he died.

6 When Shet had lived five years and a hundred years, he
   begot Enosh,
7 and Shet lived after he begot Enosh seven years and eight
   hundred years, and begot other sons and daughters.
8 And all the days of Shet were twelve years and nine
   hundred years,
   then he died.

9 When Enosh had lived ninety years, he begot Kenan,
10 and Enosh lived after he begot Kenan fifteen years and
   eight hundred years, and begot other sons and daughters.
11 And all the days of Enosh were five years and nine hundred
   years,
   then he died.

12 When Kenan had lived seventy years, he begot Mehalalel,
13 and Kenan lived after he begot Mehalalel forty years and
   eight hundred years, and begot other sons and daughters.

14 And all the days of Kenan were ten years and nine hundred
   years,
   then he died.

15 When Mehalalel had lived five years and sixty years, he
   begot Yered.
16 and Mehalalel lived after he begot Yered thirty years and
   eight hundred years, and begot other sons and daughters.
17 And all the days of Mehalalel were ninety-five years and
   eight hundred years,
   then he died.

18 When Yered had lived sixty-two years and a hundred years,
   he begot Hanokh,
19 and Yered lived after he begot Hanokh eight hundred years,
   and begot other sons and daughters.
20 And all the days of Yered were sixty-two years and nine
   hundred years,
   then he died.

From Adam to Noah (5): The extraordinary numbers in this section are
significant, not so much for their length as for their message. Cassuto has
tried to fit them into a defined scheme, showing that the purpose, and
achieved effect, of our text is to convey that human history follows a
meaningful pattern. Pride of place on the list is occupied by the seventh
member, Hanokh, who is portrayed as the first man of God. He serves as
a preparation for Noah, who also "walks in accord with God" (6:9).
Hanokh's life span, 365 years, exemplifies the number scheme of Genesis: as an expression of numerical perfection (the number of days in a
year), it symbolizes moral perfection.

26 **called out the name of YHWH:** I.e., worshipped God.
5:1 **On the day . . . :** The language is reminiscent of the earlier poem in 1:27.
   In this case, however, the Hebrew creates a rhyming effect. The cola of the
   poem here end thus: *bera'am / otam / shemam: Adam/ hibare'am.* Such a
   rhyming scheme is rare in biblical Hebrew, and usually endows a passage
   with particular significance (see also, for instance, II Sam. 12:11).
18 **Hanokh:** Trad. English "Enoch."

21 When Hanokh had lived sixty-five years, he begot
   Metushelah,
22 and Hanokh walked in accord with God after he begot
   Metushelah three hundred years, and begot other sons
   and daughters.
23 And all the days of Hanokh were sixty-five years and three
   hundred years.
24 Now Hanokh walked in accord with God,
   then he was no more,
   for God had taken him.

25 When Metushelah had lived eighty-seven years and a
   hundred years, he begot Lemekh,
26 and Metushelah lived after he begot Lemekh eighty-two
   years and seven hundred years, and begot other sons and
   daughters.
27 And all the days of Metushelah were sixty-nine years and
   nine hundred years,
   then he died.

28 When Lemekh had lived eighty-two years and a hundred
   years, he begot a son.
29 He called his name: Noah!
   saying:
   Zeh yenahamenu/May he comfort-our-sorrow
   from our toil, from the pains of our hands
   coming from the soil, which YHWH has cursed.

30 And Lemekh lived after he begot Noah ninety-five years
   and five hundred years, and begot other sons and
   daughters.
31 And all the days of Lemekh were seventy-seven years and
   seven hundred years,
   then he died.

32 When Noah was five hundred years old,
   Noah begot Shem, Ham, and Yefet.

6:1 Now it was when humans first became many on the face of
       the soil
     and women were born to them,
   2 that the divine beings saw how beautiful the human women
       were,
     so they took themselves wives, whomever they chose.

   3 YHWH said:
     My breath shall not remain in humankind for ages, for they
       too are flesh;
     let their days be then a hundred and twenty years!

Antiquity and the Preparation for the Flood (6:1–8): The final pre-Flood
section of the text includes a theme common to other ancient tales: the
biological mixing of gods and men in dim antiquity. Perhaps this fragment, which initially seems difficult to reconcile with biblical ideas about
God, has been retained here to round out a picture familiar to ancient
readers, and to recall the early closeness of the divine and the human
which, according to many cultures, later dissolved. It is also possible that
the episode serves as another example of a world that has become dis-
ordered, thus providing further justification for a divinely ordered
destruction.
   The stage is set for the Flood by means of a powerful sound reference.

22 **and Hanokh walked in accord with God . . . three hundred years:** The
   variation from the rigid formulations of this chapter draws attention to this
   key figure, the first pious man (similarly with Noah, 5:29). "Walked in
   accord with God" means walked in God's ways, led a righteous life.
24 **then he was no more:** He died. Later interpreters found the phrase ambiguous, and fantastic postbiblical legends arose concerning Hanokh (see Ginzberg).
31 **seventy-seven years and seven hundred years:** As in 4:24, a man named
   Lemekh is linked to multiples of seven.
6:2 **divine beings:** Or "godlings."
   3 **for they too are flesh:** Hebrew difficult. The text uses the singular. **a
   hundred and twenty years:** Some early interpreters take this to specify a
   "grace period" for mankind before the Flood. The text seems to be setting
   the limits of the human life span.

4 The giants were on earth in those days,
and afterward as well,
when the divine beings came in to the human women
and they bore them (children)—
they were the heroes who were of former ages, the men of
name.

5 Now YHWH saw
that great was humankind's evildoing on earth
and every form of their heart's planning was only evil all the
day.
6 Then YHWH was sorry
that he had made humankind on earth,
and it pained his heart.
7 YHWH said:
I will blot out humankind, whom I have created, from the
face of the soil,
from human to animal, to crawling thing and to the fowl of
the heavens,
for I am sorry that I made them.
8 But Noah found favor in the eyes of YHWH.

9 These are the begettings of Noah.
Noah was a righteous, whole man in his generation,
in accord with God did Noah walk.
10 Noah begot three sons: Shem, Ham, and Yefet.

11 Now the earth had gone to ruin before God, the earth was
filled with wrongdoing.
12 God saw the earth, and here: it had gone to ruin,
for all flesh had ruined its way upon the earth.

13 God said to Noah:
An end of all flesh has come before me,
for the earth is filled with wrongdoing through them;
here, I am about to bring ruin upon them, along with the
earth.
14 Make yourself an Ark of *gofer* wood,
with reeds make the Ark,

In 5:29 Noah was named, ostensibly to comfort his elders' "sorrow" over human "pains" in tilling the soil. Here (6:6), however, the meaning of the name has been ironically reversed. The one who was supposed to bring comfort only heralds God's own being "sorry" and "pained" (vv. 6–7). A similar ironic word-play, where the audience knows what the name-bestower does not, occurs in Ex. 2:3; curiously, the hero of that passage, the baby Moses, is also connected with an "ark"—the term for the little basket in which he is set adrift.

The Deluge (6:9–8:19): The biblical account of the Flood is replete with echoes and allusions which point to three clear motifs: God's justice, the totality of punishment, and a new beginning patterned after Genesis 1.

The first of these is brought out in 6:11–13: the repetition of the word "ruin" indicates not only the sorry state of society but also the principle of just retaliation, for God is to "bring ruin" upon the earth (v.13).

The totality of the disaster is conveyed by the repeated use of the word "all" in 7:21–23, as well as by the completeness of the list of those destroyed (7:21–23). Humans, as befits their place in the order of creation, appear last, but actually it is they who drag virtually all of creation down with them. This reflects a deeply held biblical idea that human

---

4 **came in to:** The common biblical term for sexual intercourse. The concept, also expressed in Arabic, is of the man entering the woman's tent for the purposes of sex.

5 **now YHWH saw . . . evildoing:** In contrast to the refrain of Chapter 1, "God saw that it was good." **every form of their heart's planning:** This lengthy phrase indicates human imagination (Speiser: "every scheme that his mind devised"). "Heart" (Heb. *lev* or *levav*) often expresses the concept of "mind" in the Bible.

9 **righteous:** A term with legal connotations; "in the right" or "just." **righteous, whole:** Foreshadowing Avraham, of whom similar vocabulary will be used (17:1). **whole:** A term used of animals fit for sacrifice: "perfect" or "unblemished." In reference to human beings it may denote "wholehearted."

11–12 **Now the earth . . . :** A poetic summary of the situation.

11 **before God:** In his sight.

12 **God saw the earth, and here: it had gone to ruin:** A bitter echo of 1:31, "Now God saw all that he had made,/ and here: it was exceedingly good!"

13 **has come before me:** Has been determined by me.

14 **Ark:** English as well as Hebrew etymology points to a box or chest, not strictly a boat. God, not human engineering, is the source of survival in the story. *gofer:* Identification unknown. **reeds:** Reading Heb. *kanim* for traditional text's *kenim* ("compartments").

and cover it within and without with a covering-of-pitch.
15 And this is how you are to make it:
Three hundred cubits the length of the Ark, fifty cubits its
breadth, and thirty cubits its height.
16 A skylight you are to make for the Ark, finishing it to a
cubit upward.
The entrance of the Ark you are to set in its side;
With a lower, a second, and a third deck you are to make
it.
17 As for me,
here, I am about to bring on the Deluge, water upon the
earth,
to bring ruin upon all flesh that has breath of life in it, from
under the heavens,
all that is on earth will perish.
18 But I will establish my covenant with you:
you are to come into the Ark, you and your sons and your
wife and your sons' wives with you,
19 and from all living-things, from all flesh, you are to bring
two from all into the Ark, to remain alive with you.
They are to be a male and a female each,
20 from fowl after their kind, from herd-animals after their
kind, from all crawling things of the soil after their kind,
two from all are to come to you, to remain alive.
21 As for you,
take for yourself from all edible-things that are eaten and
gather it to you,
it shall be for you and for them, for eating.
22 Noah did it,
according to all that God commanded him, so he did.

7:1 YHWH said to Noah:
Come, you and all your household, into the Ark!
For you I have seen as righteous before me in this
generation.
2 From all ritually pure animals you are to take seven and
seven each, a male and his mate,
and from all the animals that are not pure, two each, a male
and his mate,

3 and also from the fowl of the heavens, seven and seven
each, male and female,
to keep seed alive upon the face of all the earth.
4 For in yet seven days
I will make it rain upon the earth for forty days and forty
nights
and will blot out all existing-things that I have made, from
the face of the soil.
5 Noah did it, according to all that YHWH had commanded
him.

6 Noah was six hundred years old when the Deluge occurred,
water upon the earth;
7 and Noah came, his sons and his wife and his sons' wives
with him, into the Ark before the waters of the Deluge.
8 From the pure animals and from the animals that are not
pure and from the fowl and all that crawls about on the
soil—
9 two and two each came to Noah, into the Ark, male and
female,
as God had commanded Noah.

---

action directly affects the orderly and otherwise neutral functioning of
nature.

There are striking parallels between the Flood narrative and the creation account of Chapter 1. Just as the animals were created, each "according to its kind," their rescue, both in boarding and leaving the Ark,

15 **cubits:** A cubit equaled a man's forearm in length, about 17½ inches.
16 **skylight:** Hebrew obscure, including the end of the phrase.
17 **Deluge:** Heb. *mabbul.* Others suggest the more conventional word
"Flood," but the term may be an Assyrian loan-word.
18 **covenant:** An agreement or pact, most notably (in the Bible) one between
God and individuals or between him and the people of Israel.
7:2 **ritually pure:** An anachronism, referring to later Israelite laws about sacrifice and eating. **seven and seven each:** The contradiction between this
and 6:19 has led scholars to posit two different sources for the
story. **male:** Lit. "a man."
4 **in yet seven days:** Seven days from now. **forty:** Used in the Bible to
denote long periods of time; also a favorite patterned number.

10 After the seven days it was
   that the waters of the Deluge were upon the earth.
11 In the six hundredth year of Noah's life, in the second
   New-Moon, on the seventeenth day of the New-Moon,
   on that day:
        then burst all the well-springs of the great Ocean
        and the sluices of the heavens opened up.
12 The torrent was upon the earth for forty days and forty
   nights.

13 On that very day came Noah, and Shem, Ham, and Yefet,
   Noah's sons, Noah's wife and his three sons' wives with
   them, into the Ark,
14 they and all wildlife after their kind, all herd-animals after
   their kind, all crawling things that crawl upon the earth
   after their kind, all fowl after their kind, all
   chirping-things, all winged-things;
15 they came to Noah, into the Ark, two and two each from all
   flesh in which there is breath of life.
16 And those that came, male and female from all flesh they
   came,
   as God had commanded him.
   YHWH closed (the door) upon him.

17 The Deluge was forty days upon the earth.
   The waters increased and lifted the Ark, so that it was
   raised above the earth;
18 the waters swelled and increased exceedingly upon the
   earth, so that the Ark floated upon the face of the waters.
19 When the waters had swelled exceedingly, yes, exceedingly
   over the earth, all high mountains that were under all the
   heavens were covered.
20 Fifteen cubits upward swelled the waters, thus the
   mountains were covered.

21 Then perished all flesh that crawls about upon the earth—
   fowl, herd-animals, wildlife, and all swarming things that
   swarm upon the earth,
   and all human beings;

22 all that had rush or breath of life in their nostrils,
   all that were on firm ground, died.
23 He blotted out all existing-things that were on the face of
   the soil,
   from human to animal, to crawling thing and to fowl of the
   heavens,
   they were blotted out from the earth.
   Noah alone remained, and those who were with him in the
   Ark.

---

is similarly worded. "Ocean" and the great "breath" which existed at
creation (1:2) return here, the former to signify a lapse into chaos and the
latter, the restoration of order and peace (7:11, 8:1). Finally, after the
Flood (9:1–3) Noah is blessed in wording that recalls Adam's blessing in
1:28–30. The world thus begins anew, with the implication of some
hope for the future.

Repetition emphasizes other aspects of the story's message. In general
the word-stem "live" occurs constantly throughout the text, highlighting
the rescue and renewal of life as well as its destruction. Noah's obedience, another major theme, is indicated by variations on the phrase
"according to all that God commanded him, so he did" (6:22). Of rhythmical, almost ritual-sounding import is the phrase "you and your sons
and your wife and your sons' wives."

Our story has often been compared, with much justification, to the
several Mesopotamian Flood accounts (e.g., in the *Gilgamesh* and *Atraha-
sis* epics), with which it shares a great deal of detail. At one time scholars

11 **then burst . . . :** Cassuto suggests that the poetic verses here and elsewhere
   in the Flood story are fragments of an Israelite epic. See also 9:11,
   15. **well-springs . . . sluices:** The normal sources of rain function here
   without any restraint (Cassuto). **Ocean:** The world returns to the primeval chaos of 1:2.
16 **YHWH closed:** Another sign of God's control over the events (and of his
   protection of Noah).
17–20 **increased . . . swelled and increased exceedingly. . . . swelled exceedingly, yes, exceedingly. . . . swelled:** The structure here mirrors the action: the surging and growing of the waters.
18 **swelled:** Lit. "grew mighty." **floated:** Lit. "went."
22 **firm ground:** Heb. *harava*, lit. "dry-land." Hebrew has two words for
   "dry" (*harev* and *yavesh*), while English uses only one.
23 **blotted out:** Twice repeated, echoing God's promise in 6:7.

24 The waters swelled upon the earth for a hundred and fifty
days.

8:1 But God paid mind to Noah and all living-things, all the
animals that were with him in the Ark,
and God brought a breath-of-wind across the earth, so that
the waters abated.
2 The well-springs of Ocean and the sluices of the heavens
were dammed up,
and the torrent from the heavens was held back.
3 The waters returned from upon the earth, continually
advancing and returning,
and the waters diminished at the end of a hundred and fifty
days.
4 And the Ark came to rest in the seventh New-Moon, on the
seventeenth day of the New-Moon, upon the mountains of
Ararat.
5 Now the waters continued to advance and diminish until the
tenth New-Moon.
On the tenth, on the first day of the New-Moon, the tops of
the mountains could be seen.

6 At the end of forty days it was: Noah opened the window of
7   the Ark that he had made,/ and sent out a raven;
it went off, going off and returning, until the waters were
dried up from upon the earth.
8 Then he sent out a dove from him, to see whether the
waters had subsided from the face of the soil.
9 But the dove found no resting-place for the sole of her foot,
so she returned to him into the Ark,
for there was water upon the face of all the earth.
He sent forth his hand and took her, and brought her to
him into the Ark.
10 Then he waited yet another seven days
and sent out the dove yet again from the Ark.
11 The dove came back to him at eventime,
and here—a freshly plucked olive leaf in her beak!
So Noah knew
that the waters had subsided from upon the earth.

12 Then he waited yet another seven days
 and sent out the dove,
 but she returned to him again no more.

13 And so it was in the six hundred and first year, in the
  beginning-month, on the first day of the New-Moon,
 that the waters left firm ground upon the earth.
 Noah removed the covering of the Ark and saw:
 here, the face of the soil was firm.
14 Now in the second New-Moon, on the twenty-seventh day
 of the New-Moon, the earth was completely dry.

15 God spoke to Noah, saying:
16 Go out of the Ark, you and your wife, your sons and your
 sons' wives with you.
17 All living-things that are with you, all flesh—fowl, animals,
 and all crawling things that crawl upon the earth,

---

were quick to concentrate on the parallels, but the differences are now recognized as being much more significant. In general one may say that in contrast to the earlier (Mesopotamian) versions the biblical one is unambiguous in both tone and intent. It has been placed in Genesis to exemplify a God who judges the world according to human behavior, punishes evil and rescues the righteous. This is a far cry from the earlier accounts, where the gods plan the destruction of the world for reasons that are unclear (or in one version, because mankind's noise is disturbing the sleep of the gods), and where the protagonist, Utnapishtim, is saved as the result of a god's favoritism without any moral judgments being passed.

8:1 **paid mind:** More than merely "remembered." **breath-of-wind:** Reminiscent of the "breath of God" at creation.
3,5 **advancing and returning. . . . advance and diminish:** Again, as in 7:17–20, the motion of the waters is suggested by means of sound.
7 **sent out:** Or "released."
8 **dove:** This bird is portrayed in the Bible as beautiful (even pure) and delicate. From this passage, of course, stems the popular use of the dove as the symbol of peace.
13 **left firm ground:** Or "were fully dried up" (see note to 7:22).

have them go out with you,
that they may swarm on earth, that they may bear fruit and
   become many upon the earth.
18 So Noah went out, his sons, his wife, and his sons' wives
   with him,
19 all living-things—all crawling things, and all fowl, all that
   crawl about upon the earth,
   according to their clans they went out of the Ark.

20 Noah built a slaughter-site to YHWH.
   He took from all pure animals and from all pure fowl
   and offered up offerings upon the slaughter-site.
21 Now YHWH smelled the soothing smell
   and YHWH said in his heart:
   I will never doom the soil again on humankind's account,
      since what the human heart forms is evil from its youth;
   I will never again strike down all living-things, as I have
      done;
22 (never) again, all the days of the earth, shall
         sowing and harvest,
         cold and heat,
         summer and winter,
         day and night
         ever cease!

9:1 Now God blessed Noah and his sons and said to them:
    Bear fruit and be many and fill the earth!
  2 Your fear, your dread shall be upon all the wildlife of the
      earth and upon all the fowl of the heavens,
    all that crawls on the soil and all the fish of the sea—
    they are given into your hand.
  3 All things crawling about that live, for you shall they be, for
      eating,
    as with the green plants, I now give you all.
  4 However: flesh with its life, its blood, you are not to eat!
  5 However, too: for your blood, of your own lives, I will
      demand satisfaction—
    from all wild-animals I will demand it,

and from humankind, from every man regarding his
  brother,
demand satisfaction for human life.
6   Whoever now sheds human blood,
    by humans shall his blood be shed,
    for in God's image he made humankind.

Aftermath (8:20–9:19): The passages immediately following the Flood
narrative speak of a God who is remarkably receptive to a human kind of
change. From having been "sorry" that he created mankind (6:6), he
now evinces a change of heart about the entire issue of human evil,
conceding mankind's imperfections (8:21). In a wonderfully structured
declaration, where "never again" moves in position from the middle to
the beginning of the phrase (8:21–22), God as it were chooses to restrain
his own ability to radically disturb the processes of nature. Where later
on in Genesis the human characters exhibit the capacity to change, here
it is God himself.

The blessing in 9:1–3 establishes Noah as a kind of second Adam (and
it might be noted that chronologically Noah is the first man born after
Adam dies). It repeats the basic formulation of the blessing in 1:28–30,
with an important exception: meat-eating is now to be allowed, as part of
God's concession to human nature. Previously only the plant world had
been accessible to humankind for food. However—and this very word
punctuates the text twice in 9:4–5—there is to be an accounting for
willful bloodshed, as if to suggest that the eating of meat is being permit-
ted only under strict conditions. To underscore the importance of this
concept, the section about bloodshed uses the vocabulary of creation:
human beings are made "in the image of God."

19 **clans:** Classifications.
20 **Slaughter-site:** Others use "altar." Etymologically the word hearkens back
    to a time when such sites were used mainly for animal sacrifice; the Bible
    cites other uses such as libations and cereal offerings. **offered up:** The
    Hebrew verb (*'alo*) implies upward movement.
21 **smelled the soothing smell:** Conveyed by the sound in Hebrew, *va-yarah et
    re'ah ha-niho'ah.* **evil from its youth:** That is, evil already begins in what
    we might call adolescence. But Speiser renders it "from the start."
22 **sowing and harvest . . . :** The solemn promise is expressed in verse.
9:6 **Whoever . . . :** A poem which plays on the sounds of "humankind" (*adam*)
    and "blood" (*dam*): *Shofekh dam ha-adam/ ba-adam damo yishafekh.* **by
    humans:** Or "for that human."

7 As for you—bear fruit and be many, swarm on earth and
become many on it!

8 God said to Noah and to his sons with him, saying:

9 As for me—here, I am about to establish my covenant with
you and with your seed after you,

10 and with all living beings that are with you: fowl,
herd-animals, and all the wildlife of the earth with you;
all those going out of the Ark, of all the living-things of the
earth.

11 I will establish my covenant with you:
> All flesh shall never be cut off again by waters of the
> Deluge,
> never again shall there be Deluge, to bring the earth
> to ruin!

12 And God said:
This is the sign of the covenant which I set
between me and you and all living beings that are with you,
for ageless generations:

13 My bow I set in the clouds,
so that it may serve as a sign of the covenant between me
and the earth.

14 It shall be:
when I becloud the earth with clouds
and in the clouds the bow is seen,

15 I will call to mind my covenant
that is between me and you and all living beings—all flesh:
> never again shall the waters become a Deluge, to bring
> all flesh to ruin!

16 When the bow is in the clouds,
I will look at it,
to call to mind the age-old covenant
between God and all living beings—
all flesh that is upon the earth.

17 God said to Noah:
This is the sign of the covenant that I have established
between me and all flesh that is upon the earth.

18 Noah's sons who went out of the Ark were Shem, Ham,
and Yefet.

Now Ham is the father of Canaan.

19 These three were Noah's sons, and from these were
    scattered abroad all the earth-folk.

20 Now Noah was the first man of the soil; he planted a
    vineyard.
21 When he drank from the wine, he became drunk and
    exposed himself in the middle of his tent.
22 Ham, the father of Canaan, saw his father's nakedness
    and told his two brothers outside.
23 Then Shem and Yefet took a cloak, they put it on the
    shoulders of the two of them,
    and walked backward, to cover their father's nakedness.
    —Their faces were turned backward, their father's
    nakedness they did not see.

With verses 8 and 9 the key concept of "covenant" appears for the
first time in the Bible. It is accompanied, as is usual in the Bible, by a
symbol or "sign" (in this case, the rainbow). We are led back to the
creation story again, as other biblical texts speak of the Sabbath as a
"sign of the covenant" between God and Israel (e.g., Ex. 31:12–17).

The sixfold repetition of the phrase "never again" provides a thematic
unity in these passages.

Drunkenness and Nakedness (9:20–29): From the lofty poetry of God's
blessings and promises, we encounter an all-too-brief description of a
bizarre event. The soil, which evidently has not entirely shaken off its
primeval curse, proves once again to be a source of trouble. The nature
of the crime mentioned here ("seeing the father's nakedness") has been
variously interpreted; Buber and others see in it a reference to the sexual
"immorality" of the Canaanites, which the Israelites found particularly
abhorrent. This would explain the emphasis on the *son* of the culprit in
the story, rather than on the perpetrator.

A similar undistinguished ancestry is traced in Chapter 19, referring to
the incestuous origins of Israel's neighbors and frequent enemies, the
Moabites and Ammonites.

18 **Now Ham is the father of Canaan:** See repetition in the story to follow,
    verses 20–27.

24 Now when Noah awoke from his wine, it became known (to
   him) what his littlest son had done to him.
25 He said:
   Cursed be Canaan,
   servant of servants may he be to his brothers!
26 And he said:
   Blessed be YHWH, God of Shem,
   but may Canaan be servant to them!
27 May God extend/*yaft*
   Yefet,
   let him dwell in the tents of Shem,
   but may Canaan be servant to them!

28 And Noah lived after the Deluge three hundred years and
   fifty years.
29 And all the days of Noah were nine hundred years and fifty
   years,
   then he died.

10:1 Now these are the begettings of the sons of Noah,
   Shem, Ham, and Yefet.
   Sons were born to them after the Deluge.

 2 The Sons of Yefet are Gomer and Magog, Madai, Yavan
   and Tuval, Meshekh and Tiras.
 3 The Sons of Gomer are Ashkenaz, Rifat, and Togarma.
 4 The Sons of Yavan are Elisha and Tarshish, Cittites and
   Dodanites.
 5 From these the seacoast nations were divided by their lands,
   each one after its own tongue:
   according to their clans, by their nations.

 6 The Sons of Ham are Cush and Mitzrayim, Put and
   Canaan.
 7 The Sons of Cush are Seva and Havila, Savta, Ra'ma, and
   Savtekha;
   the Sons of Ra'ma—Sheva and Dedan.
 8 Cush begot Nimrod; he was the first mighty man on earth.
 9 He was a mighty hunter before YHWH,

therefore the saying is:
Like Nimrod, a mighty hunter before YHWH.
10 His kingdom, at the beginning, was Bavel, and Erekh,
Accad and Calne, in the land of Shinar;
11/12 from this land Ashur went forth and built Nineveh—along
with the city squares and Calah,/ and Resen between
Nineveh and Calah—that is the great city.
13 Mitzrayim begot the Ludites, the Anamites, the Lehavites,
14   the Naftuhites,/ the Patrusites, and the Casluhites, from
where the Philistines come, and the Caftorites.

The Table of the Nations (10): Genesis, with its typically ancient Near
Eastern emphasis on "begettings," now traces the development of humanity from the sons of Noah. The key formula throughout is "their
lands, their nations." Commentators have noted numerical unity in the
list, citing a total of seventy nations (once repetitions are omitted) laid
out in multiples of seven. That number, as we have indicated, represents
the concept of totality and perfection in the Bible. Thus the stage is set
for the Babel story of the next chapter, with its condemnation of man's
attempt to forestall the divinely willed "scattering" into a well-ordered
world.

Many of the names in this chapter have been identified (see Speiser),
but some are still not known with certainty. Israel is conspicuous in its
absence; despite the biblical narrative's ability to trace Israel's origins,
those origins are meant to be seen not solely in biological terms but
rather in God's choice. Similarly, Israel arises from women who begin as
barren—thus pointing to divine intervention in history, rather than the
perfectly normal account that we have here.

24 **littlest:** Or "youngest," difficult in the light of verse 18.
26 **to them:** Others use "to him."
10:2 **Sons:** Here, and later, it may mean "descendants."
4 **Dodanites:** Some read "Rodanites," following I Chron. 1:7.
6 **Mitzrayim:** The biblical name for Egypt (the modern Egyptian name is
Misr).
8 **mighty man:** Three times here; clearly Nimrod was well known as an
ancient hero.
10 **Calne:** Some read *culanna*, "all of them."
11 **city squares:** Some read this as a name, "Rehovot-Ir."
14 **Casluhites . . . Caftorites:** Some reverse the order; the Bible often speaks
of the origins of the Philistines in Caftor (Crete).

15/16 Canaan begot Tzidon his firstborn and Het,/ along with the
   17   Yevusite, the Amorite and the Girgashite,/ the Hivvite,
   18   the Arkite and the Sinite,/ the Arvadite, the Tzemarite
         and the Hamatite.
         Afterward the Canaanite clans were scattered abroad.
   19 And the Canaanite territory went from Tzidon, then as you
         come toward Gerar, as far as Gaza, then as you come
         toward Sedom and Amora, Adma, and Tzevoyim, as far
         as Lasha.
   20 These are the Sons of Ham after their clans, after their
         tongues, by their lands, by their nations.

   21 (Children) were also born to Shem,
         the father of all the Sons of Ever (and) Yefet's older
         brother.
   22 The Sons of Shem are Elam and Ashur, Arpakhshad, Lud,
         and Aram.
   23 The Sons of Aram are Utz and Hul, Geter and Mash.
   24 Arpakhshad begot Shelah, Shelah begot Ever.
   25 Two sons were born to Ever:
         the name of the first one was Peleg/Splitting, for in his days
         the earth-folk were split up,
         and his brother's name was Yoktan.
26/27 Yoktan begot Almodad and Shelef, Hatzarmavet and Yera,/
28/29   Hadoram, Uzal and Dikla,/ Oval, Avimael and Sheva,/
         Ofir, Havila, and Yovav—all these are the Sons of
         Yoktan.
   30 Now their settlements went from Mesha, then as you come
         toward Sefar, to the mountain-country of the east.
   31 These are the Sons of Shem after their clans, after their
         tongues, by their lands, after their nations.

   32 These are the clan-groupings of the Sons of Noah, after
         their begettings, by their nations.
         From these the nations were divided on earth after the
         Deluge.

11:1 Now all the earth was of one language and one set-of-words.

2 And it was when they migrated to the east that they found a
valley in the land of Shinar and settled there.
3 They said, each man to his fellow:
Come-now! Let us bake bricks and let us burn them
well-burnt!
So for them brick-stone was like building-stone, and
raw-bitumen was for them like red-mortar.
4 Now they said:
Come-now! Let us build ourselves a city and a tower, its
top in the heavens,
and let us make ourselves a name,
lest we be scattered over the face of all the earth!
5 But YHWH came down to look over the city and the tower
that the humans were building.

The Unfinished Citadel (11:1–9): At its most obvious, in an isolated
context, this famous story is about the overweening pride of man, as
represented by his technology. God's actions here recall the ending of the
garden story, where humanity was also within reach of the divine.

Yet more is involved than a threat. Buber felt that this episode has
been inserted at this point to show that mankind has failed again, as at
the time of the Flood. It has not spread out and divided into nations, as
in Chapter 10. The failure paves the way for a new divine plan, which is
to be realized through one man (Avraham) and his descendants.

Structurally, the story is a tiny literary masterpiece. It utilizes numerous plays on sound which make meaningful and often ironic linkages
between sections and ideas in the text. Most significant is how the general message—that God's response occurs in exactly the same terms as
the human challenge (i.e., divine justice)— is transmitted by means of
form. Fokkelman has provided a detailed study; it will suffice here to
indicate only the outline. The divine "Come-now!" of verse 7 clearly
stands as an answer to mankind's identical cry in verses 3 and 4. In

15 **Yevusite,** etc.: Collective names.
11:1 **language;** Lit. "lip."
3 **so . . . brick-stone . . . :** An explanation of Mesopotamian building techniques for the Hebrew audience. The text plays on sound (*levena . . .
le-aven, hemer . . . la-homer*). **raw-bitumen:** Asphalt, used for making ce-
ment.
4 **make . . . a name:** That is, make sure that we and our works will endure.

6 YHWH said:
Here, (they are) one people with one language for them all,
and this is merely the first of their doings—
now there will be no barrier for them in all that they devise
to do!
7 Come-now! Let us go down and there let us baffle their
language,
so that no man will understand the language of his fellow.
8 So YHWH scattered them from there over the face of all
the earth,
and they had to stop building the city.
9 Therefore its name was called Bavel/Babble,
for there YHWH baffled the language of all the earth-folk,
and from there, YHWH scattered them over the face of all
the earth.

10 These are the begettings of Shem:
Shem was a hundred years old, then he begot Arpakhshad,
two years after the Deluge,
11 and Shem lived after he begot Arpakhshad five hundred
years, and begot other sons and daughters.
12 Arpakhshad lived thirty-five years, then he begot Shelah,
13 and Arpakhshad lived after he begot Shelah three years and
four hundred years, and begot other sons and daughters.
14 Shelah lived thirty years, then he begot Ever,
15 and Shelah lived after he begot Ever three years and four
hundred years, and begot other sons and daughters.
16 When Ever had lived thirty-four years, he begot Peleg,
17 and Ever lived after he begot Peleg thirty years and four
hundred years, and begot other sons and daughters.
18 When Peleg had lived thirty years, he begot Re'u,
19 and Peleg lived after he begot Re'u nine years and two
hundred years, and begot other sons and daughters.
20 When Re'u had lived thirty-two years, he begot Serug,
21 and Re'u lived after he begot Serug seven years and two
hundred years, and begot other sons and daughers.
22 When Serug had lived thirty years, he begot Nahor,
23 and Serug lived after he begot Nahor two hundred years,
and begot other sons and daughters.

24 When Nahor had lived twenty-nine years, he begot Terah,
25 and Nahor lived after he begot Terah nineteen years and a
   hundred years, and begot other sons and daughters.
26 When Terah had lived seventy years, he begot Avram,
   Nahor, and Haran.

27 Now these are the begettings of Terah:

---

addition man, who congregated in order to establish a "name" and to avoid being "scattered over the face of all the earth" (v.4), is contravened by the action of God, resulting in the ironic name "Babble" and a subsequent "scattering" of humanity (v.9). The text is thus another brilliant example of biblical justice, a statement about a world view in which the laws of justice and morality are as neatly balanced as we like to think the laws of nature are.

There is an important cultural background to the story. "Shinar" refers to Mesopotamia, and the "tower," undoubtedly, to the ubiquitous *ziggurratu* (now unearthed by archeologists) which served as man-made sacred mountains (i.e., temples). By portraying an unfinished tower, by dispersing the builders, and by in essence making fun of the mighty name of Babylon, the text functions effectively to repudiate the culture from which the people of Israel sprang (Avram's "Ur" of 11:28 was probably the great Mesopotamian metropolis). From Chapter 12 on, a new world view is created.

Noah to Avram (11:10–32): Here are enumerated another ten generations, making the orderly connection between the origins of the world (Noah was viewed as a second Adam) and the origins of the people of Israel. The life spans are considerably shorter than those of Chapter 5, yet some sort of careful number scheme seems evident here as well (see Cassuto).

Beginning with verse 26 we are introduced to Avram, with little hint of what is to come in his momentous life. For the moment he is only a son, a brother, and a husband, and a man whose early life is marked principally by the death of the old world (Haran and Terah), with little hope for the new (his wife is barren).

10 **two years after the Deluge:** Possibly a typical popular way of telling time
   (see Amos 1:1, "two years after the earthquake").
26 **Avram:** Trad. English "Abram."

Terah begot Avram, Nahor, and Haran;
and Haran begot Lot.

28 Haran died in the presence of Terah his father in the land
of his kindred, in Ur of the Chaldeans.

29 Avram and Nahor took themselves wives;
the name of Avram's wife was Sarai,
the name of Nahor's wife was Milca—daughter of Haran,
father of Milca and father of Yisca.

30 Now Sarai was barren, she had no child.

31 Terah took Avram his son and Lot son of Haran, his son's
son, and Sarai his daughter-in-law, wife of Avram his son,
they set out together from Ur of the Chaldeans, to go to the
land of Canaan.
But when they had come as far as Harran, they settled
there.

32 And the days of Terah were five years and two hundred
years,
then Terah died,
in Harran.

---

28 **in the presence of Terah his father:** During his father's lifetime. **Chalde-**
ans: An anachronism; see Speiser.

30 **barren, she had no child:** This doubling is characteristic of biblical style
(formal poetry in the Bible uses parallelism of lines).

31 **Harran:** An important city and center of moon worship, like Ur. The name
means "crossroads."

The Patriarchal Narratives
(PARTS II–IV)

T HE STORIES about the fathers and mothers of Israel, as a collection, are almost contrapuntal in their richness. Life experiences are repeated and common themes recur; yet at the same time there is a remarkable variety of personalities.

Two prominent themes throughout are God's promises (of land and descendants) and his blessing. The texts revolve around the question of whether and how God will fulfill his promises, and how man will effect the transfer of the blessing. Each generation portrayed in the narratives must deal with the inherent tensions raised by these questions, since their resolution does not occur easily.

The stories are also marked by each figure's struggle to develop a concept of the religious life, of "walking in accord with God." Each one carves out his own distinct path, to arrive at a mature understanding of what it means to be a father of the people of Israel. In order to bring about such an understanding, God apparently "tests" them in both obvious and more oblique ways, often against a backdrop of bitter sibling rivalry. One also observes a physical unsettledness about the Patriarchs' quest; only Yitzhak is spared the wanderings that occur so regularly in the stories.

Rather interestingly, although the texts purport to be about "fathers," it is God himself who most consistently fits that role for the characters. God acts *in loco parentis* for each of the Patriarchs, always, significantly, after the loss of the human father. He first appears to Avraham after the death of Terah; to Yitzhak after that of Avraham; to Yaakov after he leaves home (and a seemingly dying father); and he helps Yosef directly, after he has left his father's home.

Numbers play an important role in the Patriarchal stories, as they did in Part I. It has been pointed out (see Sarna) that the life spans of the Patriarchs fit into a highly ordered pattern. Avraham lives for 175 years,

45

equaling 7×5^2; Yitzhak, for 180 years, equaling 5×6^2; and Yaakov, for 147 years, or 3×7^2. This is unmistakably a purposeful scheme, meant to convey that human history is orderly and meaningful. Similarly an examination of the stories reveals that Avraham lives for 75 years in the lifetime of his father and 75 years in the lifetime of his son, while Yaakov spends 20 years away from his father, with Yosef roughly following suit in the next generation.

Last, it should be noted that the Patriarchal stories in various details anticipate the later Exodus of the Israelites from Egypt. The specific references will be mentioned in the Notes.

PART II Avraham
(12–25:18)

ALTHOUGH Avraham is the biological father of Israel, the diverse traditions about him which have been collected and connected to form a cycle of stories give evidence of much more. The cycle portrays an active *Homo religiosis* who converses with God, sometimes with an air of doubt and questioning, who proclaims God's name at various sacred sites, who is concerned about justice and the treatment of the oppressed, and who makes dramatic life decisions without flinching. The stories thus reveal struggle, despite the fact that Avraham often appears to be the "perfect" man, always obeying God's bidding and prospering.

Buber, noting the unifying effect of the verb "see" throughout the cycle, understood Avraham as the father of the Prophets of Israel (formerly called "seers"). He also viewed the cycle as based around the series of tests that Avraham must undergo, tests quite different, we might add, from the labors of Hercules and other such ancient challenges.

Other than "see," a number of leading-words launch the major concerns of the Patriarchs: "bless," "seed," and "land." At the same time the cycle contains previously encountered motifs, albeit with interesting refinements: punishment for sin (this time, with man's questioning), intimacy with God (here through visions), and sibling rivalry (with more complex results than murder). Above all we note the singling out of one man to perform the will of God, a man very different from the rather passive Noah.

Avraham stands at the core of the entire book of Genesis, as his experiences will in many ways be reflected in those who follow him. At the core of both the book and the cycle looms the disturbing Chapter 22, which brings together and resolves, for the moment, the major themes encountered so far.

12:1 YHWH said to Avram:
Go-you-forth
from your land,
from your kindred,
from your father's house,
to the land that I will let you see.
  2 I will make a great nation of you
and will give-you-blessing
and will make your name great.
Be a blessing!
  3 I will bless those who bless you,
he who reviles you, I will curse.
All the clans of the soil will find blessing through you!

  4 Avram went, as YHWH had spoken to him, and Lot went
with him.
And Avram was five years and seventy years old when he
went out of Harran.
  5 Avram took Sarai his wife and Lot his brother's son, all
their property that they had gained, and the persons
whom they had made-their-own in Harran,
and they went out to go to the land of Canaan.
When they came to the land of Canaan,
  6 Avram passed through the land, as far as the Place of
Shekhem, as far as the Oak of Moreh.
Now the Canaanite was then in the land.

  7 YHWH was seen by Avram and said:
I give this land to your seed!
He built a slaughter-site there to YHWH who had been
seen by him.
  8 He moved on from there to the mountain-country, east of
Bet-El,
and spread his tent, Bet-El toward the sea and Ai toward
the east.
There he built a slaughter-site to YHWH
and called out the name of YHWH.
  9 Then Avram journeyed on, continually journeying to the
Negev/ the Southland.

10 Now there was a famine in the land,
and Avram went down to Egypt, to sojourn there,
for the famine was heavy in the land.

11 It was when he came near to Egypt that he said to Sarai his
wife:
Now here, I know well that you are a woman fair to look
at.

12 It will be, when the Egyptians see you and say: She is his
wife,
that they will kill me, but you they will allow to live.

The Call and the Journey (12:1–9): The Avraham cycle begins decisively,
with a command from God to leave the past behind and go to an un-
named land. Prominent in this speech, clearly, is the concept of blessing,
which will be realized by the gifts of land (Canaan) and seed (Yitzhak,
the son).

The classic mythological motif of the journey, where the hero meets
such dangers as monsters and giants, has here been avoided. All that the
text wishes us to know about is God's speech and Avram's immediate
obedience; as in Chapter 22, all other details of the actual trip have been
omitted.

The Wife—I (12:10–20): Almost immediately upon his arrival in the
promised land Avram is forced to leave it. It will be his son Yitzhak's
task to remain there on a more permanent basis.

This is the first of three such stories which are practically identical (see
Chapters 20 and 26). All pose a challenge for the interpreter. An honored

12:1 **kindred:** Others use "birthplace."
3 **find blessing:** Or "seek to be blessed (as you)."
5 **property . . . gained:** Heb. *rekhusham . . . rakhashu.*
6 **Place:** Possibly with the implication of "sacred place." **Oak:** Some read
"valley." **Moreh:** Some, like Buber, interpret this as "sage." **the Canaanite:** The peoples inhabiting the land at the time of the Israelite conquest under Joshua; see also 13:7.
7 **was seen:** Others use "appeared to," which is more comfortable in English. "See" has been kept here as a leading word in the Avraham cycle.
8 **toward the sea:** West.
10 **sojourn:** To reside temporarily, as an alien. **heavy:** Severe.

13 Pray say that you are my sister
so that it may go well with me on your account, that I
myself may live thanks to you.

14 It was when Avram came to Egypt, that the Egyptians saw
how exceedingly fair the woman was;

15 when Pharaoh's courtiers saw her, they praised her to
Pharaoh,
and the woman was taken away into Pharaoh's house.

16 It went well with Avram on her account,
sheep and oxen, he-asses, servants and maids, she-asses and
camels, became his.

17 But YHWH plagued Pharaoh with great plagues, and also
his house, because of Sarai, Avram's wife.

18 Pharaoh had Avram called, and said:
What is this that you have done to me!
Why did you not tell me that she is your wife?

19 Why did you say: She is my sister?
—So I took her for myself as a wife.
But now, here is your wife, take her and go!

20 So Pharaoh put men in charge of him, who escorted him
and his wife and all that was his.

13:1 Avram traveled up from Egypt, he and his wife and all that
was his, and Lot with him, to the Southland.

2 And Avram was exceedingly heavily laden with livestock,
with silver and with gold.

3 He went on his journeyings from the Southland as far as
Bet-El, as far as the place where his tent had been at the
first, between Bet-El and Ai,

4 to the place of the slaughter-site that he had made there at
the beginning.
There Avram called out the name of YHWH.

5 Now also Lot, who had gone with Avram, had sheep and
oxen and tents.

6 And the land could not support them, to settle together,
for their property was so great that they were not able to
settle together.

7 So there was a quarrel between the herdsmen of Avram's
   livestock and the herdsmen of Lot's livestock.
   Now the Canaanite and the Perizzite were then settled in
   the land.
8 Avram said to Lot:
   Pray let there be no quarreling between me and you,
     between my herdsmen and your herdsmen,
   for we are brother men!

---

man of God seeks to save his own skin by passing his wife off as his
sister; in each case the Patriarch emerges safely and with increased
wealth.

Speiser has tried to use the analogy of Hurrian (i.e., from Harran) law
in which a wife can be elevated to the status of "sister" as one element in
the expansion of her status. The legal background, however, is unclear
and may not be decisive here. Coming as it does after God's promise to
biologically found "a great nation" (v.2) through Avram, the story in its
first version is probably best understood as an example of God's protection not only of the key male figure, but of the Matriarch as well.
Harming Sarai, or even the threat of violating her sexuality, brings with
it divine punishment. In addition the story also enables Avram to expand
his wealth—itself a sign of God's favor and the Patriarch's importance or
"weightiness" (see Polzin).

Lot; The Land (13): We return to the theme of the land. Not for the last
time, Avram's nephew Lot is used as a foil. Their "parting" shows how
Lot makes a bad choice—the "wicked and sinful" area of Sedom and
Amora—while Avram settles "in the land of Canaan," which had been
promised to him. From here (vv.14ff.), Avram is given God's twofold
promise again, with that of descendants being spelled out more vividly
this time.

This section is linked to the previous one by the repetition of the
phrase "he and his wife and all that was his."

15 **Pharaoh:** Heb. *Par'o*. This is an Egyptian title, "(Lord of) the Great
    House," and not a name.
13:2 **heavily laden:** Rich.
   8 **brother men:** Relatives.

9 Is not all the land before you?
Pray part from me!
If to the left, then I go to the right,
if to the right, then I to the left.

10 Lot lifted up his eyes and saw all the plain of the Jordan—
how well-watered was it all, before YHWH brought ruin
upon Sedom and Amora,
like YHWH's garden, like the land of Egypt, as you come
toward Tzo'ar.

11 So Lot chose for himself all the plain of the Jordan.
Lot journeyed eastward, and they parted, each man from
the other:

12 Avram settled in the land of Canaan, while Lot settled in
the cities of the plain, pitching-his-tent near Sedom.

13 Now the men of Sedom were exceedingly wicked and sinful
before YHWH.

14 YHWH said to Avram, after Lot had parted from him:
Pray lift up your eyes and see from the place where you are,
northward, southward, eastward, seaward:

15 indeed, all the land that you see, I give it to you
and to your seed, for the ages.

16 I will make your seed like the dust of the ground,
so that if a man were able to measure the dust of the
ground, so too could your seed be measured.

17 Up, walk about through the land in its length and in its
breadth,
for I give it to you.

18 Avram moved-his-tent and came and settled by the oaks of
Mamre, which are by Hevron.
There he built a slaughter-site to YHWH.

14:1 Now it was in the days of Amrafel king of Shinar, Aryokh
king of Ellasar, Kedorla'omer king of Elam, and Tidal
king of Goyim:

2 They prepared for battle against Bera king of Sedom, Birsha
king of Amora, Shinav king of Adma, Shemever king of
Tzevoyim, and the king of Bela—that is now Tzo'ar.

3 All these joined together in the valley of
Siddim/Limestone—that is now the Salt Sea.

4 For twelve years they had been subservient to
   Kedorla'omer,
   and in the thirteenth year they had revolted,
5 but then in the fourteenth year came Kedorla'omer and the
   kings who were with him,
   they struck the Refaites in Ashterot-Karnayim, the Zuzites
6   in Ham, the Emites in Shaveh-Kiryatayim, and the/
   Horites in their mountain-country of Se'ir near El Paran,
   which is by the wilderness.
7 As they returned, they came to En Mishpat/Judgment
   Spring—that is now Kadesh,
   and struck all the territory of the Amalekites and also the
   Amorites, who were settled in Hatzatzon-Tamar.

War and Rescue (14): Abruptly Avram is presented in a new light: that of
successful warrior (see Muffs). Consistent with his character as we will
come to know it, he stands by his kinsman, acts intrepidly, and refuses
the spoils of war. Equally important, he is respected by foreigners, a
theme will will return both in Genesis and later. Perhaps this very different story has been included here as part of the early sections of the cycle
in order to establish Avram's status and stature. He is no longer merely a
wanderer but well on the road to becoming a powerful local figure.

The whether the events described in this chapter are historical or part of
an elaborate symbolic or mythical scheme has been the subject of debate
among biblical scholars. The issue, barring unexpected archeological
finds, is likely to remain unsolved.

The story is constructed around a geographical framework, using the
formula "—that is now *x*—" to identify older sites for a contemporary
audience. The one place which is *not* identified, the "Shalem" of verse
18, may well be Jerusalem. If so, this would substantiate the city's claim
to holiness. Historically it was not conquered until King David's reign in
the tenth century B.C.E.

9 **before you:** Possibly a legal term concerning boundaries. **left . . . right:**
   North and south.
10 **YHWH brought ruin:** See Chapter 19. **Sedom and Amora:** Trad. English "Sodom and Gomorrah."
14 **seaward:** Westward.
14:3 **the Salt Sea:** The Dead Sea.

8 Then out marched the king of Sedom, the king of Amora,
   the king of Adma, the king of Tzevoyim, and the king of
   Bela—that is now Tzo'ar;
   they set-their-ranks against them in battle in the valley of
   Siddim,
9 against Kedorla'omer king of Elam, Tidal king of Goyim,
   Amrafel king of Shinar, and Aryokh king of Ellasar—
   four kings against the five.
10 Now the valley of Siddim is pit after pit of bitumen,
   and when the kings of Sedom and Amora fled, they flung
   themselves therein,
   while those who remained fled to the mountain-country.
11 Now they took all the property of Sedom and Amora and all
   their food, and went away,
12 and they took Lot and all his property—the son of Avram's
   brother—and went away,
   for he had settled in Sedom.
13 One who escaped came and told Avram the Hebrew—
   he was dwelling by the Oaks of Mamre the Amorite,
   brother of Eshcol and brother of Aner,
   they were Avram's covenant-allies.
14 When Avram heard that his brother had been taken
   prisoner,
   he drew out his retainers, his house-born slaves, eighteen
   and three hundred, and went in pursuit as far as Dan.
15 He split up (his forces) against them in the night, he and
   his servants, and struck them and pursued them as far as
   Hova, which is to the north of Damascus.
16 But he returned all the property, and he also returned his
   brother Lot and his property, and also the women and the
   other people.
17 The king of Sedom went out to meet him upon his return
   from the strike against Kedorla'omer and against the
   kings that were with him, to the valley of Shaveh—that is
   now the King's Valley.

18 Now Malki-Tzedek, king of Shalem, brought out bread and
   wine,

—for he was priest of God Most-High,
19 and gave him blessing and said:
Blessed be Avram by God Most-High,
Founder of Heaven and Earth!
20 And blessed be God Most-High,
who has delivered your oppressors into your hand!
He gave him a tenth of everything.

21 The king of Sedom said to Avram:
Give me the persons, and the property take for yourself.
22 Avram said to the king of Sedom:
I raise my hand in the presence of YHWH, God
Most-High,
Founder of Heaven and Earth,
23 if from a thread to a sandal-strap—if I should take from
anything that is yours . . . !
So that you should not say: I made Avram rich.
24 Nothing for me!
Only what the lads have consumed,
and the share of the men who went with me—Aner, Eshcol,
and Mamre,
let them take their share.

---

10 **bitumen:** Asphalt.   **flung themselves:** Others use "fell."
12 **—the son of Avram's brother—:** The Hebrew places the phrase after
"property," not after "Lot," as would be comfortable in English.   **for he
had settled:** The story abounds in similar explanatory phrases, which could
almost be put in parentheses.
14 **brother:** Kinsman.
15 **North:** lit., "left."
18 **Malki-Tzedek:** Trad. English "Melchizedek." The name is a Hebrew one,
and the character appears as if from nowhere.   **Shalem:** Identified with the
later Jerusalem.   **God Most-High:** Heb. *El Elyon*.
20 **a tenth:** Like the tithe later given to Israelite priests.
22 **I raise my hand:** I swear.
23 **from a thread to a sandal-strap:** As in "from A to Z," or "anything at all."
24 **lads:** Servants.

15:1 After these event YHWH's word came to Avram in a
    vision,
    saying:
    Be not afraid, Avram,
    I am a delivering-shield to you,
    your reward is exceedingly great.
  2 Avram said:
    My Lord, YHWH,
    what would you give me—
    for I am going (to die) disgraced,
    and the Son Domestic of My House is Damascan Eliezer.
  3 And Avram said further:
    Here, to me you have not given seed,
    here, the Son of My House must be my heir.
  4 But here, YHWH's word (came) to him, saying:
    This one shall not be heir to you,
    rather, the one that goes out from your own body, he shall
      be heir to you.
  5 He brought him outside and said:
    Pray look toward the heavens and count the stars,
    can you count them?
    And he said to him:
    So shall your seed be.
  6 Now he trusted in YHWH,
    and he deemed it as righteousness on his part.

  7 Now he said to him:
    I am YHWH
    who brought you out of Ur of the Chaldeans
    to give you this land, to inherit it.
  8 But he said:
    My Lord, YHWH,
    by what shall I know that I will inherit it?
  9 He said to him:
    Fetch me a calf of three, a she-goat of three, a ram of three,
      a turtle-dove, and a fledgling.
 10 He fetched him all these.

He halved them down the middle, putting each one's half
   toward its fellow,
but the birds he did not halve.
11 Vultures descended upon the carcasses,
   but Avram drove them back.
12 Now it was, when the sun was setting,
   that deep slumber fell upon Avram—
   and here, fright and great darkness falling upon him!

The Covenant between the Pieces (15): Amid scenes of great drama and
almost mystery, a number of significant motifs are presented: (1) Avram's expressions of doubt that God will keep his promise about descendants (thus heightening the tension and final miracle of Yitzhak's birth);
(2) the linking of the Patriarch to the event of the Exodus centuries later;
and (3) the "cutting" of a covenant, in a manner well known in the
ancient world. This last motif, especially with its setting of "great darkness" and "night-blackness," takes Avram far beyond the earlier figure
of Noah into a special and fateful relationship with God.

15:1 **YHWH's word came:** A formula often used by the Prophets. Avram is
   portrayed as their spiritual ancestor (Buber).
2 **disgraced:** Heb. *ariri;* B-R uses "bare-of-children." **Son Domestic . . .
   Damascan:** Hebrew difficult. The translation here reflects the play on
   sound (Heb. *"ben meshek . . . dammesek"*).
3 **Son of My House:** The chief servant, who could inherit the estate in
   certain circumstances. Note the play on "son": the Hebrew here is *ben beti,*
   while *ben* alone means "son." **heir:** Three times here, indicating Avram's
   main concern.
6 **he deemed it:** "He" refers to God.
7 **who brought you out:** Like the later "I am YHWH your God, who
   brought you out of the land of Egypt" (Ex. 20:2). The language is undoubtedly intentional.
8 **But he said:** Avram, having just demonstrated trust in verse 6, now expresses deep doubt.
9 **of three:** I.e., three years old, and presumably mature and ritually fit for
   sacrifice.
12 **deep slumber:** Not the conventional sleep, it is almost always sent by God
   in the Bible (see 2:21, for example). The result here is "fright and great
   darkness."

13 And he said to Avram:
   You must know, yes, know
   that your seed will be sojourners in a land not theirs;
   they will put them in servitude and afflict them
   for four hundred years.
14 But the nation to which they are in servitude—I will bring
      judgment on them,
   and after that they will go out with great property.
15 As for you, you will go to your fathers in peace;
   you will be buried at a good ripe-age.
16 But in the fourth generation they will return here,
   for the punishment of the Amorite has not been paid-in-full
      heretofore.
17 Now it was, when the sun had set,
   that there was night-blackness,
   and here, a smoking oven, a fiery torch
   that crossed between those pieces.

18 On that day
   YHWH cut a covenant with Avram,
   saying: I give this land to your seed,
   from the River of Egypt to the Great River, the river
      Euphrates,
19 the Kenite and the Kenizzite and the Kadmonite,
20 and the Hittite and the Perizzite and the Refaites,
21 and the Amorite and the Canaanite and the Girgashite and
      the Yevusite.

16:1 Now Sarai, Avram's wife, had not borne him (children).
   She had an Egyptian maid—her name was Hagar.
 2 Sarai said to Avram:
   Now here, YHWH has obstructed me from bearing;
   pray come in to my maid,
   perhaps I may be built-up-with-sons through her!
   Avram hearkened to Sarai's voice:
 3 Sarai, Avram's wife, took Hagar the Egyptian-woman, her
      maid,
   at the end of ten years of Avram's being settled in the land
      of Canaan,

and gave her to her husband Avram as a wife for him.
4 He came in to Hagar, and she became pregnant.
But when she saw that she was pregnant, her mistress
   became of light worth in her eyes.
5 Sarai said to Avram:
The wrong done me is upon you!
I myself gave my maid into your bosom,
but now that she sees that she is pregnant, I have become of
   light worth in her eyes.
May YHWH see-justice-done between me and you!

The Firstborn Son (16): In the face of Sarai's inability to bear children,
Avram is given the legitimate option of producing an heir through her
maid, Hagar. Somewhat embarrassing to later interpreters, this practice
was nevertheless common in the ancient Near East (see also 30:3ff.,
30:9ff.). Hagar abuses her temporarily exalted position (as her son Yishmael apparently does in a parallel story, in Chapter 21), but is saved by
God's intervention. The motif of "affliction" is continued from Chapter
15 (here, in vv.6, 9, and 11); also mentioned three times is God's "hearkening" (hence the name Yishmael/God Hearkens). Buber understood this
vocabulary to allude to the Exodus story, which in its early chapters uses
the same terms.
  Although Yishmael is not ultimately the chosen heir, he is nonetheless
protected by God (see 21:20) and is eventually made into "a great nation" (17:20), as befits a child of Avram.

13 **afflict:** Looking toward the "affliction" of the Israelites in Egypt (Ex. 1:11,
   12).
15 **ripe-age:** Lit. "grayness" or "hoariness."
16 **But in the fourth generation . . . :** God here speaks of the future conquest
   of Canaan by Avram's descendants. The natives (here termed "Amorites")
   are viewed as having forfeited their right to the land by their immorality
   (see Lev. 18:25–8).
18 **cut:** Concluded; the usage is influenced by the act of cutting animals by the
   parties involved, as in this story.
19 **the Kenite . . . :** Canaanite tribes, here presented as a round ten in number.
16:2 **built-up-with-sons:** Heb. *ibbane,* a play on *bano* (build) and *ben* (son).
   3 **wife:** Or "concubine."
   4 **became of light worth in her eyes:** A Hebrew idiom. *New Jewish Version:*
   "was lowered in her esteem."

6 Avram said to Sarai:
   Here, your maid is in your hand, deal with her however
   seems good in your eyes.
   Sarai afflicted her, so that she had to flee from her.
7 But YHWH's messenger found her by a spring of water in
   the wilderness, by the spring on the way to Shur.
8 He said:
   Hagar, Sarai's maid, whence do you come, whither are you
   going?
   She said:
   I am fleeing from Sarai my mistress.
9 YHWH's messenger said to her:
   Return to your mistress and let yourself be afflicted under
   her hand!
10 And YHWH's messenger said to her:
   I will make your seed many, yes, many, it will be too many
   to count!
11 And YHWH's messenger said to her:
   Here, you are pregnant,
   you will bear a son;
   call his name: Yishmael/God Hearkens,
   for God has hearkened to your being afflicted.
12 He shall be a wild-ass of a man,
   his hand against all, hand of all against him,
   yet in the presence of all his brothers shall he dwell.
13 Now she called the name of YHWH, the one who was
      speaking to her:
   You God of Seeing!
   For she said:
   Have I actually gone on seeing here
   after his seeing me?
14 Therefore the well was called:
   Well of the Living-One Who-Sees-Me.
   Here, it is between Kadesh and Bered.

15 Hagar bore Avram a son,
   and Avram called the name of the son whom Hagar bore:
   Yishmael.
16 Avram was eighty years and six years when Hagar bore
   Yishmael to Avram.

17:1 Now whem Avram was ninety years and nine years,
     YHWH was seen by Avram and said to him:
     I am God Shaddai.
     Walk in my presence! And be whole!
   2 I set my covenant between me and you,
     I will make you exceedingly, exceedingly many.

The Covenant of Circumcision (17): As Plaut notes, up to this point the covenant betwen God and Avram has been rather one-sided. In this chapter Avram is given a command to perform—not only of circumcision, but to be moral and upright (v.1, expanded in 18:19). Circumcision is but the symbol of the ongoing imperative to do "what is just."

In many societies circumcision has been connected directly to puberty and marriage, usually taking place (as it does here to Yishmael) at around the age of thirteen. Our passage's moving back of the rite essentially to birth is a daring reinterpretation, at once defusing the act of exclusively sexual content while at the same time suggesting that the covenant, a lifelong commitment, is nevertheless passed down biologically through the generations. The males of the tribe are not simply made holy for marriage. They bear the mark upon their bodies as a sacred reminder of their mission.

The chapter echoes with repetition: "exceedingly, exceedingly" (vv.6

6 **afflicted:** Or "abused," "maltreated."
7 **YHWH's messenger:** Traditionally "angel," but the English word stems from the Greek *angelos,* which also means "messenger." In Genesis God's messengers seem to be quite human in appearance, and are sometimes taken for God himself (see 18:2ff.).
10 **too many to count:** Apparently fulfilling God's blessing and promise to Avram in 15:5. Until 17:16, nothing indicates that Yishmael is not Avram's long-awaited heir.
11 **Yishmael:** Trad. English "Ishmael."
13 **Have I actually gone on seeing . . . :** Heb. obscure. Hagar possibly is expressing surprise that she survived her encounter with God.
17:1 **Ninety years and nine years:** Thirteen years have elapsed since the events of the previous chapter. Now that Yishmael is entering puberty, God can no longer conceal that he is not the promised heir. See verses 16, 18. **Shaddai:** Hebrew obscure. Traditionally translated "Almighty"; others use "of the mountains." In Genesis the name is most often tied to promises of human fertility, as in verse 2. **Walk . . . be whole:** Contrasted to Noah (6:9), Avram is a genuine religious man who lives his faith actively.
2 **set:** Heb. *va-ettena.* The root *ntn* is repeated throughout the chapter (as "make" in verses 5 and 6, and as "give" in verses 8 and 16).

3 Avram fell upon his face.
God spoke with him,
saying:
4 As for me,
here, my covenant is with you,
so that you will become the father of a throng of nations.
5   No longer shall your name be called Avram,
rather shall your name be Avraham,
for I will make you *Av Hamon Goyyim*/Father of a
Throng of Nations!
6 I will cause you to bear fruit exceedingly, exceedingly,
I will make nations of you,
(yes,) kings will go out from you!
7 I establish my covenant between me and you and your seed
after you, into their generations as a covenant for the
ages,
to be God to you and to your seed after you.
8 I will give to you and to your seed after you, the land of
your sojournings, all the land of Canaan, as a holding for
the ages,
and I will be God to them.
9 God said to Avraham:
As for you,
you are to keep my covenant, you and your seed after you,
into their generations.
10 This is my covenant which you are to keep, between me
and you and your seed after you:
every male among you shall be circumcised.
11 You shall circumcise the flesh of your foreskin,
so that it may serve as a sign of the covenant between me
and you.
12 At eight days old, every male among you shall be
circumcised, into your generations,
whether house-born or bought with money from any
foreigner, who is not your seed.
13 Circumcised, yes, circumcised shall be your house-born and
your money-bought (slaves),
so that my covenant may be in your flesh as a covenant for
the ages.

14 But a foreskinned male,
   who does not have the foreskin of his flesh circumcised,
   that person shall be cut off from his kinspeople—
   he has broken my covenant!
15 God said to Avraham:
   As for Sarai your wife—you shall not call her name Sarai,
   for Sara/Princess is her name!
16 I will bless her, and I will give you a son from her,
   I will bless her
   so that she becomes nations,
   kings of peoples shall come from her!
17 But Avraham fell on his face and laughed,
   he said in his heart:
            To a hundred-year-old man shall there be (children)
              born?
            Or shall ninety-year-old Sara give birth?

---

and 20, referring to the fruitfulness of Avram's descendants), "you and
your seed after you" (vv.7, 10; see also v.19), "for the ages" (covenant
and land, vv.7, 8, 13, 19), and "into your generations" (vv.7, 9, 12).
   Preparatory to Avram's assumption of fatherhood—of an individual
and of a people—his name is changed (v.5), as is that of Sarai (v.15).
This act is of the utmost significance in the biblical world. Since a
person's name was indicative of personality and fate, the receiving of a
new one signified a new life or a new stage in life. Similarly, Yaakov (and
in a sort of coronation, Yosef) will undergo a change of name. Such a
practice still survives among kings and popes.

   4 **throng:** The word suggests the sound of a crowd, rather than merely a large
     number.
   5 **Avraham:** Trad. English "Abraham."
   8 **I will be God to them:** Often reiterated as part of the biblical covenant
     (e.g., 28:21).
  12 **house-born or bought with money:** I.e., slaves. The entire household, as
     an extension of the man's personality, is to be brought into the covenant.
  15 **you shall not call her name Sarai:** Significantly, Sara is the only woman in
     the Bible to have her name changed by God.
  16 **so that she becomes nations:** Sara in essence shares the blessing of God.
     She is not merely the biological means for its fulfillment.
  17 **laughed:** Laughter becomes the key word of most of the stories about
     Yitzhak.

18 Avraham said to God:
   If only Yishmael might live in your presence!
19 God said:
   Nevertheless,
   Sara your wife is to bear you a son,
   you shall call his name: Yitzhak/He Laughs.
   I will establish my covenant with him as a covenant for the
      ages, for his seed after him.
20 And as for Yishmael, I hearken to you:
   Here, I will make him blessed, I will make him bear fruit, I
      will make him exceedingly, exceedingly many—
   he will beget twelve princes, and I will make a great nation
      of him.
21 But my covenant I will establish with Yitzhak, whom Sara
      will bear to you at this set-time, another year hence.
22 When he had finished speaking with Avraham,
   God went up, from beside Avraham.

23 Avraham took Yishmael his son and all those born in his
      house and all those bought with his money,
   all the males among Avraham's household people,
   and circumcised the flesh of their foreskins on that very
      day,
   as God had spoken to him.
24 Avraham was ninety-nine years old when he had the flesh of
      his foreskin circumcised,
25 and Yishmael his son was thirteen years old when he had
      the flesh of his foreskin circumcised.
26 On that very day
   were circumcised Avraham and Yishmael his son,
27 and all his household people, whether house-born or
      money-bought from a foreigner, were circumcised with
      him.

18:1 Now YHWH was seen by him by the oaks of Mamre
      as he was sitting at the entrance to his tent at the heat of
         the day.
   2 He lifted up his eyes and saw:
      here, three men standing over against him.

When he saw them, he ran to meet them from the entrance
   to his tent and bowed to the earth
3 and said:
My lords,
pray if I have found favor in your eyes,
pray do not pass by your servant!
4 Pray let a little water be fetched, then wash your feet and
   recline under the tree;
5 let me fetch (you) a bit of bread, that you may refresh your
   hearts,
then afterward you may pass on—
for you have, after all, passed your servant's way!
They said:
Do thus, as you have spoken.

Visit and Promise (18:1–15): The announcement of Sara's impending
child is set in the familiar ancient garb of a tale about divine travelers
who visit an old couple. Central, as is usual in folklore, is the idea of
hospitality, emphasized in the text by the threefold use of "pray"
(please) (vv.3–4), "pass on/by" (vv.3–5), and by Avraham's flurry of
activity (he himself "runs" twice, "hastens" three times, and "fetches"
four times in serving his guests).

19 **Yitzhak:** Trad. English "Isaac."
20 **make him blessed . . . make him bear fruit . . . make him . . . many:**
   Heb. *berakhti oto ve-hifreti oto ve-hirbeti oto.* **twelve princes:** Thus equaling the twelve sons/tribes of Israel?
21 **another year:** Not nine months (Sara does not immediately become pregnant). Again the events seem to take place in a realistic framework, rather
   than in a strictly supernatural one.
22 **God went up, from beside Avraham:** Perhaps a formula used to signify the
   end of the conversation.
23 **on that very day:** Underlining Avraham's customary obedience. **as God
   had spoken to him:** Like Noah in 6:22, 7:5, and 7:9, Avraham scrupu-
   lously follows God's commands without question (so too in 21:4 and 22:3).
18:1 **entrance to his tent:** Also used in verses 2 and 10, it may hint at the
   important events being portrayed: the "entrance to the tent" is often a
   sacred spot in subsequent books of the Bible.
2 **three men:** See note on 16:7. **over against him:** Heb. *alav* could mean
   "over" or "next to" him.
3 **My lords:** Some use "My Lord."
4 **wash your feet:** Customary for weary travelers in the ancient world.

6 Avraham hastened into his tent to Sara and said:
Make haste! Three measures of choice flour! Knead it,
  make bread-cakes!
7 Avraham ran to the oxen,
he fetched a young ox, tender and fine, and gave it to a
  serving-lad, that he might hasten to make it ready;
8 then he fetched cream and milk and the young ox that he
  had made ready, and placed it before them.
Now he stood over against them under the tree while they
  ate.
9 They said to him:
Where is Sara your wife?
He said:
Here in the tent.
Now he said:
10 I will return, yes, return to you when time revives,
and Sara your wife will have a son!
Now Sara was listening at the entrance to the tent, which
  was behind him.
11 And Avraham and Sara were old, advanced in days,
the way of women had ceased for Sara.
12 Sara laughed within herself, saying:
After I have become worn, is there to be pleasure for me?
  And my lord is old!
13 But YHWH said to Avraham:
Now why does Sara laugh and say: Shall I really give birth,
  now that I am old?
14 Is anything beyond YHWH?
At that set-time I will return to you, when time revives,
and Sara will have a son.
15 Sara pretended otherwise, saying:
No, I did not laugh.
For she was afraid.
But he said:
No, indeed you laughed.

16 The men arose from there, and looked down upon the face
  of Sedom,
and Avraham went with them to escort them.

17 Now YHWH had said to himself:
Shall I cover up from Avraham what I am about to do?

18 For Avraham is to become, yes, become a great and
numerous nation,
and all the nations of the earth will find blessing through
him.

19 Indeed, I have known him,
in order that he may charge his sons and his household after
him:
they shall keep the way of YHWH,
to do what is right and just,
in order that YHWH may bring upon Avraham what he
spoke concerning him.

The Great Intercession (18:16–33): With verse 17 the narrative is inter-rupted, and there begins a remarkable scene in which man confronts God. As if to emphasize the importance of this encounter, the text pre-sents God as thinking out loud, and using the intimate term "know" (see 4:1) to describe his relationship to Avraham. And Avraham, the man through whom the nations "will find blessing" (v.18; see 12:3), the progenitor of "a great . . . nation" (v.18; see 12:2) that will see in justice its great goal, is now confronted with an urgent question of justice. While Avraham seems to be testing God in this story, it may in fact be precisely the reverse that is intended. Perhaps here more than anywhere else in the entire cycle (with the possible exception of Chapter 22), Avraham appears as the worthy father of his people, the one who will "charge his sons and his household . . . to do what is right and just" (v.19). Without this story Avraham would be a man of faith but not a man of compassion and moral outrage, a model consistent with Moses and the Prophets of Israel.

The tightly structured, almost formal dialogue allows us to focus to-tally on the issue at hand. Predominating as refrains are the words "inno-cent" and "guilty," along with the expected versions of "just/justice" that pervade Avraham's remarks.

10 **when time revives:** An idiom for "next year." B-R uses "at the time of life-bestowing."

11 **the way of women:** The menstrual period.

12 **pleasure:** Sexual.

20 So YHWH said:
   The outcry in Sedom and Amora—how great it is!
   And their sin—how exceedingly heavily it weighs!
21 Now let me go down and see:
   if they have done according to its cry that has come to me—
   destruction!
   And if not—
   I wish to know.
22 The men turned from there and went toward Sedom,
   but Avraham still stood in the presence of YHWH.
23 Avraham came close and said:
   Will you really sweep away the innocent along with the
       guilty?
24 Perhaps there are fifty innocent within the city,
   will you really sweep it away?
   Will you not bear with the place because of the fifty
       innocent that are in its midst?
25 Heaven forbid for you to do a thing like this,
   to deal death to the innocent along with the guilty,
   that it should come about: like the innocent, like the guilty,
   Heaven forbid for you!
   The judge of all the earth—will he not do what is just?
26 YHWH said:
   If I find in Sedom fifty innocent within the city,
   I will bear with the whole place for their sake.
27 Avraham answered, and said:
   Now pray, I have ventured to speak to my Lord,
   and I am but earth and ashes:
28 Perhaps of the fifty innocent, five will be lacking—
   will you bring ruin upon the whole city because of the five?
   He said:
   I will not bring ruin, if I find there forty-five.
29 But he continued to speak to him, and said:
   Perhaps there will be found there only forty!
   He said:
   I will not do it, for the sake of the forty.
30 But he said:
   Pray let not my Lord be enraged that I speak further:
   Perhaps there will be found there only thirty!

He said:
I will not do it, if I find there thirty.
31 But he said:
Now pray, I have ventured to speak to my Lord:
Perhaps there will be found there only twenty!
He said:
I will not bring ruin, for the sake of the twenty.
32 But he said:
Pray let my Lord not be enraged that I speak further just
    this one time:
Perhaps there will be found there only ten!
He said:
I will not bring ruin, for the sake of the ten.
33 YHWH went, as soon as he had finished speaking to
    Avraham, and Avraham returned to his place.

19:1 The two messengers came to Sedom at evening,
as Lot was sitting at the gate of Sedom.
When Lot saw them, he arose to meet them and bowed
    low, brow to the ground
2 and said:
Now pray, my lords,
pray turn aside to your servant's house,
spend the night, wash your feet;
early tomorrow you may continue on your journey.

---

21 **destruction:** Some read "altogether (according to its cry)."
22 **but Avraham still stood in the presence of YHWH:** Some manuscripts
read "But YHWH still stood in the presence of Avraham." The subject of
the sentence has been reversed by scribes who were uncomfortable with the
passage's human portrayal of God.
25 **Heaven forbid:** Lit. "May you have a curse," an ironic turn of phrase in
this situation. **like the innocent, like the guilty:** Or "innocent and guilty
alike."
26 **bear with:** Or "bear the sin," "forgive."
27 **earth and ashes:** Heb. *afar va-efer,* traditionally "dust and ashes." The
phrase, while common in English, is used in the Bible again only in Job
(30:19, 42:6).
33 **YHWH went:** See note on 17:22.

They said:

No, rather we will spend the night in the square.

3 But he pressed them exceedingly hard,
so they turned in to him and came into his house.
He made them a meal-with-drink and baked flat-cakes, and
they ate.

4 They had not yet lain down, when the men of the city, the
men of Sedom, encircled the house,
from young lad to old man, all the people (even) from the
outskirts.

5 They called out to Lot and said to him:
Where are the men who came to you tonight?
Bring them out to us, we want to know them!

6 Lot went out to them, to the entrance, shutting the door
behind him

7 and said:
Pray, brothers, do not be so wicked!

8 Now pray, I have two daughters who have never known a
man,
pray let me bring them out to you, and you may deal with
them however seems good in your eyes;
only to these men do nothing,
for they have, after all, come under the shadow of my
roof-beam!

9 But they said:
Step aside!
and said:
This one came to sojourn, and here he would act-the-judge
and adjudicate?!
Now we will treat you more wickedly than them!
And they pressed exceedingly hard against the man, against
Lot, and stepped closer to break down the door.

10 But the men put out their hand and brought Lot in to
them, into the house, and shut the door.

11 And the men who were at the entrance to the house, they
struck with dazzling-light—(all men) great and small,
so that they were unable to find the entrance.

12 The men said to Lot:
Whom else have you here—a son-in-law, sons, daughters?

Bring anyone whom you have in the city out of the place!
13 For we are about to bring ruin on this place,
   for how great is their outcry before YHWH!
   And YHWH has sent us to bring it to ruin.
14 Lot went out to speak to his sons-in-law, those who had
      taken his daughters (in marriage), and said:
   Up, out of this place, for YHWH is about to bring ruin on
      the city!
   But in the eyes of his sons-in-law, he was like one who
      jests.
15 Now when the dawn rose,
   the messengers pushed Lot on, saying:
   Up, take your wife and your two daughters who are here,
   lest you be swept away in the punishment of the city!
16 When he lingered,
   the men seized his hand, his wife's hand, and the hand of
      his two daughters
   —because YHWH's pity was upon him—
   and, bringing him out, they left him outside the city.

The End of Sedom and Amora (19): The detailed and colorful story of Lot
in Sedom and in flight from it adds a great deal to the Avraham cycle.
On the one hand there is the portrayal of Lot's continuing his uncle's
tradition of hospitality (vv.1–3), even to the extent of being willing to
sacrifice his own daughters' virginity. On the other hand Lot comes
across as timid (vv.7–8) and fearful (vv.18–20). In fact the word "pray"
(which we noted in Chapter 18 as a "hospitality term," and which serves
that function in verse 2 here as well) is used later in this chapter in a way
that almost suggests whining. He thus once again brings Avraham's
personality into sharper focus.

The crimes of Sedom and Amora are at last indicated more openly:
abuse of the sacred duty of hospitality, and sexual immorality (v.5). The

19:5 **we want to know them:** The meaning is unmistakably sexual.
   8 **pray let me bring them out to you . . . :** For a similar story, see Judges 19.
      There the offer of rape is accepted by the townspeople.
   9 **act-the-judge and adjudicate:** Heb. *shafot yishpot.*
  10 **the men:** The messengers.
  11 **(all men) great and small:** Lit. "from small to great."

17 It was, when they had brought him outside, that (one of
   them) said:
   Escape for your life, do not gaze behind you, do not stand
   still anywhere in the plain:
   to the mountain-country escape, lest you be swept away!
18 Lot said to them:
   No, pray, my lord!
19 Now pray, your servant has found favor in your eyes,
   you have shown great faithfulness in how you have dealt
   with me, keeping me alive—
   but I, I am not able to escape to the mountain-country,
   lest the wickedness cling to me, and I die!
20 Now pray, that town is near enough to flee to, and it is so
   tiny;
   pray let me escape there—is it not tiny?—and stay alive!
21 He said to him:
   Here then, I lift up your face in this matter as well,
   by not overturning this town of which you speak.
22 Make haste, escape there,
   for I am not able to do anything until you come there.
   Therefore the name of the town was called: Tzo'ar/Tiny.
23 (Now) the sun was going out over the earth as Lot came to
   Tzo'ar.
24 But YHWH rained down brimstone and fire upon Sedom
   and Amora, coming from YHWH, from the heavens,
25 he overturned those cities and all of the plain, all those
   settled in the cities and the vegetation of the soil.
26 Now his wife gazed behind him, and she became a pillar of
   salt.

27 Early in the morning Avraham (arose) to the place where he
   had stood in YHWH's presence,
28 he looked down upon the face of Sedom and Amora and
   upon the whole face of the plain-country
   and saw:
   here, the dense-smoke of the land ascended like the
   dense-smoke of a furnace!

29 Thus it was, when God brought ruin on the cities of the
   plain,

that God kept Avraham in mind and sent out Lot from the
   overturning,
when he overturned the cities where Lot had settled.

30 Lot went up from Tzo'ar and settled in the
      mountain-country, his two daughters with him,
   for he was afraid to settle in Tzo'ar.
   So he settled in a cave, he and his two daughters.

---

latter theme returns at the end of the story, with the incestuous incident
that takes place at the instigation of Lot's daughters.

The story uses some stylized vocabulary. In verse 13, the messengers
talk of "bringing ruin," just as we encountered in the Flood narrative
(6:13). The narrative also gives negative twists to words which were
positive in the previous chapter: "know" and "just" are changed to
indicate illicit sex (v.5) and a condemnation of the alien Lot (v.9, "act-
the-judge and adjudicate"). Here too, "door/entrance" is transformed
from a place of contact with God to one of confrontation with men.

The account of the destruction itself is terse and mysterious, but it also
reveals the predicament of an all-too-human man, Lot.

The final section of the Sedom and Amora story recounts the origins of
two of Israel's neighbors, the Moabites and Ammonites. As traditional
enemies, they are not treated very kindly, any more than was the ancestor of the Canaanites in 9:20–27.

17 **Escape:** Heb. *himmalet,* used five times here. Perhaps it is a pun on Lot's
   name; he is "the escaper" in a number of situations.
19 **lest the wickedness cling to me:** The expression of an idea common to
   many cultures: that evil is like a disease, a physical rather than purely moral
   entity.
20 **tiny:** Or "a trifle."
21 **lift up your face:** A similar Assyrian phrase means "save" or "cheer."
   overturning: Overthrowing. The word is used later in the Bible to describe
   the fate of the two cities again (e.g., Lam. 4:6).
22 **I am not able . . . until you come there:** In deference to Avraham (see
   verse 29).
26 **she became a pillar of salt:** An old folklore motif of what happens when
   humans see God (or his actions), made popular by the many mineral pillars
   in the region around the Dead Sea.
27 **Early in the morning Avraham (arose):** Or "In the morning Avraham
   hurried" (Speiser).

31 Now the firstborn said to the younger:
Our father is old,
and there is no man in the land to come in to us as befits
   the way of all the earth!
32 Come, let us have our father drink wine and lie with him
so that we may keep seed alive by our father.
33 So they had their father drink wine that night,
then the firstborn went in and lay with her father—
but he knew nothing of her lying down or her rising up.
34 It was on the morrow that the firstborn said to the younger:
Here, yesternight I lay with father.
Let us have him drink wine tonight as well,
then you go in and lie with him,
so that we may keep seed alive by our father.
35 They had their father drink wine that night as well,
then the younger arose and lay with him,
but he knew nothing of her lying down or her rising up.
36 And Lot's two daughters became pregnant by their father.
37 The firstborn bore a son and called his name: Mo'av/By
   Father,
he is the tribal-father of Mo'av of today.
38 The younger also bore a son, and called his name:
   Ben-Ammi/Son of My Kinspeople,
he is the tribal-father of the Sons of Ammon of today.

20:1 Avraham traveled from there to the Southland, and settled
   between Kadesh and Shur, sojourning in Gerar.
  2 Avraham said of Sara his wife: She is my sister.
So Avimelekh king of Gerar sent and had Sara taken.
  3 But God came to Avimelekh in a dream of the night and
   said to him:
Here, you must die because of the woman whom you have
   taken,
for she is a wedded wife!
  4 Avimelekh had not come near her. He said:
My Lord,
Would you kill a nation, though it be innocent?
  5 Did he not say to me: She is my sister,
and also she, she said: He is my brother!

With a whole heart and with clean hands have I done this.

6 God said to him in the dream:
I also know that it was with a whole heart that you did this,
and so I also held you back from being at fault against me,
therefore I did not let you touch her.

7 But now, return the man's wife
—indeed, he is a prophet, he can intercede for you—
and live!
But if you do not return her:
know that you must die, yes, die, you and all that is yours!

8 Avimelekh (arose) early in the morning and called all his
servants,
he spoke all these words in their ears, and the men became
exceedingly afraid.

9 Then Avimelekh had Avraham called and said to him:
What have you done to us?
In what did I fail you,
that you have brought me and my kingdom into such great
fault?
Deeds which are not to be done, you have done to me!

10 And Avimelekh said to Avraham:
What did you foresee, that you did this thing?

The Wife—II (Chap. 20): The second occurrence of "The Matriarch
Protected" comes immediately before the story of Yitzhak's birth, as if to
emphasize God's hand in the process one more time. In this long variation on the theme, God is most active and Avraham most revealing of his
past. He emerges from danger as a man who clearly enjoys God's full
protection and bounty.

The story almost draws a web of magic around Sara. Avimelekh is
nearly killed by God, and Sara's childlessness is inflicted upon all the
women in the king's household—even though there is not the slightest
doubt of his innocence (he "had not come near her").

35 **but he knew nothing . . . :** The repetition of the phrase from verse 33 is
meant either to absolve Lot or to ridicule him.
37 **Mo'av:** Trad. English "Moab."
20:3 **wedded wife:** Heb. *be'ulat ba'al.*
5 **With a whole heart:** Lit. "In the wholeness of my heart."
6 **being at fault:** Or "sinning," which is perhaps too theological a translation.

11 Avraham said:
   Indeed, I said to myself:
   Surely there is no fear of God in this place,
   they will kill me on account of my wife!
12 Then, too, she is truly my sister, my father's daughter,
   however not my mother's daughter—so she became my
   wife.
13 Now it was, when the power-of-God caused me to roam
   from my father's house,
   that I said to her:
   Let this be the faithfulness that you do me:
   in every place that we come, say of me: He is my brother.
14 Avimelekh took sheep and oxen, servants and maids, and
   gave them to Avraham,
   and returned Sara his wife to him.
15 Avimelekh said:
   Here, my land is before you,
   settle wherever seems good in your eyes.
16 And to Sara he said:
   Here, I have given a thousand pieces of silver to your
   brother,
   here, it shall serve you as a covering for the eyes for all who
   are with you
   and with everyone, that you have been decided for.
17 Avraham interceded with God
   and God healed Avimelekh: his wife and his slave-women,
   so that they gave birth.
18 For YHWH had obstructed, obstructed every womb in
   Avimelekh's household
   on account of Sara, the wife of Avraham.

21:1 Now YHWH took account of Sara as he had said,
         YHWH dealt with Sara as he had spoken.
   2 Sara became pregnant and bore Avraham a son in his old
      age,
      at the set-time of which God had spoken to him.
   3 And Avraham called the name of his son, who was born to
      him, whom Sara bore to him:
      Yitzhak/He Laughs.

4 And Avraham circumcised Yitzhak his son at eight days
   old, as God had commanded him.
5 Avraham was a hundred years old when Yitzhak his son was
   born to him.
6 Now Sara said:
   God has made laughter for me,
   all who hear of it will laugh for me.
7 And she said:
   Who would have declared to Avraham:
   Sara will nurse sons?
   Well, I have borne him a son in his old age!
8 The child grew and was weaned,
   and Avraham made a great drinking-feast on the day that
      Yitzhak was weaned.

9 Once Sara saw the son of Hagar the Egyptian-woman,
   whom she had borne to Avraham, laughing. . . .

Yitzhak Born (21:1–8): Two principal ideas punctuate this climax for
which we have waited since Chapter 12: God keeps his promises (hence
the poem in verse 1), and the key word in the stories about Yitzhak:
"laughter" (here the result of the actual birth).

Yishmael Banished (21:9–21): Once Yitzhak has been born, separation
must be made between heir and firstborn. Despite Avraham's obvious
love for him, Yishmael must leave; his mother must repeat her ordeal of

11 **fear:** Awe; often used of God in the Bible.
13 **roam:** A word which in Genesis suggests a wandering that is nevertheless
   directed by God. See 21:14 and 37:15 for other examples. This passage
   gives us a fascinating glimpse of Avraham's own perception of the events in
   Chapter 12. It is not unusual for the biblical storyteller to give out informa-
   tion in this manner (in a later speech of the protagonist).   **faithfulness:** Or
   "favor."
16 **a covering for the eyes:** Hebrew obscure; apparently it has legal connotations (see also "decided for" at the end of the verse).
18 **YHWH had obstructed:** On account of Sara, the "obstructed" one of 16:2.
21:6 **laugh for me:** Out of joy or disbelief. Some suggest "laugh at."
   9 **laughing:** Perhaps mockingly. The theme of Yitzhak's life continues.

10 She said to Avraham:
Drive out this slave-woman and her son,
for the son of this slave-woman shall not share inheritance
with my son, with Yitzhak!

11 The matter was exceedingly bad in Avraham's eyes because
of his son.

12 But God said to Avraham:
Do not let it be bad in your eyes concerning the lad and
concerning your slave-woman;
in all that Sara says to you, hearken to her voice,
for it is through Yitzhak that seed will be called by your
(name).

13 But also the son of the slave-woman—a nation will I make
of him,
for he too is your seed.

14 Avraham (arose) early in the morning,
he took some bread and a skin of water
and gave them to Hagar—placing them upon her shoulder—
together with the child and sent her away.
She went off and roamed in the wilderness of Be'er-Sheva.

15 Now when the water in the skin was at an end, she cast the
child under one of the bushes,

16 and went and sat by herself, opposite, as far away as a
bowshot,
for she said to herself:
Let me not see the child die!
So she sat opposite, and lifted up her voice and wept.

17 But God heard the voice of the lad,
God's messenger called to Hagar from heaven and said to
her:
What ails you, Hagar? Do not be afraid,
for God has heard the voice of the lad there where he is.

18 Arise, lift up the lad and grasp him with your hand,
for a great nation will I make of him!

19 God opened her eyes, and she saw a well of water;
she went, filled the skin with water, and gave the lad to
drink.

20 And God was with the lad as he grew up,
he settled in the wilderness, and became an archer, a
bowman.

21 He settled in the wilderness of Paran, and his mother took
    him a wife from the land of Egypt.

22 It was at about that time that Avimelekh, together with
        Pikhol the commander of his army, said to Avraham:
    God is with you in all that you do.
23 So now, swear to me here by God:
    If you should ever deal falsely with me, with my progeny
        and my posterity . . . !
    Rather, faithfully, as I have dealt with you, deal with me,
    and with the land in which you have sojourned.
24 Avraham said:
    I so swear.
25 But Avraham rebuked Avimelekh
    because of a well of water that Avimelekh's servants had
        seized.
26 Avimelekh said:
    I do not know who did this thing,
    nor have you ever told me, nor have I heard of it apart from
        today.

Chapter 16 as well. Nonetheless the text emphasizes that God is there
"with the lad" (v.20); twice the Yishamel motif of "God hearkening"
resounds (v.17); and God promises that the boy will eventually attain the
same exalted status as his brother (vv.13, 18).

Structurally, this brief tale foreshadows the next chapter, the ordeal of
Yitzhak. It speaks of a journey into the unknown, a child at the point of
death, the intervention of God's "messenger," the parent's sighting of
the way out, and the promise of future blessing. Of course the differences between the two stories are equally important.

Treaty (21:22–34): This interlude, which usefully separates the life
threats to Avraham's two sons (for a similar example, see I Samuel 25), is
one of many scenes demonstrating Avraham's relationship with local
princes.

11 **bad in Avraham's eyes:** Displeasing or upsetting to him.
12 **seed will be called:** I.e., your line will be continued.
14 **Be'er-Sheva:** Trad. English "Beersheba."
23 **with my progeny and my posterity:** Heb. *u-le-nini u-le-nekhdi.*

27 So Avraham took sheep and oxen and gave them to
   Avimelekh,
   and the two of them cut a covenant.
28 Then Avraham set seven ewe-lambs of the flock aside.
29 Avimelekh said to Avraham:
   What mean these seven ewe-lambs that you have set aside?
30 He said:
   Indeed, these seven ewe-lambs you should take from my
      hand,
   so that they may be a witness for me that I dug this well.
31 Therefore that place was called Be'er-Sheva/Well of the
      Seven-Swearing,
   for there the two of them swore (an oath).
32 Thus they cut a covenant in Be'er-Sheva.
   Then Avimelekh and Pikhol the commander of his army
      arose
   and returned to the land of the Philistines.
33 Now he planted a tamarisk in Be'er-Sheva
   and there he called out the name: YHWH God of the Ages.
34 And Avraham sojourned in the land of the Philistines for
      many days.

22:1 Now after these events it was
   that God tested Avraham
   and said to him:
   Avraham!
   He said:
   Here I am.
 2 He said:
   Pray take your son,
   your only-one,
   whom you love,
   Yitzhak,
   and go-you-forth to the land of Moriyya/Seeing,
   and offer him up there as an offering-up
   upon one of the mountains
   that I will tell you of.
 3 Avraham (arose) early in the morning,
   he saddled his ass,

he took his two serving-lads with him and Yitzhak his son,
he split wood for the offering-up
and arose and went to the place that God had told him of.
4 On the third day Avraham lifted up his eyes
and saw the place from afar.
5 Avraham said to his lads:
You stay here with the ass,
and I and the lad will go yonder,
we will bow down and then return to you.

The Great Test (22): This story is certainly one of the masterpieces of
biblical literature. In a famous article by Erich Auerbach it is remarked
how biblical style as exemplified here, in contradistinction to that of
Homer and other epic bards, eschews physical and psychological details
in favor of one central preoccupation: a man's decision in relation to
God. The result of this style is a terrible intensity, a story which is so
stark as to be almost unbearable.

Chapter 22 is a tale of God's seeming retraction of his promise (of
"seed") to Avraham. The fact that other issues may be involved here
(i.e., Israel's rejection of local and widely practiced ideas of child sacrifice) may be quite beside the point. Coming just one chapter after the
birth of the long-awaited son, the story completely turns around the
tension of the whole cycle and creates a new, frightening tension of its
own. The real horror of the story lies in this threatened contradiction to
what has gone before.

Most noticeable in the narrative is Avraham's silence, his mute accep-
tance of, and acting on, God's command. We are told of no sleepless

30 **take:** Accept.
33 **tamarisk:** A tree rarely mentioned in the Bible, it may indicate a holy place,
similar to the oaks where Avraham dwells earlier. **God of the Ages:** A
name unique to this passage.
34 **Philistines:** Another anachronism. The Philistines appear first in the days
of the Conquest (Joshua and Judges).
22:1 **after these events:** Others use "Some time afterward." **Here I am:** A
term frequently used to convey readiness, usually in relation to God's command or address.
2 **Yitzhak:** The name is left until the end of the phrase, to heighten tension.
Similarly, see 27:32. **Moriyya:** Trad. English "Moriah." The mountain
here is later identified with the site of Solomon's Temple.
5 **bow down:** Worship.

6 Avraham took the wood for the offering-up,
  he placed them upon Yitzhak his son,
  in his hand he took the fire and the knife.
  Thus the two of them went together.
7 Yitzhak said to Avraham his father, he said:
  Father!
  He said:
  Here I am, my son.
  He said:
  Here are the fire and the knife,
  but where is the lamb for the offering-up?
8 Avraham said:
  God will select for himself the lamb for the offering-up,
  my son.
  Thus the two of them went together.
9 They came to the place that God had told him of;
  there Avraham built the slaughter-site
  and arranged the wood
  and bound Yitzhak his son
  and placed him on the slaughter-site atop the wood.
10 Avraham stretched out his hand,
  he took the knife to slay his son.
11 But YHWH's messenger called to him from heaven
  and said:
  Avraham! Avraham!
  He said:
  Here I am.
12 He said:
  Do not stretch out your hand against the lad,
  do not do anything to him!
  For now I know
  that you are God-fearing—
  you have not withheld your son, your only-one, from me.
13 Avraham lifted up his eyes and saw:
  there, a ram caught behind in the thicket by its horns!
  Avraham went,
  he took the ram
  and offered it up as an offering-up in place of his son.
14 Avraham called the name of that place: YHWH Sees.
  As the saying is today: On YHWH's mountain (it) is seen.

15 Now YHWH's messenger called to Avraham a second time
   from heaven
16 and said:
   By myself I swear
   —YHWH's utterance—
   indeed, because you have done this thing, have not withheld
   your son, your only-one,

---

night, nor does he ever say a word to God. Instead he is described with a series of verbs: arising, saddling, taking, splitting, arising, going (v.3; similarly in vv.6 and 9–10). Avraham the bargainer, so willing to enter into negotiations with relations (Chapter 13), allies (Chapter 14), local princes (Chapter 20), and even God himself (Chapter 18), here falls completely silent.

The chapter serves an important structural function in the Avraham cycle, framing it in conjunction with Chapter 12. The triplet in verse 2 ("Pray take your son,/ your only-one,/ whom you love") recalls "from your land/ from your kindred/ from your father's house" in 12:1; "go-you-forth" and "the land that I will tell you of" (v.2; the latter, three times in the story) similarly point back to Avraham's call (12:1, "Go-you forth . . . to the land that I will let you see"). There he had been asked to give up the past (his father); here, the future (his son). Between the two events lies Avraham's active life as man of God, ancestor, and intercessor. After this God will never speak with him again.

In many ways this story is the midpoint of Genesis. It brings the central theme of continuity and discontinuity to a head in the strongest possible way. After Moriyya, we can breathe easier, knowing that God will come to the rescue of his chosen ones in the direst of circumstances. At the same time we are left to ponder the difficulties of being a chosen one, subject to such an incredible test.

The story is also the paradigmatic narrative of the entire book. The

---

6, 8 **Thus the two of them went together:** Between these two statements is Avraham's successful deflection of Yitzhak's question, and perhaps the hint of a happy ending.
7 **fire:** I.e., a torch or brand.
8 **select for himself:** Heb. *yir'e lo;* see the name of the mountain in verse 14, "YHWH Sees" (*yir'e*).   **offering-up,/ my son:** One might read it with a dash instead of a comma, to preserve what may be an ironic answer.
13 **a ram caught behind:** Some read "one ram caught."
16 **YHWH's utterance:** A phrase often found in the Prophetic books. See note on 15:1.

17 indeed, I will bless you, bless you,
    I will make your seed many, yes, many,
    like the stars of the heavens and like the sand that is on the
        shore of the sea;
    your seed shall inherit the gate of their enemies,
18 all the nations of the earth shall enjoy blessing through your
        seed,
    in consequence of your hearkening to my voice.
19 Avraham returned to his lads,
    they arose and went together to Be'er-Sheva.
    And Avraham stayed in Be'er-Sheva.

20 Now after these events it was, that it was told to Avraham,
        saying:
    Here, Milca too has borne, sons to Nahor your brother:
21 Utz his firstborn and Buz his brother, Kemuel father of
22   Aram, and/ Cesed, Hazo, Pildash, Yidlaf, and Betuel.
23 Now Betuel begot Rivka.—
    These eight Milca bore to Nahor, Avraham's brother.
24 And his concubine—her name was Re'uma—bore too:
    Tevah, Gaham, Tahash and Maakha.

23:1 Now Sara's life was one hundred years and twenty years
        and seven years, (thus) the years of Sara's life.
  2 Sara died in Arba-Town, that is now Hevron, in the land of
        Canaan.
     Avraham set about to lament for Sara and to weep over her;
  3 then Avraham arose from the presence of his dead
     and spoke to the Sons of Het, saying:
  4 I am a sojourner settled among you;
     give me title to a burial holding among you,
     so that I may bury my dead from my presence.
  5 The Sons of Het answered Avraham, saying to him:
  6 Hear us, my lord!
     You are one exalted by God in our midst—
     in the choicest of our burial-sites you may bury your dead,
     no man among us will deny you his burial-site
     for burying your dead!
  7 Avraham arose,

he bowed low to the People of the Land, to the Sons of
Het,
8 and spoke with them, saying:
If it be then according to your wish
that I bury my dead from my presence,
hear me and interpose for me to Efron son of Tzohar,
9 that he may give me title to the cave of Makhpela, that is
his, that is at the edge of his field,
for the full silver-worth let him give me title in your midst
for a burial holding.

Patriarch passes the test, and we know that the fulfillment of the divine
promise is assured. Yet there is an ominous note: love, which occurs here
by name for the first time, leads almost to heartbreak. So it will be for
the rest of Genesis.

Purchase and Burial (23): Even though he is now secure in God's covenant, Avraham must still live and function in the human world. His
purchase of a burial plot for Sara shows us once more his dealings with
his neighbors, here as their equal, and also establishes at last his legal

17 **indeed, I will bless you:** Avraham has received such blessings before, but
never before "because you have hearkened to my voice" (v.18). **inherit
the gate:** I.e., possess or take the city.
18 **all the nations . . . :** See 12:3.
19 **Avraham returned:** The fact that Yitzhak is not mentioned here has given
rise to speculation for centuries (see Shalom Spiegel, *The Last Trial*). The
omission may simply arise from the fact that Yitzhak as a personality is not
important to the story, which is first and foremost a test of Avraham.
23 **Rivka:** Trad. English "Rebecca."
23:1 **(thus) the years of Sara's life:** She is the only biblical woman whose life
span is given, again as a sign of importance.
3 **Sons of Het:** Or "Hittites," not to be confused with the great Hittite
empire in Asia Minor. Here the name describes a Canaanite group.
4 **a sojourner:** Even after many years, Avraham is still acutely aware of his
nonnative status in the land.
5–6 **saying to him:/ Hear us:** Others use "saying:/ No, hear us."
6 **one exalted:** Others use "a prince."
7 **People of the Land:** Possibly a title indicating notables, not, as in later
usage, the "common folk."

10 Now Efron had a seat amidst the Sons of Het,
   and Efron the Hittite answered Avraham in the ears of the
      Sons of Het,
   of all who had entry to the council-gate of his city,
   saying:
11 Not so, my lord, hear me!
   The field I give to you,
   and the cave that is therein, to you I give it;
   before the eyes of the Sons of My People I give it to you—
   bury your dead!
12 Avraham bowed before the People of the Land
13 and spoke to Efron in the ears of the People of the Land,
   saying:
   But if you yourself would only hear me out!
   I will give the silver-payment for the field,
   accept it from me,
   so that I may bury my dead there.
14 Efron answered Avraham, saying to him:
15 My lord—hear me!
   A piece of land worth four hundred silver weight,
   what is that between me and you!
   You may bury your dead!
16 Avraham hearkened to Efron:
   Avraham weighed out to Efron the silver-worth
   of which he had spoken in the ears of the Sons of Het—
   four hundred silver weight at the going merchants' rate.
17 Thus was established the field of Efron, that is in
      Makhpela, that faces Mamre,
   the field as well as the cave that is in it, and the trees that
      were in all the field, that were in all their territory round
      about,
18 for Avraham as an acquisition,
   before the eyes of the Sons of Het, of all who had entry to
      the council-gate of his city.
19 Afterward Avraham buried Sara his wife
   in the cave of the field of Makhpela, facing Mamre, that is
      now Hevron, in the land of Canaan.
20 Thus was established the field as well as the cave that is in
      it for Avraham as a burial holding, from the Sons of Het.

24:1 Now Avraham was old, advanced in days,
　　and YHWH had blessed Avraham in everything.
　2 Avraham said to his servant, the elder of his household,
　　who ruled over all that was his:
　　Pray put your hand under my thigh!
　3 I want you to swear by YHWH, the God of Heaven and the
　　God of Earth,
　　that you will not take a wife for my son from the women of
　　the Canaanites, among whom I am settled;

---

foothold in Canaan, albeit with a small piece of land. The long conversations and considerable formality of the chapter, which are not unusual in an ancient Near Eastern context, contrast with the extreme brevity of the previous chapter.

The narrative strikes a curious balance between the emotional reality of the situation (e.g., the repetition of "dead," "presence," and "bury") and the requirements of legal procedure ("Hear me," "give title," and "holding").

The Betrothal Journey (24): The last full episode of the Avraham cycle is the longest in the book. Its leisurely pace, attention to detail, and concentration on speeches as well as action belie the importance of what is being recounted: the finding of a wife for Yitzhak, who is biologically to continue the line. Yet after all that has happened in the previous chapters, we know that this will be taken care of by God. That is implied in Avraham's assured "he himself [God] will send his messenger on before you" (v.7).

Many meeting/betrothal scenes in the Bible take place at a well (e.g., Jacob, Moses); this was probably a literary convention (see Culley and Alter for a discussion of the significance of such a phenomenon). Like other crucial moments in Avraham's life the chapter involves a journey, albeit one made by his emissary. It is therefore natural that the key words of the chapter are "go," "journey," and "grant success." "Take" also appears frequently, as the biblical term often used for "marry."

10 **of all who had entry:** Similar to "People of the Land"—the aristocrats.
20 **established:** Others use "made over."
24:1 **put your hand under my thigh:** A symbol used in taking of an oath (see also 47:29). The use of "thigh" might allude to a curse of childlessness as the punishment for not keeping the oath.

4 rather, you are to go to my land and to my kindred, and
take a wife for my son, for Yitzhak.

5 The servant said to him:
Perhaps the woman will not be willing to go after me to this
land;
may I then bring your son back there,
back to the land from which you once went out?

6 Avraham said to him:
Watch out that you do not ever bring my son back there!

7 YHWH, the God of Heaven,
who took me from my father's house and from my kindred,
who spoke to me,
who swore to me, saying:
I give this land to your seed—
he himself will send his messenger on before you,
so that you take a wife for my son from there.

8 Now if the woman is not willing to go after you,
you will be clear from this sworn-oath of mine,
only: You are not to bring my son back there!

9 The servant put his hand under the thigh of Avraham his
lord,
and swore to him (an oath) about this matter.

10 The servant took ten camels from his lord's camels and
went, all kinds of good-things from his lord in his hand.
He arose and went to Aram Of-Two-Rivers, to Nahor's
town.

11 He had the camels kneel outside the town at the water well
at eventime, at the time when the water-drawers go out,

12 and said:
YHWH, God of my lord Avraham,
pray let it happen today for me, and deal faithfully with my
lord Avraham!

13 Here, I have stationed myself by the water spring as the
women of the town go out to draw water.

14 May it be
that the maiden to whom I say: Pray lower your pitcher that
I may drink,
and she says: Drink, and I will also give your camels to
drink—

let her be the one that you have decided on for your
 servant, for Yitzhak,
by means of her may I know that you have dealt faithfully
 with my lord.

15 And it was: Not yet had he finished speaking,
when here, Rivka came out,
—she had been born to Betuel, son of Milca, wife of Nahor,
 brother of Avraham—
her pitcher on her shoulder.

16 The maiden was exceedingly beautiful to look at,
a virgin—no man had known her.
Going down to the spring, she filled her pitcher and came
 up again.

17 The servant ran to meet her and said:
Pray let me sip a little water from your pitcher!

18 She said:
Drink, my lord!
And in haste she let down her pitcher on her arm and gave
 him to drink.

19 When she had finished giving him to drink, she said:
I will also draw for your camels, until they have finished
 drinking.

20 In haste she emptied her pitcher into the drinking-trough,
then she ran to the well again to draw,
and drew for all his camels.

21 The man kept staring at her,
(waiting) silently to find out whether YHWH had granted
 success to his journey or not.

22 It was, when the camels had finished drinking,

---

5 **back there:** The Hebrew text has "there" in the next line; it has been
 moved up in the English text for reasons of style. The word occurs four
 times in verses 5–8, as a signal of what is most important to Avraham: that
 his son must stay in the land of Canaan.

7 **I give this land to your seed:** Quoting 12:7.

10 **Aram Of-Two-Rivers:** Others leave untranslated, "Aram-Naharayim."

11 **water-drawers:** Female.

12 **let it happen:** Or "let it go well."

that the man took a gold nose-ring, a half-coin in weight,
and two bracelets for her wrists, ten gold pieces in weight,

23 and said:
Whose daughter are you? Pray tell me!
And is there perhaps in your father's house a place for us to
spend the night?

24 She said to him:
I am the daughter of Betuel, son of Milca, whom she bore
to Nahor.

25 And she said to him:
Yes, there is straw, yes, plenty of fodder with us, (and) yes,
a place to spend the night.

26 In homage the man bowed low before YHWH

27 and said:
Blessed be YHWH, God of my lord Avraham,
who has not relinquished his faithfulness and his
trustworthiness from my lord!
While as for me, YHWH has led me on the journey to the
house of my lord's brothers!

28 The maiden ran and told her mother's household according
to these words.

29 Now Rivka had a brother, his name was Lavan.
Lavan ran to the man, outside, to the spring:

30 and it was,
as soon as he saw the nose-ring, and the bracelets on his
sister's wrists,
and as soon as he heard Rivka his sister's words, saying:
Thus the man spoke to me,
that he came out to the man—there, he was still standing by
the camels, by the spring—

31 and said:
Come, you who are blessed by YHWH, why are you
standing outside?
I myself have cleared out the house and a place for the
camels!

32 The man came into the house and unbridled the camels,
they gave straw and fodder to the camels
and water for washing his feet and the feet of the men that
were with him.

33 (Food) was put before him to eat, but he said:
   I will not eat until I have spoken my words.
   He said: Speak!
34 He said:
   I am Avraham's servant.
35 YHWH has blessed my lord exceedingly, so that he has
   become great,
   he has given him sheep and oxen, silver and gold, servants
   and maids, camels and asses.
36 Sara, my lord's wife, bore my lord a son after she had
   grown old,
   and he has given him all that is his.
37 Now my lord had me swear, saying:
   You are not to take a wife for my son from the women of
   the Canaanites, in whose land I am settled!
38 No! To my father's house you are to go, to my clan,
   and take a wife for my son.
39 I said to my lord:
   Perhaps the woman will not go after me!
40 He said to me:
   YHWH, in whose presence I have walked, will send his
   messenger with you,
   he will grant sucess to your journey,
   so that you take a wife for my son from my clan and from
   my father's house.

---

25 **Yes, there is straw:** Not until Rivka has extended the offer of hospitality
   (and enthusiastically, with the triple "yes") is the servant sure that
   "YHWH has granted success to my journey." Hospitality, once again, is
   the determinant, over and above beauty or virginity.
27 **his faithfulness and his trustworthiness:** Others combine and translate as
   "steadfast kindness." The phrase is often found in the Psalms, describing
   God.   **brothers:** Relatives.
29 **Lavan:** Trad. English "Laban." He will be a key figure in the story of
   Rivka's son Yaakov.
34 **He said . . . :** The servant's speech diplomatically omits certain emotional
   details of Avraham's speech, most notably his warning against Yitzhak
   himself's going back "there."
40 **will send his messenger:** Speaking figuratively.

41 Only then will you be clear from my binding-oath:
When you come to my clan,
if they do not give her to you, you will be clear from my
binding-oath.

42 Now I came to the well today and said:
YHWH, God of my lord Avraham,
pray, if you wish to grant success to the journey on which I
am going,

43 here: I have stationed myself by the water spring;
may it be
that the girl who comes out to draw,
to whom I say: Pray give me a little water from your pitcher
to drink,

44 and she says to me: You drink, and I will also draw for
your camels—
let her be the woman whom YHWH has decided on for the
son of my lord.

45 (And) I, even before I had finished speaking in my heart,
here, Rivka came out, her pitcher on her shoulder,
she went down to the spring and drew.
I said to her: Pray give me to drink!

46 In haste she let down her pitcher from herself and said:
Drink, and I will also give your camels to drink.
I drank, and she also gave the camels to drink.

47 Then I asked her, I said: Whose daughter are you?
She said: The daughter of Betuel, son of Nahor, whom
Milca bore to him.
I put the ring on her nose and the bracelets on her wrists,

48 and in homage I bowed low before YHWH, and blessed
YHWH, God of my lord Avraham,
who led me on the true journey to take the daughter of my
lord's brother for his son.

49 So now, if you wish to deal faithfully and truly with my
lord, tell me,
and if not, tell me,
that I may (know to) turn right or left.

50 Lavan and Betuel answered, they said:
The matter has come from YHWH;
we cannot speak anything to you evil or good.

51 Here is Rivka before you,

take her and go, that she may be a wife for the son of your
    lord,
as YHWH has spoken.

52 It was
when Avraham's servant heard their words, that he bowed
    to the ground before YHWH.

53 And the servant brought out objects of silver and objects of
    gold and garments, and gave them to Rivka,
and he gave presents to her brother and to her mother.

54 They ate and drank, he and the men that were with him,
    and spent the night.
When they arose in the morning, he said:
Send me off to my lord.

55 But her brother and her mother said:
Let the maiden stay with us a few days, perhaps ten— after
    that she may go.

56 He said to them:
Do not delay me, for YHWH has granted success to my
    journey;
send me off, that I may go back to my lord.

57 They said:
Let us call the maiden and ask (for an answer from) her
    own mouth.

58 They called Rivka and said to her:
Will you go with this man?
She said:
I will go.

59 They sent off Rivka their sister with her nurse, and
    Avraham's servant with his men,

-----

41 **binding-oath:** Changed from Avraham's simple "sworn-oath," perhaps because it is reported from the servant's point of view.

50 **YHWH:** The family apparently worships the God of Avraham, in addition
to others (see 31:19, 30).

53 **objects of silver . . . and gold and garments:** A stock biblical phrase (see,
similarly, Ex. 3:22) for wealth or presents.

55 **a few days, perhaps ten:** Some interpret as "a year or ten months."

59 **with her nurse:** Yitzhak's life as the father of his people begins with the
marriage arranged in this chapter; curiously, when he dies in Chapter 35,
the nurse dies as well, perhaps to hint that Rivka dies too.

60 and they gave Rivka farewell-blessing and said to her:
   Our sister, may you become thousandfold myriads!
   May your seed inherit the gate of those who hate him!
61 Rivka and her maids arose, they mounted the camels and
   went after the man.
   The servant took Rivka and went away.

62 Now Yitzhak had come from where you come to the Well
   of the Living-One Who-Sees-Me—for he had settled in
   the Southland.
63 And Yitzhak went out to stroll in the field around eventide.
   He lifted up his eyes and saw: here, camels coming!
64 Rivka lifted up her eyes and saw Yitzhak;
65 she got down from the camel and said to the servant:
   Who is the man over there that is walking in the field to
   meet us?
   The servant said:
   That is my lord.
   She took a veil and covered herself.
66 Now the servant recounted to Yitzhak all the things that he
   had done.
67 Yitzhak brought her into the tent of Sara his mother,
   he took Rivka and she became his wife, and he loved her.
   Thus was Yitzhak comforted after his mother.

25:1 Now Avraham had taken another wife, her name was
   Ketura.
   2 She bore him Zimran and Yokshan, Medan and Midyan,
   Yishbak and Shuah.
   3 Yokshan begot Sheva and Dedan,
   Dedan's sons were the Ashurites, the Letushites, and the
   Leummites.
   4 Midyan's sons (were) Efa, Efer, Hanokh, Avida, and Eldaa.
   All these (were) Ketura's sons.
   5 But Avraham gave over all that was his to Yitzhak.
   6 And to the sons of the concubines that Avraham had,
   Avraham gave gifts, and he sent them away from Yitzhak
   his son while he was still alive, eastward, to the Eastland.

   7 Now these are the days and years of the life of Avraham,
   which he lived:

8 A hundred years and seventy years and five years, then he
    breathed-his-last.
  Avraham died at a good ripe-age, old and abundant (in
    days),
  and was gathered to his kinspeople.
9 Yitzhak and Yishmael his sons buried him, in the cave of
    Makhpela, in the field of Efron son of Tzohar the Hittite,
    that faces Mamre,
10 the field that Avraham had acquired from the Sons of
    Het.
  There were buried Avraham and Sara his wife.

11 Now it was after Avraham's death, that God blessed
    Yitzhak his son.
  And Yitzhak settled by the Well of the Living-One
    Who-Sees-Me.

12 Now these are the begettings of Yishmael son of Avraham,
    whom Hagar the Egyptian-woman, Sara's maid, bore to
    Avraham.
13 And these are the names of the sons of Yishmael, by their
    names after (the order of) their begettings:

Avraham's Descendants and Death (25:1–18): Avraham's death is bracketed by two passages dealing with his offspring: first, through Ketura (a
concubine), and then through Hagar (Yishmael's line). God's promise is
on the way to fulfillment, although Yitzhak is as yet childless and only a
small portion of the land has been permanently acquired.

60 **May your seed inherit the gate:** See Avraham's blessing in 22:17. Again,
    the matriarch shares in the blessing.
62 **Well of the Living-One:** Already a site of God's activity (16:14).
63 **stroll:** Hebrew obscure; some use "ponder."
67 **Sara:** As the story opened with Yitzhak's father in his last active moments,
    it closes with the memory of his mother. Yitzhak is on his own.
25:7 **days and years:** Lit. "days of the years."
   8 **A hundred years . . . :** See "The Patriarchal Narratives," pp. 45–6.
    breathed-his-last: Lit. "expired." It is translated as "perished" in
    7:21. **abundant:** Or "full." For the complete expression, see 35:29.
  11 **God blessed Yitzhak:** This is the first detail reported about Yitzhak after
    his father's death—lest there be any doubt about the continuation of God's
    care.

14 Yishmael's firstborn, Nevayot; and Kedar, Adbe'el,
   Mivsam, Mishma, Duma, Massa,
15 Hadad and Tema, Yetur, Nafish and Kedma.
16 These are the sons of Yishmael, these their names, in their
   villages and in their corrals,
   twelve princes for their tribes.
17 And these are the years of the life of Yishmael: a hundred
   years and thirty years and seven years, then he
   breathed-his-last.
   He died and was gathered to his kinspeople.
18 Now they dwelt from Havila to Shur, which faces Egypt,
   back to where you come toward Assyria;
   in the presence of all his brothers did (his inheritance) fall.

16 **corrals:** Others (including Buber) use "circled encampments." **twelve
princes:** See 17:20.
18 **did (his inheritance) fall:** Hebrew difficult. Others interpret negatively,
"made raids against" or "fell upon" (his kinsmen).

PART III Yaakov

(25:19–36:43) see also 37–50

BEFORE COMMENTING on the Yaakov cycle, it is appropriate to consider why his father Yitzhak, the second of the Patriarchs, receives no true separate group of stories on his own.

Yitzhak functions in Genesis as a classic second generation—that is, as a transmitter and stabilizing force, rather than as an active participant in the process of building the people. There hardly exists a story about him in which he is anything but a son and heir, a husband, or a father. His main task in life seems to be to take roots in the land of Canaan, an admittedly important task in the larger context of God's promises in Genesis. What this means, unfortunately, is that he has almost no personality of his own. By Chapter 27, a scant two chapters after his father dies, he appears as (prematurely?) old, blind in both a literal and figurative sense, and as we will see, he fades out of the text entirely, only to die several chapters, and many years, later.

The true dynamic figure of the second generation here is Rivka. It is she to whom God reveals his plan, and she who puts into motion the mechanism for seeing that it is properly carried out. She is ultimately the one responsible for bridging the gap between the dream, as typified by Avraham, and the hard-won reality, as realized by Yaakov.

Avraham is a towering figure, almost unapproachable as a model in his intimacy with God and his ability to hurdle nearly every obstacle. Adding to this the fact that Yitzhak is practically a noncharacter, and that Yosef, once his rise begins, also lacks dimension as a personality, it becomes increasingly clear that it is Yaakov who emerges as the most dynamic and most human personality in the book. The stories about him cover fully half of Genesis, and reveal a man who is both troubled and triumphant. Most interestingly, he, and not Avraham, gives his name to the people of Israel.

Distinctive themes of the cycle include physical struggle, deception, and confrontation. These are expressed through the key words of Yaakov's name ("Heel-Holder" and "Heel-Sneak," then Yisrael, "God-Fighter"), "deceive" and similar words, and "face." Also recurring are the terms "love," "bless," "firstborn-right," and "wages/hire" (one word in Hebrew). The cycle is structured partly around etiologies (folk explanations of place-names and personal names) and also around Yaakov's use of stones in several of the stories.

Continuing from the Avraham cycle are such earlier themes as wandering, sibling rivalry, the barren wife, wives in conflict, the renaming of the protagonist, God perceived in dreams and visions; and particular geographical locations such as Bet-El, Shekhem, and the Negev (Cassuto)..

Finally, it should be mentioned that the Yaakov stories are notable in the manner in which they portray the two levels of biblical reality: divine and human. Throughout the stories human beings act according to normal (though often strong) emotions, which God then uses to carry out his master plan. In this cycle one comes to feel the interpretive force of the biblical mind at work, understanding human events in the context of what God wills. It is a fascinating play between the ideas of fate and free will, destiny and choice—a paradox which nevertheless lies at the heart of the biblical conception of God and humankind.

19 Now these are the begettings of Yitzhak, son of Avraham.
    Avraham begot Yitzhak.
20 Yitzhak was forty years old when he took Rivka daughter of
    Betuel the Aramean, from the country of Aram, sister of
    Lavan the Aramean, for himself as a wife.
21 Yitzhak entreated YHWH on behalf of his wife, for she was
    barren,
    and YHWH granted-his-entreaty:
    Rivka his wife became pregnant.
22 But the children almost crushed one another inside her,
    so she said:
    If this be so,
    why do I exist?
    And she went to inquire of YHWH.

23 YHWH said to her:
>   Two nations are in your body,
>   two tribes from your belly shall be divided;
>   tribe shall be mightier than tribe,
>   elder shall be servant to younger!
24 When her days were fulfilled for bearing, here: twins were
     in her body!
25 The first one came out ruddy, like a hairy mantle all over,
     so they called his name: Esav/Rough-One.
26 After that his brother came out, his hand grasping Esav's
     heel,
>   so they called his name: Yaakov/Heel-Holder.
>   Yitzhak was sixty years old when she bore them.

Rivka's Children (25:19–34): Two stories of sibling confrontation begin the Yaakov cycle. From the first, verses 19–28, all the necessary conditions are introduced for what is to come: struggle in the womb (foreshadowing Yaakov's wrestling match in Chapter 32, the structural resolution of this earlier one), God's plan for the younger son to outdo the older one, the importance of names as clues to personalities, and parental preference. This last point seals the fate of the two boys.

The second story (vv.29–34) is Yaakov's first act of stealth, and sets the pattern for his whole life. Note at the same time the text's emphasis on Esav's role (v.34), "Thus did Esav despise the firstborn-right."

20 **forty years old:** Another schematic number. Twenty years later (see verse 26), his wife will bear him children. **Aramean:** Three times in this verse the root "Aram" confirms what we learned in the previous chapter—the importance of family and lineage here. **country of Aram:** Others leave this untranslated, as "Padan-Aram."

22 **almost crushed:** Others use "struggled." **inquire:** Consult an oracle. Note that there is no indication that Yitzhak is aware of what God wants.

23 **tribes:** Heb. *le'ummim*, a poetic term for "peoples."

24 **here:** The text speaks from the point of view of the onlookers, not of Rivka, who is perfectly aware that she has twins.

25 **Esav:** Trad. English "Esau." **Rough-One:** A conjectural interpretation from Arabic *'athaya.*

26 **Yaakov:** Trad. English "Jacob." **Heel-Holder:** A popular reinterpretation of the name Yaakov, which may have meant originally "May (God) protect."

27 The lads grew up:
   Esav became a man who knew the hunt, a man of the field,
   but Yaakov was a plain man, staying among the tents.
28 Yitzhak grew to love Esav, for (he brought) hunted-game
       for his mouth,
   but Rivka loved Yaakov.

29 Once Yaakov was boiling boiled-stew,
   when Esav came in from the field, and he was weary.
30 Esav said to Yaakov:
   Pray give me a gulp of the red-stuff, that red-stuff,
   for I am so weary!
   Therefore they called his name: Edom/Red-One.
31 Yaakov said:
   Sell me your firstborn-right here-and-now.
32 Esav said:
   Here, I am on my way to dying, so what good to me is a
       firstborn-right?
33 Yaakov said:
   Swear to me here-and-now.
   He swore to him and sold his firstborn-right to Yaakov.
34 Yaakov gave Esav bread and boiled lentils;
   he ate and drank and arose and went off.
   Thus did Esav despise the firstborn-right.

26:1 Now there was a famine in the land, aside from the former
       famine which there had been in the days of Avraham,
     so Yitzhak went to Avimelekh, king of the Philistines, to
       Gerar.
   2 And YHWH was seen by him and said:
     Do not go down to Egypt;
     continue to dwell in the land that I tell you of,
   3 sojourn in this land, and I will be with you and will give
       you blessing—
     for to you and to your seed I give all these lands
     and will fulfill the sworn-oath that I swore to Avraham your
       father:
   4 I will make your seed many, like the stars of the heavens,
     and to your seed I will give all these lands;

all the nations of the earth shall enjoy blessing through your
   seed—
5 in consequence of Avraham's hearkening to my voice
   and keeping what I would have him keep: my
   commandments, my laws, and my instructions.
6 So Yitzhak stayed in Gerar.

As before, these episodes point in two temporal directions. Esav resembles Yishmael, the man of the bow; and parental preference will
launch the initially tragic action in the Yosef story (Chapter 37).

In the Land (26:1–6): As we have suggested, there is no true collection of
stories about Yitzhak. That is, virtually nowhere does Yitzhak appear in
a tale where, as a distinct individual, he is a central character. And
unlike Yaakov and Yosef, Yitzhak never directly receives his father's
blessing. This is bestowed by God, and one gets the impression that even
Avraham does not deal with his son as an individual. This is not surprising, given Yitzhak's function in his father's life.

For the narrative, his main purpose, as we have stressed above, is
simply to remain in the land (note the repetition of the word "land" in
this section). It is almost as if Avraham, the man who lives in the shadow
of sacred trees, plants one in the person of his son. In this chapter
Yitzhak is forbidden to go beyond the borders of Canaan. Even his
death, so seemingly out of place in Chapter 35, occurs after Yaakov has
returned home from his wanderings: only when it is assured that there
will be continuity in the land is he allowed to die—despite the fact that as
a result the text must leave him blind and dying for twenty years.

27 **plain:** Hebrew unclear. Others use "simple."
28 **(he brought) hunted-game:** Hebrew difficult.
29 **boiling boiled-stew:** This phrase may connote plotting, as in our English
   "cook up," "brew," "concoct," or "stir up" trouble. Other forms of the
   Hebrew verb denote "insolence."
31 **here-and-now:** Others use "at once"; apparently a legal term.
34 **he ate . . . :** Esav's impulsive personality is brilliantly portrayed by the use
   of four rapid-fire verbs. **despise:** Others use "belittle."
26:1 **a famine . . . Yitzhak went to Avimelekh:** Parallel to the story in Chapter
   20.
   5 **in consequence of Avraham's hearkening . . . :** The blessing mirrors
   22:17ff. **my commandments . . . :** These are not specified; this is probably a poetic phrase describing a general idea.

7 Now when the men of the place asked about his wife, he
   said: She is my sister,
   for he was afraid to say: my wife—
   (thinking): Otherwise the people of the place will kill me on
   account of Rivka, for she is beautiful to look at.
8 But it was, when he had been there a long time,
   that Avimelekh, king of the Philistines, looked out through
   a window
   and saw: there was Yitzhak laughing-and-loving with Rivka
   his wife!
9 Avimelekh had Yitzhak called and said:
   But here, she must be your wife!
   Now how could you say: She is my sister?
   Yitzhak said to him:
   Indeed, I said to myself: Otherwise I will die on account of
   her!
10 Avimelekh said:
   What is this that you have done to us!
   One of the people might well have lain with your wife,
   and then you would have brought guilt upon us!
11 Avimelekh charged the entire people, saying:
   Whoever touches this man or his wife must be put to death,
   yes, death!

12 Yitzhak sowed in that land, and reaped in that year a
   hundred measures;
   thus did YHWH bless him.
13 The man became great, and went on, went on becoming
   greater, until he was exceedingly great:
14 he had herds of sheep and herds of oxen and a large retinue
   of servants,
   and the Philistines envied him.
15 And all the wells which his father's servants had dug in the
   days of Avraham his father, the Philistines stopped up
   and filled with earth.
16 Avimelekh said to Yitzhak:
   Go away from us, for you have become exceedingly more
   numerous than we!

17 So Yitzhak went from there, he encamped in the wadi of
   Gerar and settled there.
18 Yitzhak again dug up the wells of water which had been
   dug in the days of Avraham his father, the Philistines
   having stopped them up after Avraham's death,
   and he called them by the names, the same names, by
   which his father had called them.
19 Yitzhak's servants also dug in the wadi, and found there a
   well of living water.
20 Now the shepherds of Gerar, quarreled with the shepherds
   of Yitzhak, saying: The water is ours!
   So he called the name of the well: Esek/Bickering, because
   they had bickered with him.
21 They dug another well, and quarreled also over it,
   so he called its name: Sitna/Animosity.

———————

The Wife—III (26:7–11): Here is the final "Yitzhak version" of the tale,
constructed around the same king whom Avraham had encountered in
Chapter 20. Its individual coloring is supplied by the "laughing-and-loving" of verse 8, playing on Yitzhak's name. Otherwise, just as in the
following episode, he is merely repeating his father's experience.

Blessing (26:12–33): Confirmation of Yitzhak's status as heir comes in
verses 12–14, in the form of material blessings (already referred to immediately after Avraham's death, 25:11). It will be Yaakov's task to reclaim
and continue the spiritual side of the tradition.
   The first episode is centered around not Yitzhak but Avraham. The
phrase "his father" reverberates; again Avimelekh returns. In the second
episode, Avraham's treaty with that king (Chapter 21) is replayed, with
the same result as before: an explanation of the name Be'er-Sheva.

8 **laughing-and-loving:** Heb. *metzahek,* which can mean laughter or sexual
   activity. Trad. English "sporting."
11 **touches:** Or "harms."
12 **reaped:** Lit. "attained."
17 **there:** The word occurs seven times through verse 25. It may be a counter-
   point to Chapter 24's usage, or stress that Yitzhak stays in the land.

22 He moved on from there and dug another well, but they did
   not quarrel over it,
   so he called its name: Rehovot/Space,
   and said: Indeed, now YHWH has made space for us, so
   that we may bear fruit in the land!
23 He went up from there to Be'er-Sheva.

24 Now YHWH was seen by him on that night and said:
   I am the God of Avraham your father.
   Do not be afraid, for I am with you,
   I will bless you and will make your seed many, for the sake
   of Avraham my servant.
25 He built a slaughter-site there
   and called out the name of YHWH.
   He spread his tent there, and Yitzhak's servants excavated a
   well there.
26 Now Avimelekh went to him from Gerar, along with
   Ahuzzat his aide and Pikhol the commander of his army.
27 Yitzhak said to them:
   Why have you come to me?
   For you hate me and have sent me away from you!
28 They said:
   We have seen, yes, seen that YHWH has been with you,
   so we say: Pray let there be a binding-oath between us,
      between us and you,
   we want to cut a covenant with you:
29 If ever you should deal badly with us . . . !
   Just as we have not harmed you and just as we have only
      dealt well with you and have sent you away in peace—
   you are now blessed by YHWH!
30 He made them a drinking-feast, and they ate and drank.
31 They (arose) early in the morning and swore to one another;
   then Yitzhak sent them off, and they went from him in
      peace.
32 Now it was on that same day
   that Yitzhak's servants came and told him about the well
      that they had been digging,
   they said to him: We have found water!

33 So he called it: Shiv'a/Swearing-Seven;
therefore the name of the city is Be'er-Sheva until this day.

34 When Esav was forty years old, he took to wife Yehudit
daughter of B'eri the Hittite and Ba'semat daughter of
Elon the Hittite.
35 And they were a bitterness of spirit to Yitzhak and Rivka.

27:1 Now when Yitzhak was old and his eyes had become too
dim for seeing,
he called Esav, his elder son, and said to him:
My son!
He said to him:
Here I am.
2 He said:
Now here, I have grown old, and do not know the day of
my death.
3 So now, pray pick up your weapons—your hanging-quiver
and your bow,
go out into the field and hunt me down some hunted-game,

Deceit and Blessing (26:34 to 28:9): Of all the stories of Genesis, this is
perhaps the most brilliantly staged. Nowhere is the narrative so vivid as
here, and nowhere, even including Chapter 22, is the tension so master-
fully drawn out.

Despite the fact that the story line is a simple one, involving deception
and the "taking" of the blessing, the text is imbued with great subtlety.
Most striking is the sensuality it invokes: seven times we hear of
"game," six of the "delicacy" (or "tasty-dish"), and three times Yitzhak
"feels" Yaakov (who "comes close" four times). In fact the story makes
use of all five of the senses. One sense—that of sight— is defective, and

26 **aide:** Lit. "friend."
30 **they ate and drank:** The cutting of a covenant is often accompanied by a
meal in biblical and other societies.
34 **forty years old:** The same age that his father was at the time of his marriage.

4 and make me a delicacy, such as I love;
    bring it to me, and I will eat it,
    that I may give you my own blessing before I die.
5 Now Rivka was listening as Yitzhak spoke to Esav his son,
    and so when Esav went off into the fields to hunt down
        hunted-game to bring (to him),
6 Rivka said to Yaakov her son, saying:
    Here, I was listening as your father spoke to Esav your
        brother, saying:
7 Bring me some hunted-game and make me a delicacy, I will
        eat it
    and give you blessing before YHWH, before my death.
8 So now, my son, listen to my voice, to what I command
        you:
9 Pray go to the flock and take me two fine goat kids from
        there,
    I will make them into a delicacy for your father, such as he
        loves;
10 you bring it to your father, and he will eat,
    so that he may give you blessing before his death.
11 Yaakov said to Rivka his mother:
    Here, Esav my brother is a hairy man, and I am a smooth
        man,
12 perhaps my father will feel me—then I will be like a
        trickster in his eyes,
    and I will bring a curse and not a blessing on myself!
13 His mother said to him:
    Let your curse be on me, my son!
    Only: listen to my voice and go, take them for me.
14 He went and took and brought them to his mother,
    and his mother made a delicacy, such as his father loved.
15 Rivka then took the garments of Esav, her elder son, the
        choicest ones that were with her in the house,
16 and clothed Yaakov, her younger son;
    and with the skins of the goat kids, she clothed his hands
        and the smooth-parts of his neck.
17 Then she placed the delicacy and the bread that she had
        made in the hand of Yaakov her son.

18 He came to his father and said:
Father!
He said:
Here I am. Which one are you, my son?
19 Yaakov said to his father:
I am Esav, your firstborn.
I have done as you spoke to me:
Pray arise, sit and eat from my hunted-game,
that you may give me your own blessing.

-----

on that deficiency will turn the action of the story. Yet another level of meaning is apparent: "to see" in ancient Israel, as in many cultures, was a term connected to prophetic powers, as we observed regarding Avraham. So here, ironically, Yitzhak's blindness leads to both deception and to the proper transferral of the blessing.

Structurally the story is framed by two references to Esav and his wives: 26:34–35 prepares the way for his loss of the blessing, by showing that he has alienated himself from his parents (and broken Avraham's charge to Yitzhak in 24:3), and 28:6–9 finds Esav obeying his father and making a rather pathetic attempt to reassure himself of his love.

Some of the story's motifs will return later. The threefold "as he loves" looks to the crucial role that the theme of "love" will play later on in Genesis (as well as being a key to the story itself). The general theme of nonrecognition will return with an interesting twist in the Yosef novella (especially in Chapters 42–44).

27:4 **delicacy:** See 25:28. Yitzhak is tied to the senses, a trait that he prizes in Esav. **my own blessing:** Or "my special blessing." Heb. *nefesh* frequently means "self" or "personality."
7 **before YHWH:** Note that Rivka adds these words to her husband's.
9 **take:** Fetch (see also verses 13, 14, 45).
13 **Let your curse be on me:** Ominously, Rivka disappears from the narrative after verse 46.
18 **Which one are you:** Three times—here, in verse 21, and in verse 24—the father asks for assurances about the son's identity. **my son:** This phrase reverberates throughout the story, underlining the confusion over the identity of the sons.
19 **Esav, your firstborn:** From the first word the lie is blatant; contrast Esav's tension-filled reply to the same question in verse 32.

20 Yitzhak said to his son:
   How did you find it so hastily, my son?
   He said: Indeed, YHWH your God made it happen for me.
21 Yitzhak said to Yaakov:
   Pray come closer, that I may feel you, my son,
   whether you are really my son Esav or not.
22 Yaakov moved closer to Yitzhak his father.
   He felt him and said:
   The voice is Yaakov's voice, the hands are Esav's hands—
23 but he did not recognize him, for his hands were like the
        hands of Esav his brother, hairy.
   Now he was about to bless him,
24 when he said:
   Are you he, my son Esav?
   He said:
   I am.
25 So he said: Bring it close to me, and I will eat from the
        hunted-game of my son,
   in order that I may give you my own blessing.
   He put it close to him and he ate,
   he brought him wine and he drank.
26 Then Yitzhak his father said to him:
   Pray come close and kiss me, my son.
27 He came close and kissed him.
   Now he smelled the smell of his garments
   and blessed him and said:
   See, the smell of my son
   is like the smell of a field
   that YHWH has blessed.
28   So may God give you
          from the dew of the heavens,
          from the fat of the earth,
          (along with) much grain and new-wine!
29   May peoples serve you,
          may tribes bow down to you;
          be master to your brothers,
          may your mother's sons bow down to you!
          Those who curse you, cursed!
          Those who bless you, blessed!

30 Now it was, when Yitzhak had finished blessing Yaakov,
   yes it was—Yaakov had just gone out, out from the
      presence of Yitzhak his father—
   that Esav his brother came back from his hunting.
31 He too made a delicacy and brought it to his father.
   He said to his father:
   Let my father arise and eat from the hunted-game of his
      son,
   that you may give me your own blessing.
32 Yitzhak his father said to him:
   Which one are you?
   He said:
   I am your son, your firstborn, Esav.
33 Yitzhak trembled with very great trembling
   and said:
   Who then was he
   that hunted down hunted-game and brought it to me—I ate
      it all before you came
   and I gave him my blessing!
   Now blessed he must remain!
34 When Esav heard the words of his father,
   he cried out with a very great and bitter cry,
   and said to his father:
   Bless me, me also, father!

---

20 **made it happen:** An appropriate expression to use with Yitzhak; see 24:12.
23 **hairy:** In the end Yitzhak relies more on the sense of touch than on his
   hearing. Yet the latter is usually regarded as the source of truth in the Bible
   (see Deut. 4:12, for example).
27 **a field:** Fitting for Esav, the "man of the field" (25:27).
29 **Those who bless you, blessed!:** Perhaps hearkening back to God's speech
   to Avraham in 12:3. Note that this blessing, at least in this particular
   wording, is never spoken to Yitzhak.
32 **Esav:** The exact identification is put off until the end of the sequence,
   heightening the drama. Similarly, see 22:2.
33,34 **very great:** Movingly, the father's terror and the son's anguish mirror one
   another via use of the same phrase (Heb. *ad me'od,* which is rare).
33 **blessed he must remain:** Once uttered, the words of blessing cannot be
   rescinded.

35 He said:
Your brother came with deceit and took away your blessing.
36 He said:
Is that why his name was called Yaakov/Heel-Sneak? For he
has now sneaked against me twice:
My firstborn-right he took, and now he has taken my
blessing!
And he said:
Haven't you reserved a blessing for me?
37 Yitzhak answered, saying to Esav:
Here, I have made him master to you,
and all his brothers I have given him as servants,
with grain and new-wine I have invested him—
so for you, what then can I do, my son?
38 Esav said to his father:
Have you only a single blessing, father?
Bless me, me also, father!
And Esav lifted up his voice and wept.
39 Then Yitzhak his father answered, saying to him:
Behold, from the fat of the earth
must be your dwelling-place,
from the dew of the heavens above.
40   You will live by your sword,
you will serve your brother.
But it will be
that when you brandish it,
you will tear his yoke from your neck.
41 Now Esav held a grudge against Yaakov because of the
blessing with which his father had blessed him.
Esav said in his heart:
Let the days of mourning for my father draw near
and then I will kill Yaakov my brother!
42 Rivka was told of the words of Esav, her elder son.
She sent and called for Yaakov, her younger son,
and said to him:
Here, Esav your brother is consoling himself about you,
with (the thought of) killing you.
43 So now, my son, listen to my voice:
Arise and flee to Lavan my brother in Harran,

44 and stay with him for a few days, until your brother's fury
has turned away,
45 until his anger turns away from you and he forgets what
you did to him.
Then I will send and have you taken from there—
for should I be bereaved of you both in a single day?
46 So Rivka said to Yitzhak:
I loathe my life because of those Hittite women;
if Yaakov should take a wife from the Hittite women—like
these, from the women of the land,
why should I have life?
28:1 So Yitzhak called for Yaakov,
he blessed him and charged him, saying to him:
You are not to take a wife from the women of Canaan;
2 arise, go to the country of Aram, to the house of Betuel,
your mother's father,
and take yourself a wife from there, from the daughters of
Lavan, your mother's brother.
3 May God Shaddai bless you,
may he make you bear fruit and make you many,
so that you become a host of peoples.
4 And may he give you the blessing of Avraham,
to you and to your seed with you,
for you to inherit the land of your sojournings,
which God gave to Avraham.

---

36 **Heel-Sneak:** In effect, Esav puts a curse on his brother's name, which will
be removed only in 32:29, twenty years later. **he has now sneaked
against me:** Or "cheated me."
37 **invested:** Or "sustained."
39 **Behold, from the fat of the earth:** Some interpret this negatively as "Behold, *away* from the fat of the earth. . . ."
40 **brandish:** I.e., a sword; Hebrew obscure.
41 **let the days . . . :** That is, wait until my father dies!
44 **days:** May be an idiomatic usage meaning "years."
45 **Then I will send:** This never occurs in the later course of the story.
28:2 **arise, go to the country of Aram:** It is curious that Yitzhak sends his son
on a journey that he himself had been forbidden to undertake.
4 **seed . . . land:** Again the two elements of the blessing given to Avraham.

5 So Yitzhak sent Yaakov off;
    he went to the country of Aram, to Lavan son of Betuel the
        Aramean,
    the brother of Rivka, the mother of Yaakov and Esav.

6 Now Esav saw
    that Yitzhak had given Yaakov farewell-blessing and had
        sent him to the country of Aram, to take himself a wife
        from there,
    (and that) when he had given him blessing, he had charged
        him, saying: You are not to take a wife from the women
        of Canaan!
7 And Yaakov had listened to his father and his mother and
        had gone to the country of Aram.
8 And Esav saw
    that the women of Canaan were bad in the eyes of Yitzhak
        his father,
9 so Esav went to Yishmael and took Mahalat daughter of
        Yishmael son of Avraham, sister of Nevayot, in addition
        to his wives as a wife.

10 Yaakov went out from Be'er-Sheva and went toward
        Harran,
11 and encountered a certain place.
    He had to spend the night there, for the sun had set.
    Now he took one of the stones of the place
    and set it at his head
    and lay down in that place.
12 And he dreamt:
    Here, a ladder was set up on the earth,
    its top reaching the heavens,
    and here: messengers of God were going up and down on it.
13 And here:
    YHWH was standing over against him.
    He said:
    I am YHWH,
    the God of Avraham your father and the God of Yitzhak.
    The land on which you lie
    I give to you and to your seed.

14 Your seed will be like the dust of the earth;
   you will burst forth, seaward, eastward, northward,
      southward.
   All the clans of the soil will find blessing through you and
      through your seed!
15 Here, I am with you,
   I will watch over you wherever you go
   and will bring you back to this soil;
   indeed, I will not leave you
   until I have done what I have spoken to you.

Yaakov Sets Out (28:10–22): Yaakov's journey takes him not only to a foreign land, but to the portals of adulthood. It begins fittingly with a dream vision, so that we will know from the start that God is with him. In fact Yaakov always encounters God at crucial life junctures, at the point of journeys (31:3—leaving Aram; 32:25ff.—meeting Esav; 35:1—returning to Bet-El; 35:9ff.—the homecoming; and 46:2ff.—on the way to Egypt).

The setting for this particular encounter is highly unusual, especially when compared to the generally nongeographical nature of the revelations to Avraham. The idea of a sacred site ("place," a biblical word with these connotations, occurs three times) is strongly suggested. The notion of a ladder or ramp (or "gateway," v.17) between the divine and human worlds is well known in ancient stories. A variation of the theme occurs in 32:2–3, where Yaakov sees "messengers" again in an "encounter"; these two stories frame the middle of the entire cycle.

As Yaakov enters his adult life, he resembles both his grandfather Avraham, the visionary, and his son Yosef, the dreamer.

5 **Yaakov and Esav:** In the end, the oracle to Rivka is confirmed, with younger son superseding elder.
6 **charged:** Or "commanded."
12 **Here:** The word (three times) emphasizes the immediacy of the report; it is the vocabulary of dreams, as in 37:7 (Andersen). **ladder:** Others use "ramp" or "stairway."
13 **over against:** See note to 18:2.
13ff. **the land,** etc.: Once again Yaakov receives the blessing of Avraham "his father" (!). See 13:14–16.

16 Yaakov awoke from his sleep
and said:
Why,
YHWH is in this place,
and I, I did not know it!

17 He was awestruck and said:
How awesome is this place!
This is none other than a house of God,
and that is the gate of heaven!

18 Yaakov (arose) early in the morning,
he took the stone that he had set at his head
and set it up as a standing-pillar
and poured oil on top of it.

19 And he called the name of the place: Bet-El/House of
God—
however, Luz was the name of the city in former times.

20 And Yaakov vowed a vow, saying:
If God will be with me
and will watch over me on this way that I go
and will give me food to eat and a garment to wear,

21 and if I come back in peace to my father's house—
YHWH shall be God to me,

22 and this stone that I have set up as a standing-pillar shall
become a house of God,
and everything that you give me
I shall tithe, tithe it to you.

29:1 Yaakov lifted his feet and went to the land of the
Easterners.

2 He looked around him, and there: a well in the field, and
there were three herds of sheep crouching near it,
for from that well they used to give the herds to drink.
Now the stone on the mouth of the well was large,

3 so when all the herds were gathered there,
they used to roll the stone from the mouth of the well, give
the sheep to drink, and put the stone back on the mouth
of the well in its place.

4 Now Yaakov said to them:
Brothers, where are you from?
They said:
We are from Harran.
5 He said to them:
Do you know Lavan, son of Nahor?
They said:
We know him.
6 He said to them:
Is all well with him?
They said:
It is well—
and here comes Rahel his daughter with the sheep!
7 He said:
Indeed, it is still broad daylight,
it is not time to gather in the livestock,
so give the sheep to drink and go back, tend them.

Arrival in Aram (29:1–14): As one might expect from the usual biblical pattern, Yaakov meets his bride-to-be at a well. As in other ancient stories (see also Ex. 2:15–17) the hero performs a feat of physical strength, this time with a large stone—continuing the use of stones as a motif in the Yaakov stories.

Lavan is once again the chief representative of the family, as he was in the betrothal account of Chapter 24.

18 **standing-pillar:** A stone marker, common to the culture of the region. **Bet-El:** Trad. English "Beth El."
21 **in peace:** Or "safely." This functions as a key word in the Yaakov cycle, extending into the Yosef story as well. Yaakov, the "sneak" and wanderer, seeks peace and safety; he does not find it until the end of his life, albeit in a foreign land.
22 **tithe:** See note to 14:20.
29:1 **lifted his feet:** Colloquially, "picked up and went."
5 **We know him:** Biblical Hebrew expresses the idea "yes" by repeating the words of the question. See also verse 6 and 24:58.
6 **Rahel:** Trad. English "Rachel." The name means "ewe."
7 **to gather in:** For the night.

8 But they said:
We cannot, until all the herds have been gathered;
only then do they roll the stone from the mouth of the well,
   and then we give the sheep to drink.
9 While he was still speaking with them,
Rahel came with the sheep that were her father's
—for she was a shepherdess.
10 Now it was when Yaakov saw Rahel, the daughter of Lavan
   and the sheep of Lavan his mother's brother,
that Yaakov came close,
he rolled the stone from the mouth of the well
and gave drink to the sheep of Lavan his mother's brother.
11 Then Yaakov kissed Rahel, and lifted up his voice and
   wept.
12 And Yaakov told Rahel
that he was her father's brother
and that he was Rivka's son.
She ran and told her father.
13 Now it was, as soon as Lavan heard the tidings concerning
   Yaakov, his sister's son,
that he ran to meet him, embraced him and kissed him, and
   brought him into his house.
And he recounted all these events to Lavan.
14 Lavan said to him:
Without doubt you are my bone, my flesh!
And he stayed with him the days of a
   Renewing-of-the-Moon.

15 Lavan said to Yaakov:
Just because you are my brother, should you serve me for
   nothing?
Tell me, what shall your wages be?
16 Now Lavan had two daughters: the name of the elder was
   Lea, the name of the younger was Rahel.
17 Lea's eyes were delicate, but Rahel was fair of form and fair
   to look at.
18 And Yaakov fell in love with Rahel.
He said:
I will serve you seven years for Rahel, your younger
   daughter.

19 Lavan said:
   My giving her to you is better than my giving her to
      another man;
   stay with me.
20 So Yaakov served seven years for Rahel,
   yet they were in his eyes as but a few days, because of his
      love for her.
21 Then Yaakov said to Lavan:
   Come-now, (give me) my wife, for my days-of-labor have
      been fulfilled,
   so that I may come in to her.
22 Lavan gathered all the people of the place together and
      made a drinking-feast.
23 Now in the evening
   he took Lea his daughter and brought her to him,
   and he came in to her.
24 Lavan also gave her Zilpa his maid,
   for Lea his daughter as a maid.
25 Now in the morning:
   here, she was Lea!
   He said to Lavan:
   What is this that you have done to me!

Deception Repaid (29:15–30): The language of the text here, as well as
the tenor of the situation, suggest that the Bible has set up Yaakov's
punishment for having stolen Yitzhak's blessing from his brother. "Deceived" (v.25) and "younger . . . firstborn" (v.26) echo the Chapter 27
narrative, and provide another example of biblical justice.

10 **his mother's brother:** Three times here, to accentuate the familial ties.
12 **brother:** Relative (so also verse 15).
14 **Renewing-of-the-Moon:** Heb. *hodesh*, a month.
16 **Lea:** Trad. English "Leah." The name means "wild cow."
17 **delicate:** Others use "weak." Either the term is meant negatively or else
   Lea is being praised for one attribute but Rahel for total beauty.
18 **seven:** Aside from forty, this is the other schematic number found often in
   Genesis and elsewhere (for instance, as the basic number of the biblical
   calendar, in days, months, and years).
19 **with me:** Or "in my service," "under me."
21 **fulfilled:** I.e., over, completed.

Was it not for Rahel that I served you?
Why have you deceived me?
26 Lavan said:
Such is not done in our place, giving away the younger
    before the firstborn;
27 just fill out the bridal-week for this one, then we shall give
    you that one also,
    for the service which you will serve me for yet another
    seven years.
28 Yaakov did so—he fulfilled the bridal-week for this one,
    and then he gave him Rahel his daughter as a wife.
29 Lavan also gave Rahel his daughter Bilha his maid,
    for her as a maid.
30 So he came in to Rahel also,
    and he loved Rahel also,
    more than Lea.
    Then he served him for yet another seven years.

31 Now when YHWH saw that Lea was hated,
    he opened her womb,
    while Rahel was barren.
32 So Lea became pregnant and bore a son;
    she called his name: Re'uven/See, a Son!
    for she said:
    Indeed, YHWH has seen my being afflicted,
    indeed, now my husband will love me!
33 She became pregnant again and bore a son,
    and said:
    Indeed, YHWH has heard that I am hated,
    so he has given me this one as well!
    And she called his name: Shim'on/Hearing.
34 She became pregnant again and bore a son,
    and said:
    Now this time my husband will be joined to me,
    for I have borne him three sons!
    Therefore they called his name: Levi/Joining.
35 She became pregnant again and bore a son,
    and said:
    This time I will give thanks to YHWH!

Therefore she called his name: Yehuda/Giving-Thanks.
Then she stopped giving birth.

30:1 Now when Rahel saw that she could not bear (children) to
     Yaakov,
     Rahel envied her sister.
     She said to Yaakov:
     Come-now, (give) me children!
     If not, I will die!
   2 Yaakov's anger raged against Rahel,
     he said:
     Am I in place of God,
     who has denied you fruit of the body?
   3 She said:
     Here is my slave-girl Bilha;
     come in to her,
     so that she may give birth upon my knees, so that I too may
        be built-up-with-sons through her.
   4 She gave him Bilha her maid as a wife,
     and Yaakov came in to her.
   5 Bilha became pregnant and bore Yaakov a son.

Love, Jealousy, and Children (29:31–30:24): The narrative now demonstrates (1) how Yaakov prospers in exile, increasing both in wealth and in
progeny, and thus (2) how God fulfills his promise to the Patriarchs to
"make them many." Characteristically for the Bible, this takes place as a
result of human emotions: the jealousy of two sisters who are married to
the same man. The emotions, interestingly, are portrayed largely
through the names given to Yaakov's sons. In the end Lea seems to be
the victor, at least in the terms of a culture that prizes the production of
male children; she becomes the mother of fully half of the sons of Israel
(Redak).

31 **hated:** Others use "rejected," "unloved."
32 **Re'uven:** Trad. English "Reuben."
33 **Shim'on:** Trad. English "Simeon."
35 **Yehuda:** Trad. English "Judah."
30:3 **give birth upon my knees:** An idiom for legal adoption (here, by Rahel).

6 Rahel said:
God has done-me-justice; yes, he has heard my voice!
He has given me a son!
Therefore she called his name: Dan/He-Has-Done-Justice.
7 And Bilha, Rahel's maid, became pregnant again and bore a
second son to Yaakov.
8 Rahel said:
A struggle of God have I struggled with my sister; yes, I
have prevailed!
So she called his name: Naftali/My Struggle.

9 Now when Lea saw that she had stopped giving birth,
she took Zilpa her maid and gave her to Yaakov as a wife.
10 Zilpa, Lea's maid, bore Yaakov a son.
11 Lea said:
What fortune!
So she called his name: Gad/Fortune.
12 And Zilpa, Lea's maid, bore a second son to Yaakov.
13 Lea said:
What happiness!
For women will deem me happy.
So she called his name: Asher/Happiness.

14 Now Re'uven went in the days of the wheat-harvest and
found some love-apples in the field,
and brought them to Lea his mother.
Rahel said to Lea:
Pray give me (some) of your son's love-apples!
15 She said to her:
Is your taking away my husband such a small thing
that you would now take away my son's love-apples?
Rahel said:
Very well, he may lie with you tonight in exchange for your
son's love-apples.
16 So when Yaakov came home from the fields in the evening,
Lea went out to meet him and said:
You must come in to me,
for I have hired, yes, hired you for my son's love-apples.
So he lay with her that night.
17 And God hearkened to Lea,

so that she became pregnant and bore Yaakov a fifth son.
18 Lea said:
God has given me my hired-wages,
because I gave my maid to my husband!
So she called his name: Yissakhar/There-Is-Hire.
19 Once again Lea became pregnant, and she bore a sixth son
     to Yaakov.
20 Lea said:
God has presented me with a good present,
this time my husband will prize me—
  for I have borne him six sons!
So she called his name: Zevulun/Prince.
21 Afterward she bore a daughter, and called her name Dina.

22 But God kept Rahel in mind,
God hearkened to her and opened her womb,
23 so that she became pregnant and bore a son.
She said:
God has removed/*asaf*
my reproach!
24 So she called his name: Yosef,
saying:
May YHWH add/*yosef*
another son to me!

---

13 **What happiness:** Others use "Happy am I!"
14 **love-apples:** Heb. *duda'im;* a plant believed to have aphrodisiac powers.
   Others use "mandrakes."
15 **taking away:** The theme of "taking," so prominent in Chapter 27, returns,
   in the context of sibling rivalry again.
18 **hired-wages:** "Wages" recurs as a theme throughout this part of the Yaakov cycle (Fokkelman). It is perhaps a veiled portrayal of the events of
   Yaakov's adulthood as "payment" for what he did to his brother. **Yissakhar:** Trad. English "Issachar."
20 **this time my husband will prize me:** Lea's six pregnancies and birthings
   are bracketed by this verse and 29:32, "Now my husband will love
   me." **Zevulun:** Trad. English "Zebulun."
23–24 **removed. . . . add:** Yosef's naming prefigures his destiny as a son lost and
   found.
24 **Yosef:** Trad. English "Joseph."

25 Now it was, once Rahel had borne Yosef, that Yaakov said
    to Lavan:
    Send me free, that I may go back to my place, to my land,
26 give over my wives and my children,
    for whom I have served you,
    and I will go.
    Indeed, you yourself know my service that I have served
    you!
27 Lavan said to him:
    Pray, if I have found favor in your eyes . . .
    I have become wealthy,
    and YHWH has blessed me on account of you.
28 And he said: Specify the wages due you from me, and I will
    give you payment.
29 He said to him:
    You yourself know
    how I have served you,
    and how it has gone with your livestock in my charge.
30 For you had but few before me,
    and they have since burst out into a multitude.
    Thus has YHWH blessed you at my every step!
    But now, when may I too do something for my household?
31 He said:
    What shall I give you?
    Yaakov said:
    You are not to give me anything—
    only do this thing for me,
    then I will return, I will tend your flock, I will keep watch:
32 Let me go over your whole flock today
    removing from there every speckled and dappled head;
    and every dark head among the lambs, and each dappled
        and speckled-one among the goats—they shall be may
        wages.
33 And may my honesty plead for me on a future day:
    when you come-to-check my wages (that are) before you,
    whatever is not speckled or dappled among the goats, or
        dark among the lambs,
    it will be as though stolen by me.
34 Lavan said:

Good, let it be according to your words.

35 And on the same day he removed the streaked and dappled
   he-goats
   and every speckled and dappled she-goat, every one that
   had any white on it,
   and every dark-one among the lambs,
   and handed them over to his sons.

36 Then he put a three-days' journey between himself and
   Yaakov.
   Now Yaakov was tending Lavan's remaining flock.

37 Yaakov took himself rods from moist poplar, almond, and
   plane trees
   and peeled white peelings in them, exposing the white that
   was on the rods,

38 then he presented the rods that he had peeled in the
   gutters, in the water troughs where the flock would come
   to drink, in front of the flock.

Yaakov in Exile: Stealth and Prosperity (30:25–32:1): The long account of
how Yaakov outwits Lavan rounds out the portrait of his personality: he
is a man at once clever, successful, and harassed. The text goes to great
lengths to describe both men in behavior and thought, and we are given
enough dialogue to be able to understand their motivations. The repeating words point to major themes: "serve," "wages," "face" (which will
become central to the whole cycle by Chapter 32), and a whole vocabulary of trickery: "steal" (with the variations "be stealthy" and "steal the
wits"), "take away" (see Chapter 27!), "snatch," and "rob."

26 **give over my wives and my children:** In the law of the region, slaves did
   not retain control of their families. Does this suggest something about
   Yaakov's treatment by Lavan? (Speiser)

27 **Pray, if I have found:** Or "May I now find." **I have become wealthy,/
   and ʾYHWH . . . :** Some interpret this as "I have divined that
   YHWH . . ."

32 **Let me go:** Some read "Go." **every speckled . . . :** This would appeal to
   Lavan, since such animals would be in the minority.

35 **white:** Heb. *lavan*. Also the word "poplar" in verse 37 is a play on Lavan
   (*livne*). The conniving father-in-law is tricked with words resembling his
   own name.

Now they would be in heat as they came to drink;

39 thus the flock came to be in heat by the rods,
and the flock bore streaked, speckled, and dappled (young).

40 But the sheep, Yaakov set apart,
and gave position among the flock to each streaked-one and
every dark-one among Lavan's flocks;
thus he made special herds for himself, but did not make
them for Lavan's flock.

41 So it was that whenever the robust flock-animals were in
heat,
Yaakov would put the rods in sight of the flock-animals, in
the gutters, to make them be in heat next to the rods.

42 But when the flock-animals were feeble, he would not put
them there.
And so it was that the feeble-ones became Lavan's, and the
robust-ones, Yaakov's.

43 The man burst-forth-with-wealth exceedingly, yes,
exceedingly, he came to have many flock-animals and
maids and servants, and camels and he-asses.

31:1 Now he heard the words of Lavan's sons, (that they) said:
Yaakov has taken away all that was our father's,
and from what was our father's he has made all this
weighty-wealth!

2 And Yaakov saw by Lavan's face:
here, he was no longer with him as yesterday and the
day-before.

3 And YHWH said to Yaakov:
Return to the land of your fathers, to your kindred!
I will be with you!

4 So Yaakov sent and had Rahel and Lea called to the field,
to his animals,

5 and said to them:
I see by your father's face:
indeed, he is no longer toward me as yesterday and the
day-before.
But the God of my father has been with me!

6 You yourselves know that I have served your father with all
my might,

7 but your father has cheated me and changed my wages ten
   times over,
   yet God has not allowed him to do me ill.

8 If he said thus: The speckled-ones shall be your wages,
   all the animals would bear speckled-ones,
   and if he said thus: The streaked-ones shall be your wages,
   all the animals would bear streaked-ones.

9 So God has snatched away your father's livestock and given
   them to me.

10 Now it was at the time of the animals' being in heat
    that I lifted up my eyes and saw in a dream:
    here, the he-goats that mount the animals—streaked,
    speckled, and spotted!

11 And God's messenger said to me in the dream: Yaakov!
    I said: Here I am.

12 He said:
    Pray lift up your eyes and see:
    All the he-goats that mount the animals—streaked,
    speckled, and spotted!
    For I have seen all that Lavan is doing to you.

---

39 **by the rods:** Folk belief holds that what the animals see as they mate will
   influence the color of their offspring.

40 **gave position:** Following the interpretation of Fokkelman.

43 **he came to have many flock-animals:** Like his father (26:14) and grandfather (12:16).

31:2 **he was no longer with him:** Others use "Lavan's manner toward him was
     no longer . . ."

3 **land of your fathers . . . your kindred:** Here, unlike 12:1, the land is
  Canaan, not Harran! **I will be with you:** Heb. *ehye immakh*, interpreted
  here and throughout by B-R as "I will be-there with you," stressing that it
  is God's presence that is indicated by the verb *hyh*, "to be." See especially
  Ex. 3:14.

4 **to the field:** As a place where such conversations would be certain to be
  private.

7 **ten times:** Many times.

10 **Now it was . . . in a dream:** Several times in this chapter we hear of
   important events secondhand, in speech rather than in action. See note to
   20:13. **streaked, speckled, and spotted:** Heb. *akuddim, nekuddim, u-ve-
   ruddim.* The rhyme (rare in biblical Hebrew) suggests a vision or a dream.

13 I am the God of Bet-El,
   where you anointed the pillar,
   where you vowed a vow to me.
   So now, arise,
   get out of this land,
   return to the land of your kindred!
14 Rahel and Lea answered him, they said to him:
   Do we still have a share, an inheritance in our father's
      house?
15 Is it not as strangers that we are thought of by him?
   For he has sold us and eaten up, yes, eaten up our
      purchase-price!
16 Indeed, all the riches that God has snatched away from our
      father—
   they belong to us and to our children.
   So now, whatever God has said to you, do!
17 So Yaakov arose, he lifted his children and his wives onto
      the camels
18 and led away all his livestock, all his property that he had
      gained,
   the acquired-livestock of his own acquiring which he had
      gained in the country of Aram,
   to come home to Yitzhak his father in the land of Canaan.
19 Now Lavan had gone to shear his flock;
   Rahel, meanwhile, stole the *terafim* that belonged to her
      father.
20 Now Yaakov stole the wits of Lavan the Aramean,
   by not telling him that he was about to flee.
21 And flee he did, he and all that was his;
   he arose and crossed the River, setting his face toward the
      mountain-country of Gil'ad.
22 Lavan was told on the third day that Yaakov had fled;
23 he took his tribal-brothers with him and pursued him, a
      seven-days' journey,
   and caught up with him in the mountain-country of Gil'ad.
24 But God came to Lavan the Aramean in a dream of the
      night
   and said to him:

Be on your watch
lest you speak to Yaakov, be it good or ill!
25 When Lavan caught up with Yaakov,
—Yaakov had pegged his tent in the mountains, and Lavan
along with his brothers had pegged (his tent) in the
mountain-country of Gil'ad—
26 Lavan said to Yaakov:
What did you mean to do
by stealing my wits and leading my daughters away like
captives of the sword?
27 Why did you secretly flee and steal away on me, without
even telling me,
—for I would have sent you off with joy and with song,
with drum and with lyre—
28 and you did not even allow me to kiss my grandchildren
and my daughters?
You have done foolishly now!
29 It lies in my hand's power to do (all of) you ill!
But yesterday night the God of your father said to me,
saying:
Be on your watch
from speaking to Yaakov, be it good or ill!
30 Well now, you had to go, yes, go, since you longed, longed
for your father's house—
Why did you steal my gods?
31 Yaakov answered and said to Lavan:
Indeed, I was afraid, for I said to myself: Perhaps you will
even rob me of your daughters!

---

19 *terafim:* Hebrew obscure; apparently some sort of idols. Others use "household gods."
20 **stole the wits:** Fooled, hoodwinked.
24 **be it good or ill:** Lit. "from good to ill."
28 **kiss:** Upon leaving; "kiss good-bye."
30 **you had to go:** Or "Suppose you had to go."
31 **Indeed, I was afraid:** Yaakov seems to be explaining why he "had to go"
first, and then answering Lavan's question in verse 32.

32 With whomever you find your gods—he shall not live;
here in front of our brothers, (see if) you recognize anything
of yours with me, and take it!
Yaakov did not know that Rahel had stolen them.

33 Lavan came into Yaakov's tent and into Lea's tent and into
the tents of the two maids, but he did not find anything.
Then he went out of Lea's tent and came into Rahel's tent.

34 Now Rahel had taken the *terafim* and had put them in the
basket-saddle of the camels, and had sat down upon them.
Lavan felt all around the tent, but he did not find anything.

35 She said to her father:
Do not let anger rage in my lord's eyes that I am not able to
rise in your presence,
for the manner of women is upon me.
So he searched, but he did not find the *terafim*.

36 Now Yaakov became enraged and took up quarrel with
Lavan,
Yaakov answered, saying to Lavan:
What is my offense, what is my sin,
that you have dashed hotly after me,

37 that you have felt all through my wares?
What have you found from all your household-wares?
Set it here in front of your brothers and my brothers,
that they may decide between us two!

38 It is twenty years now that I have been under you:
your ewes and your she-goats have never miscarried,
the rams from your flock I never have eaten,

39 none torn-by-beasts have I ever brought you—
I would make good the loss,
at my hand you would seek it,
stolen by day or stolen by night.

40 (Thus) I was:
by day, parching-heat consumed me, and cold by night,
and my sleep eluded my eyes.

41 It is twenty years for me now in your house:
I have served you fourteen years for your two daughters,
and six years for your animals,
yet you have changed my wages ten times over.

42 Had not the God of my father,

the God of Avraham and the Terror of Yitzhak,
been-there for me,
indeed, you would have sent me off now, empty-handed!
But God has seen my being afflicted and the toil of my
    hands,
and yesterday night he decided.

43 Lavan gave answer, he said to Yaakov:
The daughters are my daughters,
the children are my children,
the animals are my animals—
all that you see, it is mine!
But to my daughters—what can I do to them today, or to
    their children whom they have borne?

44 So now, come,
let us cut a covenant, I and you,
and let (something here) serve as a witness between me and
    you.

45 Yaakov took a stone and erected it as a standing-pillar.

46 And Yaakov said to his brothers:
Collect stones!
They fetched stones and made a mound.
And they ate there by the mound.

47 Now Lavan called it: *Yegar Sahaduta,*
while Yaakov called it: Gal-Ed.

---

32 **with me:** In my possession.

34 **sat down upon them:** Ridiculing the pagan gods, at least to the audience. **felt all around:** Recalling the "feeling" of Yitzhak in Chapter 27.

35 **manner of women:** The menstrual period.

37 **felt all through:** Or "rifled."

39 **seek:** I.e., seek restitution.

41 **twenty years:** Yosef will be away from Yaakov for approximately the same
period of time.

42 **Terror:** The intent of the Hebrew is unclear; it could be something like
"Yitzhak's champion" or "the One who inspired terror in Yitzhak."

43 **to my daughters:** Others use "for my daughters."

46 **And they ate:** See note to 26:30.

47 *Yegar Sahaduta:* Aramaic for "Mound-Witness" (Yaakov's Gal-Ed of the
next verse). Aramaic was the *lingua franca* of the area from the First Millennium B.C.E. on, and still exists in some forms today.

48 Lavan said:
This mound is witness between me and you from today.
Therefore they called its name: Gal-Ed/Mound-Witness,
49 and also: Mitzpa/Guardpost,
because he said:
May YHWH keep guard between me and you, when we are
hidden from one another!
50 If you should ever afflict my daughters,
if you should ever take wives besides my daughters . . . !
No man is here with us,
(but) see, God is witness between me and you!
51 And Lavan said to Yaakov:
Here is this mound, here is the pillar that I have sunk
between me and you:
52 witness is this mound, witness is the pillar
that I will not cross over this mound to you
and you will not cross over this mound and this pillar to
me,
for ill!
53 May the God of Avraham and the God of Nahor
keep-justice between us—the God of their father.
And Yaakov swore by the Terror of his father Yitzhak.
54 Then Yaakov slaughtered a slaughter-meal on the mountain
and called his brothers to eat bread.
They ate bread and spent the night on the mountain.
32:1 Lavan (arose) early in the morning, kissed his grandchildren
and his daughters and blessed them,
and Lavan went to return to his place.

2 As Yaakov went on his way,
messengers of God encountered him.
3 Yaakov said when he saw them:
This is a camp of God!
And he called the name of that place:
Mahanayim/Double-Camp.

4 Now Yaakov sent messengers on ahead of him to Esav his
brother in the land of Se'ir, in the territory of Edom,

5 and charged them, saying:
Thus say to my lord, to Esav:
Thus says your servant Yaakov:
I have sojourned with Lavan and have tarried until now.
6 Ox and ass, sheep and servant and maid have become mine.
I have sent to tell my lord, to find favor in your eyes.
7 The messengers returned to Yaakov, saying:
We came to your brother, to Esav—
but he is already coming to meet you, and four hundred
men are with him!
8 Yaakov became exceedingly afraid and was distressed.
He divided the people that were with him and the sheep
and the oxen and the camels into two camps,
9 saying to himself:
Should Esav come against the one camp and strike it, the
camp that is left will escape.

Preparations for Esav (32:2–24): As if to portend something momentous, Yaakov's first act upon setting out for home is an encounter with "messengers of God." From this starting point everything is subsequently a matter of "two camps" (v.8) or two levels: the divine and the human. This is the key to understanding the meeting between Yaakov and his brother in its entirety: Yaakov will have to deal with God before he can resolve his problem with Esav.

With an obsequiousness whose language reflects both the culture and the emotional setting, Yaakov prepares a gift for Esav, but finds to his dismay that his brother is "coming to meet him," with seemingly hostile intent. Once again stealth (or at least extreme caution) is the rule, with Yaakov taking elaborate precautions.

49 **when we are hidden:** Even when I cannot verify your behavior.
50 **God:** Or "a god."
54 **bread:** Or more generally, "food."
32:1 **Lavan (arose)** . . . : The verse numbering follows the Hebrew; some English translations number 32:1 as 31:55.
7 **four hundred men:** A considerable fighting force. Even if the number is schematic (as ten times forty), it still represents something formidable.

10 Then Yaakov said:
God of my father Avraham,
God of my father Yitzhak,
O YHWH,
who said to me: Return to your land, to your kindred, and
    I will deal well with you!—

11 Too small am I for all the faithfulness and trust that you
    have shown your servant.
For with only my rod did I cross this Jordan, and now I
    have become two camps.

12 Pray save me from the hand of my brother, from the hand
    of Esav!
For I am in fear of him,
lest he come and strike me down, mothers and children
    alike!

13 But you, you have said:
I will deal well, well with you,
I will make your seed like the sand of the sea, which is too
    much to count!

14 Spending the night there that night,
he took a gift from what was at hand, for Esav his brother:

15 she-goats, two hundred, and kids, twenty,
ewes, two hundred, and rams, twenty,

16 nursing camels and their young, thirty,
cows, forty, and bulls, ten,
she-asses, twenty, and colts, ten;

17 he handed them over to his servants, herd by herd
    separately,
and said to his servants:
Cross on ahead of me, and leave room between herd and
    herd.

18 He charged the first group, saying:
When Esav my brother meets you
and asks you, saying: To whom do you belong, where are
    you going, and to whom do these ahead of you belong?

19 Then say:
—to your servant, to Yaakov, it is a gift sent to my lord, to
    Esav,

and here, he himself is also behind us.

20 Thus he charged the second, and thus the third, and thus
   all that were walking behind the herds, saying:
   According to this word shall you speak to Esav when you
   come upon him:

21 You shall say: Also—here, your servant Yaakov is behind
   us.
   For he said to himself:
   I will wipe (the anger from) his face
   with the gift that goes ahead of my face;
   afterward, when I see his face,
   perhaps he will lift up my face!

22 The gift crossed over ahead of his face,
   but he spent the night on that night in the camp.

23 He arose during that night,
   took his two wives, his two maids, and his eleven children
   to cross the Yabbok crossing.

24 He took them and brought them across the river; he
   brought across what belonged to him.

25 And Yaakov was left alone—
   Now a man wrestled with him until the dawn rose.

26 When he saw that he could not prevail against him,
   he touched the socket of his thigh;
   the socket of Yaakov's thigh had been dislocated as he
   wrestled with him.

---

11 **Too small:** This is the first indication of the change in Yaakov's personality. Now he relies on God (although he still uses his wits, by diplomatically
   and strategically preparing for his meeting with Esav).

13 **you have said:** I.e., you have promised. See also note on 31:10. **like the
   sand:** In fact, this is God's promise to Avraham, in 22:17.

15: **she-goats . . . :** The gift is a special one, promising increase (females with
   their young).

21 **lift up my face:** Or "be gracious to me."

23 **Yabbok:** A traditional natural boundary, it creates a wild gorge which is the
   perfect setting for this incident.

25 **left alone:** In a psychological sense Yaakov has not yet crossed the river.

26 **touched:** Perhaps in homage, for the injury had already occurred (Ehrlich).

27 Then he said:
Let me go,
for the dawn has risen!
But he said:
I will not let you go
unless you bless me.
28 He said to him:
What is your name?
And he said: Yaakov.
29 Then he said:
Not as Yaakov/Heel-Sneak shall your name be henceforth
    uttered,
but rather as Yisrael/God-Fighter,
for you have fought with God and men
and have prevailed.
30 Then Yaakov asked and said:
Pray tell me your name!
But he said:
Now why do you ask after my name?
And he gave him farewell-blessing there.
31 Yaakov called the name of the place: Peniel/Face of God,
for: I have seen God,
face to face,
and my life has been saved.
32 The sun shone on him as he crossed by Penuel,
and he was limping on his thigh.
33 —Therefore the Sons of Israel do not eat the sinew that is
    on the socket of the thigh until this day,
for he had touched the socket of Yaakov's thigh at the
    sinew.

33:1 Yaakov lifted up his eyes and saw:
there was Esav coming, and with him, four hundred men!
He divided the children among Lea, Rahel, and the two
    maids:
2 he put the maids and their children first,
Lea and her children behind them,
and Rahel and Yosef behind them,

The Mysterious Stranger: Struggle at the Yabbok (32:25–33): Unexpectedly there is a break in the narrative. The stage has been set for something mysterious to happen with a nighttime backdrop and accented references to "crossing" (vv.23–24), which clearly refers to more than just the river.

The great wrestling scene at the Yabbok both symbolizes and resolves beforehand Yaakov's meeting with Esav, much as Shakespeare's pre-battle dream scenes (e.g., *Julius Caesar, Richard III, Macbeth*) will do with his characters. Struggle, the motif already introduced in the mother's womb (Chapter 25), returns here, but that is not the only consideration. At issue is Yaakov's whole life and personality, which despite his recent material successes are still under the pall of Esav's curse (27:36). Central, then, is the change of name in verse 29, which suggests both a victorious struggle and the emergence of a new power. This is further supported by the Hebrew plays on sound: *Y'KB* (Yaakov), *YBK* (Yabbok), and *Y'BK* (wrestling).

The story may have originated as the well-known tale of a hero fighting a river divinity, but it clearly has been transformed into something much broader by its position and vocabulary.

Resolution (33:1–17): Once the Yabbok crisis is past, there is hope for reconciliation of the brothers. Even so, Yaakov exercises caution, behaving like a man who is presenting tribute to a king. The narrative is brought full circle in verses 10 and 11, where "face" is once again highlighted and where Yaakov's gift is termed a "token-of-blessing." At last the tension of Yaakov's early life seems resolved.

27 **dawn has risen:** In folklore, supernatural beings often must disappear with the break of day.

28–29 **What is your name? . . . Not as Yaakov:** As if to say "You cannot be blessed with such a name!" The "man" in effect removes Esav's curse.

29 **God-Fighter:** The name may actually mean "God fights." Buber further conjectured that it means "God rules," containing the kernel of ancient Israel's concept of itself, but he retained "Fighter of God" in the translation. **God and men:** Others use "beings divine and human."

30 **Now why do you ask:** In folklore the name of a divine being is often withheld, for to know it would be to acquire power over him. See also Judges 13:18: "Now why do you ask after my name? For it is wondrous!"

31 **Peniel/Face of God:** See verse 21, and 33:10, for the important allusions.

32 **The sun shone:** A sign of favor. **Penuel:** A variant spelling of Peniel.

33 **sinew:** The sciatic nerve.

3 while he himself advanced ahead of them.
And he bowed low to the ground seven times, until he had
come close to him, to his brother.

4 Esav ran to meet him,
he embraced him, flung himself upon his neck, and kissed
him.
And they wept.

5 Then he lifted up his eyes and saw the women and the
children, and said:
What are these to you?
He said:
—the children with whom God has favored your servant.

6 Then the maids came close, they and their children, and
bowed low.

7 Then Lea and her children came close and bowed low.
Afterward Yosef and Rahel came close and bowed low.

8 He said:
What to you is all this camp that I have met?
He said:
—to find favor in my lord's eyes.

9 Esav said:
I have plenty, my brother, let what is yours remain yours.

10 Yaakov said:
No, I pray!
Pray, if I have found favor in your eyes,
then take this gift from my hand.
For I have, after all, seen your face, as one sees the face of
God,
and you have been gracious to me.

11 Pray take my token-of-blessing that is brought to you,
for God has shown me favor—for I have everything.
And he pressed him, so he took it.

12 Then he said:
Let us travel on, and I will go on at your side.

13 But he said to him:
My lord knows
that the children are frail,
and the sheep and the oxen are suckling in my care;
if we were to push them for a single day, all the animals
would die!

14 Pray let my lord cross on ahead of his servant,
   while as for me, I will travel slowly,
   at the pace of the gear ahead of me and at the pace of the
      children,
   until I come to my lord, in Se'ir.
15 Esav said:
   Pray let me leave with you some of the people who are
      mine.
   But he said:
   For what reason?
   May I only find favor in my lord's eyes!
16 So Esav started back that same day on his journey to Se'ir,
17 while Yaakov traveled to Succot.
   He built himself a house there, and for his livestock he
      made sheds.
   Therefore they called the name of the place: Succot/Sheds.

18 Yaakov came home in peace to the city of Shekhem, which
      is in the land of Canaan,
   on his homecoming from the country of Aram,
   and he encamped facing the city.

Home: Peace and Violence (33:18–34:31): "Yaakov came home in peace
to the city of Shekhem" (33:18) continues the theme of resolution. Not
only has Esav accepted his gift, but Yaakov has arrived home safely, in
fulfillment of his prayer in 28:21. Like Avraham he purchases land;
again like him he builds an altar.

   Chapter 34, however, shatters the newly created atmosphere of secu-
rity and peace ("peaceably disposed" in verse 21 is a bitter twist).
Whereas Avraham and Yitzhak had been able to conclude treaties with
the inhabitants of Canaan, Yaakov winds up in the opposite position.
The text implies, as usual, that Canaanite sexual behavior is odious (v.7,
"such [a thing] is not to be done!"), and this provides the spring for the

33:8 **What to you is:** I.e., What does it mean to you?
   9 **my brother:** The phrase suggests that they are now reconciled.
   15 **leave with you:** Or "station with you," "put at your disposal."   **mine:** Lit.
   "with me."   **For what reason?:** Yaakov still seems cautious.

19 And he acquired the piece of territory where he had spread
   out his tent, from the Sons of Hamor, Shekhem's father,
   for a hundred lambs'-worth.
20 There he set up a slaughter-site
   and called it:
   El/God, the God of Yisrael!

34:1 Now Dina, Lea's daughter, whom she had borne to
   Yaakov, went out to see the women of the land.
 2 And Shekhem son of Hamor the Hivvite, the prince of the
   land, saw her:
   he took her and lay with her, forcing her.
 3 But his emotions clung to Dina, Yaakov's daughter—he
   loved the girl,
   and he spoke to the heart of the girl.
 4 So Shekhem said to Hamor his father, saying:
   Take me this girl as a wife!
 5 Now Yaakov had heard that he had defiled Dina his
   daughter,
   but since his sons were with his livestock in the fields,
   Yaakov kept silent until they came home.
 6 Hamor, Shekhem's father, went out to Yaakov, to speak
   with him.
 7 But Yaakov's sons came back from the fields when they
   heard,
   and the men were pained, they were exceedingly enraged,
   for he had done a disgrace in Israel by lying with Yaakov's
   daughter,
   such (a thing) is not to be done!
 8 Hamor spoke with them, saying:
   My son Shekhem—
   his emotions are so attached to your daughter,
   (so) pray give her to him as a wife!
 9 And make marriage-alliances with us:
   give us your daughters, and our daughters take for
   yourselves,
10 and settle among us!
   The land shall be before you:
   settle down, travel about it, obtain holdings in it!

11 And Shekhem said to her father and to her brothers:
   May I only find favor in your eyes!
   However much you say to me, I will give-in-payment,
12 to whatever extreme you multiply the bride price and the
      marriage gift,
   I will give however much you say to me—
   only give me the girl as a wife!
13 Now Yaakov's sons answered Shekhem and Hamor his
      father with deceit,
   speaking (thus) because he had defiled Dina their sister,
14 they said to them:
   We cannot do this thing,
   give our sister to a man who has a foreskin,
   for that would be a reproach for us!

---

action. Interestingly, Yaakov's sons act somewhat like their father had, "with deceit" (v.13); and love once again leads to an unfortunate end.

The vengefulness and brutality of Yaakov's sons in this story antici- pates their later behavior in the Yosef story (Chapter 37); surprisingly, it is for the present crime and not the sale of Yosef that their father con- demns them on his deathbed (49:5–7).

The chapter is notable for the latitude it allows its characters to ex- press their thoughts and emotions: Shekhem's desire and love, the sons' anger and cunning, the Hivvites' gullibility and greed, and Yaakov's fear. Like other stories in the Yaakov cycle, it presents us with a some- what ambiguous situation, where right and wrong are not always simple and the putative heroes are not always heroic.

19 **he acquired:** Like his grandfather Avraham, Yaakov must purchase the land. **lambs'-worth:** Hebrew obscure.
34:1 **to see:** To visit.
   2 **Hamor:** Heb. "ass." Some take the name to prove that they were donkey- drivers, while others see it as an insult to the character.
   7 **disgrace:** A different Hebrew word from the one rendered "disgraced" in 15:2.
   8 **his emotions are so attached:** Speiser uses "has his heart set on." **pray give:** The repetition of "give" suggests a greediness on their part.
   10 **travel about:** Or "trade."
   13 **with deceit:** Another example of a key word in the Yaakov stories; see 27:35 and 29:25.

15 Only on this (condition) will we comply with you:
   if you become like us, by having every male among you
       circumcised.
16 Then we will give you our daughters, and your daughters
       we will take for ourselves,
   and we will settle among you, so that we become a single
       people.
17 But if you do not hearken to us, to be circumcised,
   we will take our daughter and go.
18 Their words seemed good in the eyes of Hamor and in the
       eyes of Shekhem son of Hamor,
19 and the young man did not hesitate to do the thing,
   for he desired Yaakov's daughter.
   Now he carried more weight than anyone in his father's
       house.
20 When Hamor and Shekhem his son came back to the gate
       of their city,
   they spoke to the men of their city, saying:
21 These men are peaceably disposed toward us;
   let them settle in the land and travel about in it,
   for the land is certainly wide-reaching enough for them!
   Let us take their daughters as wives for ourselves, and let
       us give them our daughters.
22 But only on this condition will the men comply with us, to
       settle among us, to become a single people:
   that every male among us be circumcised, as they are
       circumcised.
23 Their acquired livestock, their acquired property and all
       their beasts—will they not then become ours?!
   Let us only comply with them, that they may settle among
       us!
24 So they hearkened to Hamor and to Shekhem his son, all
       who go out (to war) from the gate of his city:
   all the males were circumcised, all who go out (to war) from
       the gate of his city.
25 But on the third day it was, when they were still hurting,
   that two of Yaakov's sons, Shim'on and Levi, Dina's
       full-brothers, took each man his sword,

they came upon the city (feeling) secure, and killed all the
     males,
26 and Hamor and Shekhem his son they killed by the sword.
    Then they took Dina from Shekhem's house and went off.
27 Yaakov's other sons came up upon the corpses and
         plundered the city,
    because they had defiled their sister.
28 Their sheep, their oxen, their asses—whatever was inside
         the city and out in the field, they took,
29 all their riches, all their little-ones and their wives they
         captured and plundered,
    as well as all that was in the houses.
30 But Yaakov said to Shim'on and to Levi:
    You have stirred-up-trouble for me,
    making me reek among the settled-folk of the land, the
         Canaanites and the Perizzites!
    For I have menfolk few in number;
    they will band together against me and strike me,
    and I will be destroyed, I and my household!
31 But they said:
    Should our sister then be treated like a whore?

35:1 Now God said to Yaakov:
    Arise,
    go up to Bet-El and stay there,
    and construct a slaughter-site there
    to the God/*El* who was seen by you when you fled from
         Esav your brother.

----

19 **desired:** Not the same Hebrew term as in 2:9.   **carried more weight:** I.e.,
    was more respected.
21 **peaceably disposed:** Or "friendly," "honest."
24 **all who go out . . . :** I.e., all able-bodied men.
25 **Shim'on and Levi:** They are condemned for this incident by Yaakov in
    49:5–7.
27 **Yaakov's other sons:** Lit. "Yaakov's sons."

2 Yaakov said to his household and to all who were with him:
Put away the foreign gods that are in your midst!
Purify yourselves! Change your garments!

3 Let us arise and go up to Bet-El,
there I will construct a slaughter-site
to the God who answered me on the day of my distress
—he was with me on the way that I went!

4 So they gave Yaakov all the foreign gods that were in their
hand, along with the sacred-rings that were in their ears,
and Yaakov concealed them under the oak/*ela* that is near
Shekhem.

5 Then they departed.
Now a dread from God lay upon the towns that were
around them,
so that they did not pursue Yaakov's sons.

6 So Yaakov came home to Luz, which is in the land of
Canaan—that is now Bet-El—he and all the people that
were with him.

7 There he built a slaughter-site
and called the place:
Godhead/*El* of Bet-El!
For there had the power-of-God been revealed to him, when
he fled from his brother.

8 Now Devora, Rivka's nurse, died.
She was buried below Bet-El, beneath the oak;
they called its name: Allon Bakhut/Oak of Weeping.

9 God was seen by Yaakov again, when he came home from
the country of Aram,
and he gave him blessing:

10 God said to him:
Yaakov is your name,
Yaakov shall your name be called no more,
for your name shall be Yisrael!
And he called his name: Yisrael!

11 God said further to him:
I am God Shaddai.
Bear fruit and be many!

Nation, yes, a host of nations shall come from you,
kings shall go out from your loins!
12 The land
   that I gave to Avraham and to Yitzhak,
   to you I give it,
   and to your seed after you I give the land.
13 God went up from beside him, at the place where he had
   spoken with him.
14 And Yaakov set up a standing-pillar at the place where he
   had spoken with him, a pillar of stone,
   he poured out a poured-offering on it and cast oil upon it.
15 And Yaakov called the name of the place where God had
   spoken with him:
   Bet-El/House of God!

Home: Blessing and Death (35): Several brief notices round out Yaakov's
return to Canaan. First (vv.1–7) there is the return to Bet-El, where he
builds an altar and has the "foreign" gods of his household people put
away—thus fulfilling his promise in Chapter 28. This passage is built
upon the Hebrew word *El,* God (related actually to an earlier Northwest
Semitic name for a god).

Apparently a second version of Yaakov's name change is recorded in
verses 9–15. As in the case of Avraham, seed and land are promised by
God. The land can be given to him and "to your seed after you" only
upon his return.

Finally, spread out through the chapter are the accounts of three
deaths: Devora, Rivka's nurse (v.8—a veiled reference to Rivka's own
death?), Rahel (vv.16–20), and finally Yitzhak (vv.28–29). Yaakov's
youth is over, with the dramatic break with those close to him in that
period.

35:2 **Change your garments:** Speiser translates this as "Put on new clothes."
   8 **Rivka's nurse, died:** See note to 24:59.
   9ff. **God was seen . . . :** Apparently a different version of the Peniel story of
        Chapter 32.
11–12 **I am God Shaddai . . . :** See God's words to Avraham in 17:6.
   13 **at the place where he had spoken with him:** The phrase occurs three times
        here and subsequently, probably to emphasize the sanctity of Bet-El.

16 They departed from Bet-El.
But when there was still a stretch of land to come to Efrat,
Rahel began to give birth,
and she had a very hard birthing.

17 It was, when her birthing was at its hardest,
that the midwife said to her:
Do not be afraid,
for this one too is a son for you!

18 It was, as her life was slipping away
—for she was dying—
that she called his name: Ben-Oni/Son-of-My-Woe.
But his father called him: Binyamin/Son-of-the-Right-Hand.

19 So Rahel died;
she was buried along the way to Efrat—that is now
Bet-Lehem.

20 Yaakov set up a standing-pillar over her burial-place,
that is Rahel's burial pillar of today.

21 Now Yisrael departed and spread his tent beyond
Migdal-Eder/Herd-Tower.

22 And it was when Yisrael was dwelling in that land: Re'uven
went and lay with Bilha, his father's concubine.
And Yisrael heard—

Now the sons of Yaakov were twelve:

23 The sons of Lea: Yaakov's firstborn, Re'uven; Shim'on,
Levi and Yehuda, Yissakhar and Zevulun.

24 The sons of Rahel: Yosef and Binyamin.

25 The sons of Bilha, Rahel's maid: Dan and Naftali.

26 The sons of Zilpa, Lea's maid: Gad and Asher.
These (were) Yaakov's sons, who were born to him in the
country of Aram.

27 Yaakov came home to Yitzhak his father at Mamre, in the
town of Arba—that is now Hevron,
where Avraham and Yitzhak had sojourned.

28 And the days of Yitzhak were a hundred years and eighty

29   years,/ then Yitzhak breathed-his-last.

He died and was gathered to his kinspeople, old and
   abundant in days.
Esav and Yaakov his sons buried him.

36:1 And these are the begettings of Esav—that is Edom.
   2 Esav took his wives from the women of Canaan:
      Ada, daughter of Elon the Hittite, and Oholivama, daughter
   3   of Ana (and) granddaughter of Tziv'on the Hivvite,/ and
      Ba'semat, daughter of Yishmael and sister of Nevayot.
   4 Ada bore Elifaz to Esav,
      Ba'semat bore Re'uel,
   5 Oholivama bore Ye'ush, Ya'lam, and Korah.
      These are Esav's sons, who were born to him in the land of
      Canaan.

Re'uven (35:21–22): The following tiny fragment, concerning Re'uven's
usurping his father's concubine, serves to presage his fall as firstborn
later on. Such an act had symbolic value in biblical society; Avshalom
(Absalom) sleeps with David's concubines as a sign of rebellion and a
desire to attain the crown (II Sam. 16:21–22).

Esav's Descendants (36): The complicated genealogies and dynasties of
this chapter close out the first part of the Yaakov cycle, strictly speaking.
Fitting in the context of a society which lay great store by kinship and
thus by careful remembering of family names, it may also indicate the
greatness of Yitzhak's line, as Chapter 25 had earlier done for Avraham.
Certainly the lists give evidence of a time when the Edomites were more
than merely Israel's neighbors, assuming great importance in historical
recollection (Speiser).

17 **this one too is a son:** This seems to be a breach birth, since the midwife
   already knew that it was a son when "her birthing was at its hardest"—that
   is, before the child had fully emerged.
18 **her life was slipping away:** Or "her life-breath was leaving (her)," paralleling a similar expression in Ugaritic. **But his father called him: Binyamin:**
   Given the power of names, it would not have been considered fortuitous for
   a child to begin life with a name such as the one Rahel gives him. **Binyamin:** Trad. English "Benjamin."
19 **Bet-Lehem:** Trad. English "Bethlehem."
29 **Then Yitzhak breathed-his-last:** See the Commentary on 26:1–6.

6 Esav took his wives, his sons and his daughters, and all the
persons in his household,
as well as his acquired livestock, all his beasts, and all his
acquisitions that he had gained in the land of Canaan,
and went to (another) land, away from Yaakov his brother;

7 for their property was too much for them to settle together,
the land of their sojourning could not support them, on
account of their acquired livestock.

8 So Esav settled in the mountain-country of Se'ir—Esav, that
is Edom.

9 And these are the begettings of Esav, the tribal-father of
Edom, in the mountain-country of Se'ir:

10 These are the names of the sons of Esav:
Elifaz son of Ada, Esav's wife, Re'uel, son of Ba'semat,
Esav's wife.

11 The sons of Elifaz were Teman, Omar, Tzefo, Ga'tam, and
Kenaz.

12 Now Timna was concubine to Elifaz son of Esav, and she
bore Amalek to Elifaz.
These are the sons of Ada, Esav's wife.

13 And these are the sons of Re'uel: Nahat and Zerah,
Shamma and Mizza.
These were the sons of Ba'semat, Esav's wife.

14 And these were the sons of Oholivama, daughter of Ana,
(and) granddaughter of Tziv'on (and) Esav's wife:
She bore Ye'ush and Ya'lam and Korah to Esav.

15 These are the families of Esav's sons:
From the sons of Elifaz, Esav's firstborn, are: the Family
Teman, the Family Omar, the Family Tzefo, the Family

16 Kenaz,/ the Family Korah, the Family Ga'tam, the
Family Amalek;
these are the families from Elifaz in the land of Edom, these
are the sons of Ada.

17 And these are the Sons of Re'uel, Esav's son: the Family
Nahat, the Family Zerah, the Family Shamma, the
Family Mizza;
these are the families from Re'uel in the land of Edom,
these the Sons of Ba'semat, Esav's wife.

18 And these are the Sons of Oholivama, Esav's wife: the
      Family Ye'ush, the Family Ya'lam, the Family Korah;
      these are the families from Oholivama, daughter of Ana,
      Esav's wife.
19 These are the Sons of Esav and these are their families.
      —That is Edom.

20 These are the sons of Se'ir the Horite, the settled-folk of the
      land:
21 Lotan and Shoval and Tziv'on and Ana and Dishon and
      Etzer and Dishan.
      These are the Horite families, the Sons of Se'ir in the land
      of Edom.
22 The sons of Lotan were Hori and Hemam, and Lotan's
      sister was Timna.
23 And these are the sons of Shoval: Alvan and Manahat and
      Eval, Shefo and Onam.
24 And these are the sons of Tziv'on: Ayya and Ana.
      —That is the Ana who found the *yemim* in the wilderness,
      as he was tending the asses of Tziv'on his father.
25 And these are the sons of Ana: Dishon—and Oholivama was
      Ana's daughter.
26 And these are the sons of Dishon: Hemdan and Eshban and
      Yitran and Ceran.
27 These are the sons of Etzer: Bilhan and Zaavan and Akan.
28 These are the sons of Dishan: Utz and Aran.
29 These are the Horite families: the Family Lotan, the Family
30   Shoval, the Family Tziv'on, the Family Ana,/ the Family
      Dishon, the Family Etzer, the Family Dishan.

36:7 **for their property was too much:** Again recalling Avraham, in his conflict
      with Lot (13:6).
  14 **Tziv'on:** The name means "hyena." Such animal names have long been
      popular in the region and occur a number of times in this chapter (Vawter).
  15 **families:** Others use "chieftains."
  24 *yemim:* Hebrew obscure; some use "hot-springs," "lakes."
  26 **Dishon:** The traditional text uses "Dishan," but see I Chron. 1:41.

These are the families of the Horites, according to their families in the land of Se'ir.

31 Now these are the kings who served as king in the land of Edom, before any king of the Sons of Israel served as king:

32 In Edom, Bela son of Be'or was king; the name of his city was Dinhava.

33 When Bela died, Yovav son of Zerah of Botzra became king in his stead.

34 When Yovav died, Husham from the land of the Temanites became king in his stead.

35 When Husham died, Hadad son of Bedad became king in his stead—who struck Midyan in the territory of Mo'av, and the name of his city was Avit.

36 When Hadad died, Samla of Masreka became king in his stead.

37 When Samla died, Sha'ul of Rehovot-by-the-River became king in his stead.

38 When Sha'ul died, Baal-Hanan son of Akhbor became king in his stead.

39 When Baal-Hanan son of Akhbor died, Hadar became king in his stead; the name of his city was Pa'u, and the name of his wife, Mehetavel daughter of Matred, daughter of Me-Zahav.

40 Now these are the names of the families from Esav, according to their clans, according to their local-places, by their names:

41 The Family Timna, the Family Alvan, the Family Yetet,/ the Family Oholivama, the Family Ela, the Family

42 Pinon,/ the Family Kenaz, the Family Teman, the Family

43 Mivtzar,/ the Family Magdiel, the Family Iram. These are the families of Edom according to their settlements in the land of their holdings.

That is Esav, the tribal-father of Edom.

PART IV Yosef
(37–50)

THE STORIES about the last Patriarch form a coherent whole, leading some to dub it a "novella." It stands well on its own, although it has been consciously and artfully woven together into both the Yaakov cycle and the entire book.

Initially the tale is one of family emotions, and it is in fact extreme emotions which give it a distinctive flavor. All the major characters are painfully expressive of their feelings, from the doting father to the spoiled son, from the malicious brothers to the lustful wife of Potifar, from the nostalgic adult Yosef to the grief-stricken old Yaakov. It is only through the subconscious medium of dreams, in three sets, that we are made to realize that a higher plan is at work which will supersede the destructive force of these emotions.

For this is a story of how "ill"—with all its connotations of fate, evil, and disaster—is changed to good. Despite the constant threat of death to Yosef, to the Egyptians, and to Binyamin, the hidden, optimistic thrust of the story is "life," a word that appears in various guises throughout. Even "face," the key word of the Yaakov cycle which often meant something negative, is here given a kinder meaning, as the resolution to Yaakov's life.

A major subtheme of the plot is the struggle for power between Re'uven and Yehuda. Its resolution has implications that are as much tribal as personal, for the tribe of Yehuda later became the historical force in ancient Israel as the seat of the monarchy.

Although many details of the narrative confirm Egyptian practices, those practices actually reflect an Egypt considerably later than the period of the Patriarchs (Redford). Of interest also is the prominence of the number five in the story, a detail that is unexplained but that gives some unity to the various sections of text.

In many ways the Yosef material repeats elements in the Yaakov traditions. A long list could be compiled, but let us at least mention here

sibling hatred, exile of the hero, foreign names, love and hate, dreams,
and deception—even so detailed as to duplicate the use of a goat-kid. But
its focusing on a classic rags-to-riches plot, with the addition of a moral-
istic theme, make the Yosef story a distinctive and always popular tale,
accessible in a way that the more difficult stories of the first three parts
of Genesis are not.

37:1 Yaakov settled in the land of his father's sojournings,
     in the land of Canaan.

2 These are the begettings of Yaakov.

   Yosef, seventeen years old, used to tend the sheep along with
      his brothers,
      for he was serving-lad with the sons of Bilha and the sons of
         Zilpa, his father's wives.
      And Yosef brought a report of them, an ill one, to their
         father.
3 Now Yisrael loved Yosef above all his sons,
      for he was a son of old age to him,
      so he made him an ornamented coat.
4 When his brothers saw that it was he whom their father
      loved above all his brothers,
      they hated him,
      and could not speak to him in peace.

5 Now Yosef dreamt a dream, and told it to his brothers
      —from then on they hated him still more—,
6 he said to them:
   Pray hear this dream that I have dreamt:
7 Here,
      we were binding sheaf-bundles out in the field,
      and here, my sheaf arose, it was standing upright,
         and here, your sheaves were circling round and bowing
            down to my sheaf!

8 His brothers said to him:
  Would you be king, yes, king over us?
  Or would you really rule, yes, rule us?
  From then on they hated him still more—for his dreams,
    for his words.

Young Yosef: Love and Hate (37): As has been the pattern with the
Avraham and Yaakov cycles, the opening chapter here introduces the
key themes of the entire story. These include the father's love, the power
of words, dreams, "ill" as a key word (here denoting evil intent but
eventually encompassing misfortune, among other concepts), and of
course, the brothers' hatred, which at first glance is the motivating force
behind the action.

But the initial blame for what happens clearly lies with the father
(vv.3–4), and is made unbearable by Yosef's own behavior. In point of
fact he is largely responsible for his own downfall, bearing tales about his
brothers (v.2) even before Yaakov's preference for him is noted. His
insistence on telling his dreams to his brothers must be galling, particularly the second time (v.9), coming as it does after the report that "they
hated him still more for his dreams" (v.8).

37:2 **begettings:** In the sense of "family history." As noted above, the Yosef
    story is a continuation of the Yaakov saga. **seventeen:** Together with
    47:28, this provides another example of numerical balance in these stories
    (see the Commentary on "The Patriarchal Narratives, p. 45). Yosef lives
    with Yaakov for the first seventeen years of his life and for the last seven-
    teen of his father's. **along with his brothers:** A hint that he would one day
    "shepherd" (rule) his brothers? The Hebrew is open to that interpretation
    (Redford). **brought a report:** Or "gossip." Although the doting father's
    love is crucial, it seems really to be Yosef's own behavior (which precedes
    the information about his coat) that causes his abuse by the brothers.
  3 **ornamented:** Hebrew obscure; B-R uses "ankle-length."
  4 **hated:** Such a violent emotion nevertheless has once before (with Lea in
    29:31) led not to disaster but to the fulfillment of the divine plan (there, the
    hatred results in the competition to have children). **in peace:** Or "civ-
    illy"—again the key Yaakov word, "peace."
  6 **hear:** Which can also mean "understand" in biblical Hebrew.
  8 **king, yes, king . . . rule, yes, rule:** The doubling might reflect the
    brothers' astonishment and bitterness. See also verse 10.

9   But he dreamt still another dream, and recounted it to his
        brothers,
    he said:
    Here, I have dreamt still (another) dream:
    Here,
    the sun and the moon and eleven stars were bowing down
        to me!
10 When he recounted it to his father and his brothers,
    his father rebuked him and said to him:
    What kind of dream is this that you have dreamt!
    Shall we come, yes, come, I, your mother and your
        brothers,
    to bow down to you to the ground?
11 His brothers envied him,
    while his father remembered the matter.

12 Now his brothers went to tend their father's sheep in
        Shekhem.
13 Yisrael said to Yosef:
    Are not your brothers tending sheep in Shekhem?
    Come, I will send you to them!
    He said to him:
    Here I am.
14 And he said to him:
    Come, pray, look into the well-being of your brothers and
        into the well-being of the sheep,
    and bring me back word.
    So he sent him out from the valley of Hevron, and he came
        to Shekhem.
15 And a man came upon him—here, he was roaming in the
        field;
    the man asked him, saying:
    What do you seek?
16 He said:
    I seek my brothers,
    pray tell me where they are tending-sheep.
17 The man said:
    They have moved on from here,
    indeed, I heard them say: Let us go to Dotan.

Yosef went after his brothers and came upon them in
Dotan.

18 They saw him from afar,
and before he had gotten near them, they plotted-cunningly
against him to cause his death.

19 They said each man to his brother:
Here comes that dreamer!

20 So now, come, let us kill him and cast him into one of these
pits
and say: An ill-tempered beast has devoured him!
Then we will see what becomes of his dreams!

21 When Re'uven heard it he tried to rescue him from their
hand, he said:
Let us not take his life!

22 And Re'uven said to them:
Do not shed blood!
Cast him into this pit that is in the wilderness,
but do not lay a hand upon him!
—in order that he might save him from their hand, to
return him to his father.

The key word of the chapter, not surprisingly, is "brother," culminating in Yehuda's ironic words (v.27): "let not our hand be upon him, for
he is our brother. . . ." Shortly afterward Yosef, their "(own) flesh," is
sold into slavery and probable death.

10 **your mother:** The fact that she had died in Chapter 35 does not detract
from the symbol of the dream.
11 **remembered:** Or "kept in mind."
12 **Shekhem:** In our text this city's name (three times here) reminds the reader
of the disastrous events of Chapter 34.
13 **Come:** Repeated in verses 20 and 27; it is ironically Yaakov's decision to
send Yosef to his brothers that sets this part of the plot into action.
14 **well-being:** Heb. *shalom,* translated as "peace" in verse 4 and elsewhere.
15 **a man:** Possibly another divine messenger (like the "man" in 32:25). See
also the note to "roaming" in 20:13.
21 **take his life:** Lit. "strike him mortally."

23 So it was, when Yosef came to his brothers,
   that they stripped Yosef of his coat,
   the ornamented coat that he had on,
24 and took him and cast him into the pit.
   Now the pit was empty—no water in it.
25 And they sat down to eat bread.

   They lifted up their eyes and saw:
   there was a caravan of Yishmaelites coming from Gil'ad,
   their camels carrying balm, balsam, and ladanum,
   traveling to take them down to Egypt.
26 Now Yehuda said to his brothers:
   What gain is there
   if we kill our brother and cover up his blood?
27 Come, let us sell him to the Yishmaelites—
   but let not our hand be upon him,
   for he is our brother, our flesh!
   And his brothers listened to him.

28 Meanwhile, some Midyanite men, merchants, passed by;
   they hauled up Yosef from the pit
   and sold Yosef to the Yishmaelites, for twenty pieces of
      silver.
   They brought Yosef to Egypt.

29 When Re'uven returned to the pit:
   here, Yosef was no more in the pit!
   He rent his garments
30 and returned to his brothers and said:
   The child is no more!
   And I—where am I to go?

31 But they took Yosef's coat,
   they slew a goat buck
   and dipped the coat in the blood.
32 They had the ornamented coat sent out
   and had it brought to their father and said:
   We found this;
   pray recognize

whether it is your son's coat or not!
33 He recognized it
and said:
My son's coat!
An ill-tempered beast has devoured him!
Yosef is torn, torn-to-pieces!
34 Yaakov rent his clothes,
he put sackcloth on his loins
and mourned his son for many days.
35 All his sons and daughters arose to comfort him,
but he refused to be comforted.
He said:
No,
I will go down to my son
in mourning, to Sheol!
Thus his father wept for him.
36 Meanwhile, the Midyanites had sold him into Egypt
to Potifar, Pharaoh's court-official,
Chief of the (palace) Guard.

---

25 **bread:** Or "food."
29 **rent his garments:** The tearing of clothing was a customary sign of mourning.
30 **And I . . . :** Heb. *va-ani, ana ani va.* The sound expresses the emotions. **Where am I to go:** I.e., what will become of me?
32 **pray recognize:** See 27:23, where Yitzhak did not "recognize" Yaakov. Yaakov's youth returns to haunt him, in a sense.
33 **My son's coat:** With the omission of "It is," the shock is conveyed more dramatically. Some ancient versions, however, include the phrase. **An ill-tempered beast . . . torn-to-pieces:** The Hebrew breaks into verse structure, with three word-beats per line: *haya ra'a akhalat'hu/ tarof toraf Yosef* (Alter).
34 **many days:** Possibly "years"; at any rate, longer than a normal mourning period (in the Bible, thirty or seventy days) (Jacob).
35 **Sheol:** The biblical underworld; others (and B-R) use "the grave."
36 **Midyanites:** The Hebrew has "Medanites." **court-official:** Lit. "eunuch," a common ancient Near Eastern title for such a position. Originally the term was applied literally, although later on the person was not necessarily a eunuch.

38:1 Now it was at about that time
that Yehuda went down, away from his brothers
and turned aside to an Adullamite man—his name was
Hira.
2 There Yehuda saw the daughter of a Canaanite man—his
name was Shua,
he took her (as his wife) and came in to her.
3 She became pregnant and bore a son, and he called his
name: Er.
4 She became pregnant again and bore a son, and she called
his name: Onan.
5 Once again she bore a son, and she called his name: Shela.
Now he was in Ceziv when she bore him.

6 Yehuda took a wife for Er, his firstborn—her name was
Tamar.
7 But Er, Yehuda's firstborn, was ill in the eyes of YHWH,
and YHWH caused him to die.
8 Yehuda said to Onan:
Come in to your brother's wife, do a brother-in-law's duty
by her,
to preserve seed for your brother!
9 But Onan knew that the seed would not be his,
so it was, whenever he came in to his brother's wife, he let
it go to ruin on the ground,
so as not to provide seed for his brother.
10 What he did was ill in the eyes of YHWH,
and he caused him to die as well.
11 Now Yehuda said to Tamar his daughter-in-law:
Sit as a widow in your father's house
until Shela my son has grown up.
For he said to himself:
Otherwise he will die as well, like his brothers!
So Tamar went and stayed in her father's house.
12 And many days passed.

Now Shua's daughter, Yehuda's wife, died.
When Yehuda had been comforted,
he went up to his sheep-shearers, he and his friend Hira the
Adullamite, to Timna.

Yehuda and Tamar (38): Chapter 38 has been the subject of many discussions, for it seems to be out of place. It interrupts the story of Yosef at a crucial dramatic spot, and is not chronologically fully consistent with it (Yehuda ages considerably; then we return to Yosef as a seventeen-year-old). Some feel that the suspension in the drama helps to raise tension; others argue that this is the only possible place to put an important tradition about the important brother. While these and other arguments may have their merit, one may discern some significant thematic connections as well, both within the context of the Yosef story and of Genesis as a whole.

The episode first of all demonstrates the growth of Yehuda as a character who is central to the Yosef novella. Already in Chapter 37 he had demonstrated active leadership, albeit in a questionable cause. There he actually saved Yosef's life, in contrast to Re'uven's unsuccessful and ultimately self-centered rescue attempt. As the one who basically assumes responsibility, he will be made to undergo an inner development in the narrative, and again becomes the one to take charge of the youngest son (Binyamin, in Chapters 43 and 44). The missing piece that begins to explain his nobility in this regard (Chapter 44) is the present chapter. Yehuda here learns what it is to lose sons, and to want desperately to protect his youngest. Although his failure to marry off Tamar to the youngest son leads to public humiliation (twice, actually), his response shows that he immediately accepts blame: "She is in-the-right more than I" (v.26). Such an interpretation is further confirmed by the restriction

---

38:1 **away from his brothers:** More than geography seems to be meant. Yehuda begins to change as a person here, in preparation for Chapter 44. Note that the place Adullam assonates with Arabic (*'adula*) "to turn aside."

5 **Ceziv:** The Hebrew root connotes "lying."

6 **Tamar:** The name means "palm tree."

6–7 **firstborn:** Perhaps parallel to the ineffectual firstborn, Re'uven, of the previous chapter.

7 **was ill:** I.e., he was evil, although we are not told specifically how.

8 **a brother-in-law's duty:** It was a well-known practice in biblical times that if a man died without leaving an heir, it was the obligation of his nearest of kin (usually his brother) to marry the widow and sire a son—who would then bear the name of the deceased man (Deut. 25:5–10).

10 **What he did was ill:** Onan dies because he does not fulfill his legal obligation to continue his brother's line. The later interpretation, that his crime was masturbation ("onanism"), has no basis in this text.

11 **Otherwise he will die:** Folk belief often regarded a woman who had outlived two husbands as a bad risk in marriage. The emotion here—a father's fear of losing a young son—will return as central in 42:36.

13 Tamar was told, saying:
Here, your father-in-law is going up to Timna to shear his
sheep.

14 She removed her widow's garments from her,
covered herself with a veil and wrapped herself,
and sat down by the entrance to Enayim/Two-Wells, which
is on the way to Timna,
for she saw that Shela had grown up, yet she had not been
given to him as a wife.

15 When Yehuda saw her, he took her for a whore, for she had
covered her face.

16 So he turned aside to her by the wayside and said:
Come-now, pray let me come in to you—
for he did not know that she was his daughter-in-law.
She said:
What will you give me for coming in to me?

17 He said:
I myself will send out a goat kid from the flock.
She said:
Only if you give me a pledge, until you send it.

18 He said:
What is the pledge that I am to give you?
She said:
Your seal, your cord, and your staff that is in your hand.
He gave them to her and then he came in to her—and she
became pregnant by him.

19 She arose and went away,
then she put off her veil from her and clothed herself in her
widow's garments.

20 Now when Yehuda sent the goat kid by the hand of his
friend the Adullamite, to fetch the pledge from the
woman's hand,
he could not find her.

21 He asked the people of her place, saying:
Where is that sacred-prostitute, the one in Two-Wells by
the wayside?
They said:
There has been no sacred-prostitute here!

22 So he returned to Yehuda and said:

I could not find her; moreover, the people of the place said:
There has been no sacred-prostitute here!
23 Yehuda said:
Let her keep them for herself, lest we become a
laughing-stock.
Here, I sent her this kid, but you, you could not find her.

---

of the word "pledge" to here and 43:9. Yehuda has learned what it
means to stake oneself for a principle.

Only after we have been informed of Yehuda's change can the narrative
resume with Chapter 39. True to biblical thinking, redemption may start
only after the crime has been punished (e.g., the Samson story, where the
hero's hair begins to grow immediately after his imprisonment).

Actually the chronology works out quite well. We are told via 41:46,
53–54, that about twenty years elapse between the sale of Yosef and his
meetings with the brothers in Egypt; this often signifies a period in
biblical parlance and could encompass a generation or a bit less. Since
Yehuda was quite possibly a father already in Chapter 37, the present
story could well end just before the events reported in Chapter 43—in
other words, Yehuda reaches full inner maturity just in time.

The other function of this story seems to be to carry out the major
theme of Genesis as we have presented it: continuity and discontinuity
between the generations. What is at stake here is not merely the line of
one of the brothers, but the line which (as the biblical audience must
have been fully aware) will lead to royalty—King David was a descen-
dant of Peretz of verse 29. This should not be surprising in a book of
origins; we noted the possible mention of Jerusalem in 14:18. Apparently
a popular early theme, connected as we have noted to the power of God
in history, continuity/discontinuity is repeated in somewhat similar circumstances in the book of Ruth (which contains the only other mention
of "begettings" outside of Genesis and Num.3:1).

The narrator has woven Chapters 38 and 37 together with great skill.
Again a man is asked to "recognize" objects, again the use of a kid, and
again a brother (this time a dead one) is betrayed.

18 **seal . . . cord . . . staff:** Individual objects of identification in the ancient
Near East, particularly the seal, which served to sign documents. See
Speiser.
21 **sacred-prostitute:** Or "cult prostitute," one attached to a shrine in Canaan.
Sex in the ancient world was often linked to religion (as part of fertility
rites), although the Hebrews sought to sever the tie.

24 Now it was, after almost three New-Moons
   that Yehuda was told, saying:
   Tamar your daughter-in-law has played-the-whore,
   in fact, she has become pregnant from whoring!
   Yehuda said:
   Bring her out and let her be burned!
25 (But) as she was being brought out,
   she sent a message to her father-in-law, saying:
   By the man to whom these belong I am pregnant.
   And she said:
   Pray recognize—
   whose seal and cords and staff are these?
26 Yehuda recognized them
   and said:
   She is in-the-right more than I!
   For after all, I did not give her to Shela my son!
   And he did not know her again.

27 Now it was, at the time of her birthing, that here: twins
   were in her body!
28 And it was, as she was giving birth, that (one of them) put
   out a hand;
   the midwife took and tied a crimson thread on his hand,
   saying:
   This one came out first.
29 But it was, as he pulled back his hand, here, his brother
   came out!
   So she said:
   What a breach you have breached for yourself!
   So they called his name: Peretz/Breach.
30 Afterward his brother came out, on whose hand was the
   crimson thread.
   They called his name: Zerah.

39:1 Now when Yosef was brought down to Egypt,
   Potifar, an official of Pharaoh, and Chief of the Guard, an
   Egyptian man, acquired him from the hand of the
   Yishmaelites who brought him down there.

2 But YHWH was with Yosef, so that he became a man of
   success:
   while he was in the house of his lord the Egyptian,
3 his lord saw that YHWH was with him,
   so that whatever he did, YHWH made succeed in his
   hands.
4 Yosef found favor in his eyes, and he waited upon him;
   he appointed him over his house, and everything belonging
   to him he placed in his hands.
5 And it was, from when he had appointed him over his
   house and over everything that belonged to him,
   that YHWH blessed the Egyptian's house because of Yosef;
   YHWH's blessing was upon everything that belonged to
   him, in the house and in the fields.

Yosef: Rise and Fall (39): This chapter prefigures Yosef's eventual rise to
power and simultaneously chronicles his lowest point, literally and figuratively. The two strands of the plot are woven together into a pattern of
success/authority → imprisonment → success/authority. This also mirrors the larger story, which progresses from favorite son → slavery →
viceroy of Egypt. The integration takes place partly through the medium
of a key word, "hand"—which also occurred four times at the end of
Chapter 38 and thus acts as a further textual connector. Yosef's success is
tied six times to the phrase "in his hands" (vv.3, 4, 6, 8, 22, 23); he is
thrown into prison because of the garments that he left in his mistress's
"hands" (vv.12, 13). Similarly, the movement of the chapter is mirrored
in the word "eyes," which is linked first to the theme of authority (v.4),

27ff. **Now it was . . . :** The scene here rather strikingly recalls Yaakov and Esav
      at birth: twins, the hand reaching out, and the struggle to be first.
 29 **breach:** Not in the sense of a "breach birth."
 30 **Zerah:** Possibly connoting "red of dawn"—connecting with the crimson
      thread of verse 28 (and possibly paralleling Esav, who was also known as
      Edom, the "Red One").
39:1 **Potifar . . . :** The narrative resumes exactly, almost literally, where it had
      left off in 37:36.
  2 **a man of success:** Or "a man blessed by success."
  4 **over his house:** Foreshadowing Yosef's eventual position and title (41:40).

6 So he left everything that was his in Yosef's hands,
  not concerning himself about anything with him there,
  except for the bread that he ate.
  Now Yosef was fair of form and fair to look at.

7 Now after these events it was
  that his lord's wife fixed her eyes upon Yosef
  and said:
  Lie with me!
8 But he refused,
  he said to his lord's wife:
  Look, my lord need not concern himself with anything in
    the house, with me here,
  and everything that belongs to him, he has placed in my
    hands.
9 He is no greater in this house than I
  and has withheld nothing from me
  except for yourself,
  since you are his wife.
  So how could I do this great ill?
  I would be sinning against God!
10 Now it was, as she would speak to Yosef day after day, that
    he would not hearken to her, to lie beside her, to be with
    her—
11 so it was, on such a day,
  when he came into the house to do his work,
  and none of the house-people was there in the house—
12 that she grabbed him by his garment, saying:
  Lie with me!
  But he left his garment in her hand and fled, escaping
    outside.
13 Now it was, when she saw that he had left his garment in
    her hand and had fled outside,
14 that she called in her house-people and said to them, saying:
  See! He has brought to us
  a Hebrew man to play around with us!
  He came to me, to lie with me,
  but I called out with a loud voice,
15 and it was, when he heard that I raised my voice and called
    out

that he left his garment beside me and fled, escaping
   outside!
16 Now she kept his garment beside her, until his lord came
   back to the house.
17 Then she spoke to him according to these words, saying:
   There came to me the Hebrew servant whom you brought
      to us, to play around with me;
18 but it was, when I raised my voice and called out,
   that he left his garment beside me and fled outside.
19 Now it was, when his lord heard his wife's words which she
      spoke to him,
   saying: According to these words, your servant did to me!—
   that his anger raged;

----

then to the attempted seduction (v.7), and finally to authority again
(v.21) (Alter).

The chapter also repeats the phrase "And it was" (in one form or
another) some twelve times, as a distinct stylistic pattern.

Yosef's temporary downfall occurs here for reasons beyond literary
balance or suspense. It is in a very real sense the punishment for the
bratty behavior of his adolescence. Once again words (this time not his
own) get him into trouble (vv.17, 19), as they did in 37:8. And once
again a garment is cited as proof of a fabricated crime.

6 **left:** Consigned; see also verse 13 for a play on words. **except for the
bread that he ate:** Since the Egyptians did not eat with foreigners (see, for
instance, 43:32). **fair of form and fair to look at:** The only other person
in the Bible described in exactly these words is Rahel, Yosef's mother
(29:17). We are thus given an indirect clue about the source of Yaakov's
doting behavior in the Yosef story.

9 **sinning:** Or "at fault." **against God:** From this point on, it is clear that
Yosef is no longer the spoiled brat of Chapter 37. At key points in his life
he consistently makes mention of God as the source of his success and good
fortune (40:8; 41:16; 45:5, 7, 9).

10 **to lie beside her, to be with her:** A curious expression. Why does not the
text say, as in verse 7, "to lie beside her"? There is an additional irony: "to
be with" usually refers to God (see verse 2, for example).

14 **play around:** A sexual reference.

15 **beside:** Three times here, the word perhaps suggests to the audience that
Yosef's garment is all that she will ever get "to lie beside her."

20 Yosef's lord took him and put him in the dungeon house,
   in the place where the king's prisoners are imprisoned.
   But while he was there in the dungeon house,
21 YHWH was with Yosef and extended kindness to him:
   he put his favor in the eyes of the dungeon warden.
22 And the dungeon warden put in Yosef's hands all the
      prisoners that were in the dungeon house;
   whatever had to be done there, it was he that did it.
23 The dungeon warden did not need to see to anything at all
      in his hands,
   since YHWH was with him,
   and whatever he did, YHWH made succeed.

40:1 Now after these events it was
   that the cupbearer and the baker of the king of Egypt fell
      afoul of their lord, the king of Egypt.
   2 Pharaoh became infuriated with his two officials, with the
      chief cupbearer and the chief baker,
   3 and he placed them in custody in the house of the chief of
      the guard, in the dungeon house, the place where Yosef
      was imprisoned.
   4 The chief of the guard appointed Yosef for them, that he
      should wait upon them.
   They were in custody for many days.
   5 And then the two of them dreamt a dream, each man his
      own dream, in a single night,
   each man according to his dream's interpretation,
   the cupbearer and the baker of the king of Egypt, who were
      imprisoned in the dungeon house.
   6 When Yosef came to them in the morning and saw them,
      here, they were dejected!
   7 So he asked Pharaoh's officials who were with him in
      custody in the house of his lord, saying:
   Why are your faces in such ill-humor today?
   8 They said to him:
   We have dreamt a dream, and there is no interpreter for it!
   Yosef said to them:
   Are not interpretations from God?
   Pray recount them to me!

9 The chief cupbearer recounted his dream to Yosef, he said
   to him:
   In my dream—
   here, a vine was in front of me,
10 and on the vine, three winding-tendrils,
   and just as it was budding, the blossom came up,
   (and) its clusters ripened into grapes.
11 Now Pharaoh's cup was in my hand—
   I picked the grapes
   and squeezed them into Pharaoh's cup
   and put the cup in Pharaoh's palm.
12 Yosef said to him:
   This is its interpretation:
   The three windings are three days—

The Rise to Power: Dreams (40:1–41:52): Continued are the themes of
Yosef's success in adversity and skill in interpreting dreams (yet his
father and brother, and not he, had done the interpreting in Chapter
37!). In Chapter 37 dreams had brought about his downfall; here
(Chapter 40) they will help the cupbearer and in Chapter 41 ultimately
save a country, his family, and himself. Yosef's self-assurance and reliance on God, already evident in 39:9, here mean that it will not be long
before he stands at the pinnacle.

Yosef's dramatic rise to power is an old and favorite motif in folklore.
The text colorfully presents Pharaoh's dreams, in great detail, especially
in his emotional retelling. All the more striking then is Yosef's simple
interpretation (41:23–27).

20 **dungeon:** Hebrew obscure.
21 **kindness:** Or "faithfulness," "loyalty." See 32:11.
40:1 **the cupbearer and the baker of the king of Egypt:** The Hebrew has "the
     cupbearer of the king of Egypt and the baker," a common construction in
     biblical Hebrew.
2 **cupbearer:** Others use "butler."
4 **appointed Yosef:** As Potifar had "appointed him over his house" (39:4).
5 **interpretation:** Or "meaning."
8 **Are not interpretations from God:** Foreshadowing 41:16, "Not I!/ God
  will answer. . . ."
11 **Pharaoh's cup:** The cup was a common symbol of fate in the ancient Near
   East.

13 in another three days
    Pharaoh will lift up your head,
    he will restore you to your position
    so that you will put Pharaoh's cup in his hand (once more),
    according to the former practice, when you were his
        cupbearer.
14 But keep me in mind with you, when it goes well for you,
    pray deal kindly with me and call me to mind to Pharaoh,
    so that you have me brought out of this house.
15 For I was stolen, yes, stolen from the land of the Hebrews,
    and here too I have done nothing
    that they should have put me in this pit.
16 Now when the chief baker saw that he had interpreted for
        good,
    he said to Yosef:
    I too, in my dream—
    here, three baskets of white-bread were on my head,
17 and in the uppermost basket, all sorts of edibles for
        Pharaoh, baker's work,
    and birds were eating them from the basket, from off my
        head.
18 Yosef gave answer, he said:
    This is its interpretation:
    The three baskets are three days—
19 in another three days
    Pharaoh will lift up your head
    from off you,
    he will hang you on a tree,
    and the birds will eat your flesh from off you.
20 And thus it was, on the third day,
    Pharaoh's birthday,
    that he made a great drinking-feast for all his servants,
    and he lifted up the head of the chief cupbearer and the
        head of the chief baker amidst his servants:
21 he restored the chief cupbearer to his cupbearership,
    so that he put the cup in Pharaoh's palm (once more),
22 but the chief baker he hanged,
    just as Yosef had interpreted to them.

23 But the chief cupbearer did not keep Yosef in mind,
he forgot him.

41:1 Now at the end of two years'-time it was
that Pharaoh dreamt:
here, he was standing by the Nile-Stream,
2 and here, out of the Nile, seven cows were coming up,
fair to look at and fat of flesh,
and they grazed in the reed-grass.
3 And here, seven other cows were coming up after them out
of the Nile,
ill to look at and lean of flesh,
and they stood beside the other cows on the bank of the
Nile.
4 Then the cows ill to look at and lean of flesh ate up
the seven cows fair to look at, the fat-ones.
Pharaoh awoke.
5 He fell asleep and dreamt a second time:
here, seven ears-of-grain were going up on a single stalk, fat
and good,
6 and here, seven ears, lean and scorched by the east wind,
were springing up after them.

---

13 **lift up your head:** A parallel expression in Assyrian means "release" or
"pardon."
14 **with you:** Possibly stressing the personal nature of the plea.
15 **stolen:** The Yaakov motif of Chapters 30–31.
16 **white-bread:** Others use "wicker."
17ff. **eating:** In Pharaoh's dreams of Chapter 41, "eating" comes to symbolize
the disaster of famine.
19 **hang . . . on a tree:** Others use "impale on a stake."
23 **he forgot him:** Here, as in Potifar's house, initial success gives way to
failure and continued imprisonment.
41:1 **two years'-time:** Lit. "two years of days."
2 **cows:** In later (Ptolemaic) Egyptian inscriptions, as here, cows represent
years.
5 **fat and good:** Referring to the ears of grain.

7 Then the lean ears swallowed up
the seven ears fat and full.
Pharaoh awoke,
and here: (it was) a dream!

8 But in the morning it was, that his spirit was agitated,
so he sent and had all of Egypt's magicians and all of its
wise-men called.
Pharaoh recounted his dream to them,
but no one could interpret them to Pharaoh.

9 Then the chief cupbearer spoke up to Pharaoh, saying:
I must call my faults to mind today!

10 Pharaoh was once infuriated with his servants
and placed me in custody, in the house of the chief of the
guard,
myself and the chief baker.

11 And we dreamt a dream in a single night, I and he,
we dreamt each man according to the interpretation of his
dream.

12 Now there was a Hebrew lad there with us, a servant of the
chief of the guard;
we recounted them to him, and he interpreted our dreams
to us,
for each man according to his dream he interpreted.

13 And thus it was: As he interpreted to us, so it was—
I was restored to my position, and he was hanged.

14 Pharaoh sent and had Yosef called.
They hurriedly brought him out of the pit;
he shaved, changed his clothes, and came before Pharaoh.

15 Pharaoh said to Yosef:
I have dreamt a dream, and there is no interpreter for it!
But I have heard it said of you
that you but need to hear a dream in order to interpret it.

16 Yosef answered Pharaoh, saying:
Not I!
God will answer what is for Pharaoh's welfare.

17 Pharaoh spoke to Yosef:
In my dream—
here, I was standing on the bank of the Nile,

18 and here, out of the Nile were coming up seven cows,

fat of flesh and fair of form,
and they grazed in the reed-grass.

19 And here, seven other cows were coming up after them,
wretched and exceedingly ill of form and lank of flesh,
in all the land of Egypt I have never seen their like for
ill-condition!

20 Then the seven lank and ill-looking cows ate up
the first seven cows, the fat-ones.

21 They entered their body, but you would not know that they
had entered their body, for they were as ill-looking as at
the beginning!
Then I awoke.

22 And I saw (again) in my dream:
here, seven ears were going up on a single stalk, full and
good,

23 and here, seven ears, hardened, lean, and scorched by the
east wind, were springing up after them.

24 Then the lean ears swallowed up
the seven good ears!
Now I have spoken with the magicians, but there is no one
that can tell me the answer!

25 Yosef said to Pharaoh:
Pharaoh's dream is one.
What God is about to do, he has told Pharaoh.

26 The seven good cows
are seven years,
the seven good ears
are seven years,
the dream is one.

---

8 **his dream:** The two dreams function as one, as Yosef explains.

19 **in all the land . . . I have never seen their like:** Pharaoh's description of
his dream is more vivid than the narrator's (vv.1–4).

25 **is one:** Or "has a single meaning."

26ff. **The seven good cows . . . :** Yosef's interpretation is highly structured.
The rhetoric emphasizes the last line of verse 27: after hearing "x are seven
years," three times, we hear "x will be seven years of famine!" See above,
40:19, where "Pharaoh will lift up your head" is followed by "from off
you."

27 And the seven lank and ill-looking cows that were coming
    up after them
    are seven years,
    and the seven ears, hollow and scorched by the east wind,
    will be seven years of famine!
28 That is the word that I spoke to Pharaoh:
    what God is about to do, he has let Pharaoh see.
29 Here,
    seven years are coming
    of great abundance in all the land of Egypt.
30 But seven years of famine will arise after them,
    when all the abundance in the land of Egypt will be
      forgotten.
    The famine will destroy the land,
31 and you will not know of that abundance in the land
    because of that famine afterward,
    for it will be exceedingly heavy.
32 Now as for the twofold repetition of the dream to Pharaoh:
    it means that the matter is determined by God,
    and God is hastening to do it.
33 So now, let Pharaoh select a discerning and wise man,
    and set him over the land of Egypt.
34 Let Pharaoh do this: let him appoint appointed-overseers
    for the land,
    dividing the land of Egypt into five parts during the seven
    years of abundance.
35 Let them collect all kinds of food from these good years
    that are coming,
    and let them pile up grain under Pharaoh's hand as
    food-provisions in the cities, and keep it under guard.
36 So the provisions will be an appointed-reserve for the land
    for the seven years of famine that will occur in the land of
    Egypt,
    so that the land will not be cut off by the famine.
37 The words seemed good in Pharaoh's eyes and in the eyes
    of all his servants,
38 and Pharaoh said to his servants:
    Could we find another like him, a man in whom is the spirit
    of a god?
39 Pharaoh said to Yosef:

Since a god has made you know all this,
there is none as wise and discerning as you;
40 you shall be the One Over My House!
To your orders shall all my people submit;
only by the throne will I be greater than you!
41 Pharaoh said further to Yosef:
See, I place you over all the land of Egypt!
42 And Pharaoh removed his signet-ring from his hand and
placed it on Yosef's hand,
he had him clothed in linen garments and put the gold
chain upon his neck;
43 he had him mount the chariot of his second-in-rank, and
they called out before him: *Avrekh!*/Attention!
Thus he placed him over all the land of Egypt.
44 Pharaoh said to Yosef:
I am Pharaoh,
but without you, no man shall raise hand or foot in all the
land of Egypt!
45 Pharaoh called Yosef's name: *Tzafenat Pane'ah*/The God
Speaks and He Lives.
He gave him Asenat, daughter of Poti Fera, priest of On, as
a wife.
And Yosef's influence went out over all the land of Egypt.

---

34 **let him appoint appointed-overseers:** We already know that Yosef is a
man often entrusted with responsibility—"appointed" (39:4, 40:4). **divid-
ing . . . into five parts:** Hebrew obscure. B-R uses "arm (the land of
Egypt)."
35 **hand:** I.e., supervision.
36 **the land:** I.e., its people.
37 **The words seemed good:** Words now bring about Yosef's rise to power.
40 **the One Over My House:** A title similar to that of Yosef's steward in
43:16ff. **submit:** Hebrew obscure. **only by the throne:** Similar to Yosef's situation in Potifar's house, "He is no greater in this house than I"
(39:9)—but he withholds his wife.
41ff. **all the land of Egypt:** A refrain here, pointing to Yosef's power.
43 *Avrekh*/**Attention:** Hebrew unclear. Some suggest that it is Hebrew for
"bend the knee," others that it resembles an Assyrian title.
45 *Tzafenat-Pane'ah*/ **The God Speaks and He Lives:** An Egyptian name
which is appropriate to the story. Yosef lives, and through him, so do
Egypt, his family, and the future People of Israel. **Yosef's influence:**
Perhaps an idiom, or merely "Yosef went out."

46 Now Yosef was thirty years old when he stood in the
   presence of Pharaoh, king of Egypt.
   Yosef went out from Pharaoh's presence and passed through
   all the land of Egypt.

47 In the seven years of abundance the land produced in
   handfuls.
48 And he collected all kinds of provisions from those seven
   years that occurred in the land of Egypt,
   and placed provisions in the cities.
   The provisions from the fields of a city, surrounding it, he
   placed in it (as well).
49 So Yosef piled up grain like the sand of the sea, exceedingly
   much, until they had to stop counting, for it was
   uncountable.

50 Now two sons were born to Yosef, before the year of famine
   came,
   whom Asenat, daughter of Poti Fera, priest of On, bore to
   him.
51 Yosef called the name of the firstborn:
   Menashe/He-Who-Makes-Forget,
   meaning: God has made-me-forget all my hardships, all my
   father's house.
52 And the name of the second he called:
   Efrayim/Double-Fruit,
   meaning: God has made me bear fruit in the land of my
   affliction.

53 There came to an end the seven years of abundance that
   had occurred in the land of Egypt,
54 and there started to come the seven years of famine, as
   Yosef had said.
   Famine occurred in all lands, but in all the land of Egypt
   there was bread.
55 But when all the land of Egypt felt the famine, and the
   people cried out to Pharaoh for bread,
   Pharaoh said to all the Egyptians:

Go to Yosef, whatever he says to you, do!

56 Now the famine was over all the surface of the earth.
Yosef opened up all (storehouses) in which there was
     (grain), and gave-out-rations to the Egyptians,
since the famine was becoming stronger in the land of
     Egypt.

57 And all lands came to Egypt to buy rations, to Yosef,
for the famine was strong in all lands.

42:1 Now when Yaakov saw that there were rations in Egypt,
Yaakov said to his sons:
Why do you keep looking at one another?

2 And he said:
Here, I have heard that there are rations in Egypt,
go down there and buy us rations from there,
that we may live and not die.

Famine: The Brothers Come (41:53–42:38): Worldwide famine creates the
backdrop for the family drama that is about to unfold. The ancients
understood famine as sent by the gods, often as punishment; and the
events of our text suggest that God is indeed the prime mover here. We
are again presented with the characters of Chapter 37, all of whom have
somehow changed. Yaakov emerges as more pitiful than ever (a shadow
of the wrestler at the Yabbok), Yosef as powerful governor, not only of
all Egypt but of his family's destiny as well, and the brothers, remarkably, are repentant (42:21–22). We also see Yosef's emotional side for the
first time. He weeps in 42:24, as he will do three times again (43:30;
45:2, 14,15).

46 **thirty:** Yosef will be in power for eighty years (2 × 40), another patterned
number.

51 **Menashe:** Trad. English "Menasseh." **made-me-forget:** Yet he does not
forget for long, any more than the cupbearer did (Chapter 41).

52 **bear fruit . . . affliction:** Two expressions from the stories about the Patriarchs.

54ff. **Famine occurred in all lands:** The repetition of "all" here brings home the
totality of the famine.

42:2 **that we may live and not die:** This becomes a refrain in the story, alternat-
ing in meaning between Yosef's family (here and 43:8) and the Egyptians
(47:19).

3 So Yosef's brothers went down, ten (of them),
    to buy some rationed grain from Egypt.
4 But Binyamin, Yosef's brother, Yaakov would not send
    with his brothers,
    for he said: Lest harm befall him!
5 The sons of Yisrael came to buy rations among those that
    came,
    for the famine was in the land of Canaan.
6 Now Yosef was the governor over the land, it was he who
    supplied rations to all the people of the land.
    And Yosef's brothers came and bowed low to him, brow to
    the ground.
7 When Yosef saw his brothers, he recognized them,
    but he pretended-no-recognition of them and spoke harshly
    with them.
    He said to them:
    From where do you come?
    They said: From the land of Canaan, to buy food-rations.
8 Now although Yosef recognized his brothers, for their part,
    they did not recognize him.
9 And Yosef was reminded of the dreams that he had dreamt
    of them.
    He said to them:
    You are spies!
    It is to see the nakedness of the land that you have come!
10 They said to him: No, my lord!
    Rather, your servants have come to buy food-rations.
11 We are all of us the sons of a single man,
    we are honest,
    your servants have never been spies!
12 But he said to them:
    No!
    For it is the nakedness of the land that you have come to
    see!
13 They said:
    Your servants are twelve,
    we are brothers,
    sons of a single man in the land of Canaan:

the youngest is with our father now,
and one is no more.

14 Yosef said to them:
It is just as I spoke to you, saying: You are spies!

15 Hereby shall you be tested:
As Pharaoh lives!
You shall not depart from this (place)
unless your youngest brother comes here!

16 Send one of you to fetch your brother,
while (the rest of) you remain as prisoners.
Thus will your words be tested, whether there is truth in
  you or not—
as Pharaoh lives, indeed, you are spies!

17 He removed them into custody for three days.

18 Yosef said to them on the third day:
Do this, and stay alive,
for I fear God:

19 if you are honest,
let one of your brothers be held prisoner in the house of
  your custody,
and as for you, go, bring back rations for the famine-supply
  of your households.

20 Then bring your youngest brother back to me,
so that your words will be proven truthful, and you will not
  die.
They (prepared to) do so.

---

4 **Yosef's brother:** His full brother, as opposed to the others who were
half-brothers.

7 **recognized:** Ironically recalling the brothers' "Pray recognize" of 37:32.
pretended-no-recognition: Others use "pretended to be a stranger."

9 **nakedness:** Vulnerability (strategically).

11 **honest:** They will be, by the end of the chapter (Redford).

13 **twelve:** At last they think of themselves as a unit, "we are brothers!"

16 **tested:** Heb. *bahan*, a different root from the word translated "tested" (*nissa*)
in 22:1. Interestingly, the English "test" and the Hebrew *bhn* originally
meant the refining of metals, separating pure from impure. **or not—:** Or
"(in you.)/ If not. . . ."

21 But they said, each man to his brother:
Truly,
we are guilty:
concerning our brother!
—that we saw his heart's distress
when he implored us,
and we did not listen.
Therefore this distress has come upon us!

22 Re'uven answered them, saying:
Did I not say to you, say: Do not sin against the child!
But you would not listen,
so for his blood—now, satisfaction is demanded!

23 Now they did not know that Yosef was listening, for a
translator was between them.

24 But he turned away from them and wept.
When he was able to return to them, he spoke to them
and had Shim'on taken away from them, imprisoning him
before their eyes.

25 Then Yosef commanded that they fill their vessels with
grain
and return their silver-pieces into each man's sack,
and give them victuals for the journey.
They did so for them.

26 Then they loaded their rations onto their asses and went
from there.

27 But as one opened his sack to give his ass fodder at the
night-camp,
he saw his silver—there it was in the mouth of his pack!

28 He said to his brothers:
My silver has been returned—yes, here in my pack!
Their hearts gave way, and they trembled to one another,
saying:
What is this that God has done to us?

29 They came home to Yaakov their father, in the land of
Canaan,
and told him all that had befallen them, saying:

30 The man, the lord of the land, spoke harshly with us,
he took us for those that spy on the land!

31 Now we said to him: We are honest, we have never been
     spies!
32 We are twelve, brothers all, sons of our father:
     one is no more, and the youngest is now with our father in
     the land of Canaan.
33 Then the man, the lord of the land, said to us:
     Hereby shall I know whether you are honest:
     Leave one of your brothers with me,
     and as for the famine-supply of your households, take it and
     go.
34 But bring your youngest brother back to me,
     so that I may know that you are not spies, that you are
     honest.
     (Then) I will give your brother back to you, and you may
     travel about the land.
35 But it was, when they emptied their sacks: there was each
     man's silver pouch in his sack!
     They looked at their silver pouches, they and their father,
     and became frightened.
36 Yaakov their father said to them:
     It is me that you bereave!
     Yosef is no more,
     Shim'on is no more,

---

21 **guilty:** Perhaps it is the phrase "youngest brother" in Yosef's words (v.20)
     that jars their memory. They must now show responsibility to their father,
     which they had evaded in Chapter 37. **distress. . . . distress:** Another
     example of strict justice in the Bible: the punishment fits the crime.
22 **Re'uven:** A replay of Chapter 37, with Re'uven again making extravagant
     but ineffective declarations. Once again Yehuda will emerge in charge.
23 **translator:** Interpreter.
24 **imprisoning:** Or "fettering." **before their eyes:** As opposed to the sale of
     Yosef, where their presence is not mentioned, strictly speaking.
25 **they fill:** "They" refers to Yosef's servants. **silver-pieces:** Yosef had been
     sold for siver (37:28).
30 **The man:** Used eight times of Yosef in Chapters 42-44, perhaps out of
     ironic anonymity. **harshly:** Paralleling their earlier attitude: they "could
     not speak to him in peace" (37:4).

now you would take Binyamin—
upon me has all this come!

37 Re'uven said to his father, saying:
My two sons you may put to death
if I do not bring him back to you!
Place him in my hands, and I myself will return him to
   you.

38 But he said:
My son is not to go down with you!
For his brother is dead,
and he alone is left!
Should harm befall him on the journey on which you are
   going,
you will bring down my gray hair in grief to Sheol!

43:1 But the famine was heavy in the land.

2 And so it was, when they had finished eating the rations
   that they had brought from Egypt,
   that their father said to them:
   Return, buy us some food-rations.

3 But Yehuda said to him, saying:
   The man warned, yes, warned us,
   saying: You shall not see my face unless your brother is
      with you.

4 If you wish to send our brother with us, we will go down
   and buy you some food-rations.

5 But if you do not wish to send him, we will not go down,
   for the man said to us: You shall not see my face unless
   your brother is with you.

6 Yisrael said:
   Why did you deal so ill with me, by telling the man that
   you have another brother?

7 They said:
   The man asked, he asked about us and about our kindred,
   saying: Is your father still alive? Do you have another
      brother?
   So we told him, according to these words.
   Could we know, know that he would say: Bring your
      brother down?

8 Yehuda said to Yisrael his father:
Send the lad with me,
and we will arise and go,
that we may live and not die,
so we, so you, so our little-ones!
9 I will act as his pledge,
at my hand you may seek him!
If I do not bring him back to you
and set him in your presence,
I will be culpable-for-sin against you all the days (of my
life).

The Test (43–44): Yosef's testing of his brothers is masterful, not only
because of the plan itself, but also because of the depth of emotion that
the text evokes in its characterizations. It demonstrates how well the
whole story has been integrated into the Yaakov material, for here as well
as there long conversations are used to reveal complex passions.

Some have questioned the morality of Yosef's actions, seeing that the
aged Yaakov might well have died while the test was progressing, without ever finding out that Yosef had survived. But that is not the point of
the story. What it *is* trying to teach (among other things) is a lesson
about crime and repentance. Only by recreating something of the original situation—the brothers are again in control of the life and death of a
son of Rahel—can Yosef be sure that they have changed. Once the
brothers pass the test, life and covenant can then continue.

37 **My two sons:** Re'uven is again spouting nonsense. **I myself will return
him:** But he did not in 37:22 (Ackerman).
38 **My son is not to go down. . . . you will bring down my gray hair in grief:**
Yaakov will indeed "go down," but to Egypt, not to Sheol, to meet his
"dead" son. The latter part of the phrase is basically repeated in 44:29 and
44:31, as a key to the father's feelings. **he alone is left:** Of his mother
Rahel (see 44:20).
43:3 **my face:** The great confrontation theme of the Yaakov stories returns.
4–5 **send:** Or "release," "let go."
9 **I will act as his pledge/ at my hand you may seek him:** Echoing Yaakov's
own language of responsibility in 31:39 ("I would make good the loss/ at
my hand you would seek it"). **in your presence:** Literally, "before your
face."

10 Indeed, had we not lingered, we would indeed have been
     back twice already!
11 Yisrael their father said to them:
     If it must be so, then, do this:
     Take some of the produce of the land in your vessels
     and bring them down to the man as a gift:
     a little balsam, a little honey, balm and ladanum, pistachio
       nuts and almonds.
12 And silver two times over take in your hand;
     and the silver that was returned in the mouth of your packs,
       return in your hand,
     perhaps it was an oversight.
13 And as for your brother, take him!
     Arise, return to the man,
14 and may God Shaddai give you mercy before the man,
     so that he releases your other brother to you, and Binyamin
       as well.
     And as for me—if I must be bereaved, I must be bereaved!
15 The men took this gift, silver two times over they took in
       their hand
     and Binyamin as well.
     They arose and went down to Egypt
     and stood in Yosef's presence.
16 When Yosef saw Binyamin with them,
     he said to the steward of his house:
     Bring the men into the house, slaughter some
       slaughter-animals and prepare them,
     for it is with me that these men shall eat at noon.
17 The man did as Yosef had said, the man brought the men
     into Yosef's house.
18 But the men were frightened that they had been brought
     into Yosef's house, and said:
     It is because of the silver that was returned in our packs
       before that we have been brought here,
     for (them to) roll upon us, and fall upon us,
     and take us into servitude, along with our asses!
19 They came close to the man, to the steward of Yosef's
     house, and spoke to him at the entrance to the house,
20 they said:

Please, my lord!

We came down, came down before to buy food-rations,

21 but it was, when we came to the night camp and opened
    our packs,

    there was each man's silver in the mouth of his pack, our
    silver by its exact weight—

    but (here) we have returned it in our hand!

22 And other silver as well we have brought down in our hand,
    to buy food.

    We do not know who put back our silver in our packs!

23 He said:

    It is well with you, do not be afraid!

    Your God, the God of your father, placed a treasure in your
    packs for you—(for) your silver has come in to me.

    And he brought Shim'on out to them.

24 Then the man had the men come into Yosef's house

    and gave them water so that they might wash their feet

    and gave them fodder for their asses.

25 They prepared the gift, until Yosef came back at noon,

    for they understood that they were to eat bread there.

26 When Yosef came into the house, they brought him the gift
    that was in their hand, into the house,

    and bowed down to him, to the ground.

27 He asked after their welfare and said:

    Is your old father well, of whom you spoke?

    Is he still alive?

---

11 **Take:** Three times, culminating in the pathetic "And as for your brother,
   take him!" (v.13). **balsam . . . honey, balm and ladanum, pistachio nuts
   and almonds:** Another example of concealment in the story. The list includes the cargo of the caravan that carried Yosef away (37:25).

12 **two times over . . . oversight:** Heb. *mishne . . . mishge.*

14 **God Shaddai:** Yaakov uses the same term for God as did his father, when
   Yaakov left for Aram (28:3). **bereaved:** Echoing the fears of his mother
   Rivka (27:45).

18 **roll upon us:** Others use "attack us." **roll upon us, and fall upon us:** The
   rhythm reflects the brothers' emotional anguish.

23 **has come in:** I.e., I have received full payment.

27 **well:** Or "at peace"—as before, a key element of the Yaakov stories.

28 They said:
Your servant, our father, is well, he is still alive—
and in homage they bowed low.

29 He lifted up his eyes and saw Binyamin his brother, his
    mother's son,
and he said:
Is this your youngest brother, of whom you spoke to me?
And he said:
May God show you favor, my son!

30 And in haste—for his feelings were so kindled toward his
    brother that he had to weep—
Yosef entered a chamber and wept there.

31 Then he washed his face and came out, he restrained
    himself, and said:
Serve bread!

32 They served him by himself and them by themselves and
    the Egyptians who were eating with him by themselves,
for Egyptians will not eat bread with Hebrews—for that is
    an abomination for Egyptians.

33 But they were seated in his presence:
the firstborn according to his rank-as-firstborn and the
    youngest according to his rank-as-youngest.
And the men stared at each other in astonishment over it.

34 He had courses taken to them from his presence,
and Binyamin's course was five times greater than all their
    courses.
Then they drank and became drunk with him.

44:1 Now he commanded the steward of his house, saying:
Fill the men's packs with food, as much as they are able to
    carry,
and put each man's silver in the mouth of his pack.

2 And my goblet, the silver goblet, put in the mouth of the
    youngest's pack, along with the silver for his rations.
He did according to Yosef's word which he had spoken.

3 At morning light, the men were sent off, they and their
    asses;

4 they were just outside the city—they had not yet gone far—
when Yosef said to the steward of his house:

Up, pursue the men, and when you have caught up with
   them, say to them:
Why have you paid back ill for good?

5 Is not this (goblet) the one that my lord drinks with?
And he also divines, yes, divines with it!
You have wrought ill in what you have done!

6 When he caught up with them, he spoke those words to
   them.

7 They said to him:
Why does my lord speak such words as these?
Heaven forbid for your servants to do such a thing!

8 Here, the silver that we found in the mouth of our packs,
   we returned to you from the land of Canaan;
so how could we steal silver or gold from the house of your
   lord?

9 He with whom it is found among your servants, he shall
   die,
and we also will become my lord's servants!

10 He said:
Now as well, according to your words, so be it:
he with whom it is found shall become my servant, but you
   shall be clear.

11 With haste each man let down his pack to the ground, each
   man opened his pack.

12 and then he searched: with the eldest he started and with
   the youngest he finished—
and the goblet was found in Binyamin's pack!

---

29 **Is this:** Or "So this is."
34 **five times:** Others use "many times." Yet the prominence of the number
   five throughout the Yosef story, as noted above, should not be overlooked.
44:2 **my goblet:** The ensuing scene is somewhat parallel to Rahel's theft of the
   terafim (compare verse 9 with 31:32).
   5 **divines:** Cups were used in predicting the future in the ancient Near East;
   see note to 40:11. The diviner would examine the shapes made by insoluble
   liquids, such as oil in water. **You have wrought ill:** Resembling Laban's
   accusation against Yaakov, "You have done foolishly" (31:28).
10 **clear:** Of punishment.

13 They rent their clothes,
   each man loaded up his ass, and they returned to the city.
14 Yehuda and his brothers came into Yosef's house
   —he was still there—
   and flung themselves down before him to the ground.
15 Yosef said to them:
   What kind of deed is this that you have done!
   Do you not know that a man like me can divine, yes divine?
16 Yehuda said:
   What can we say to my lord?
   What can we speak, by what can we show ourselves
      innocent?
   God has found out your servants' crime!
   Here we are, servants to my lord, so we, so the one in
      whose hand the goblet was found.
17 But he said:
   Heaven forbid that I should do this!
   The man in whose hand the goblet was found—he shall
      become my servant,
   but you—go up in peace to your father!
18 Now Yehuda came closer to him and said:
   Please, my lord,
   pray let your servant speak a word in the ears of my lord,
   and do not let your anger rage against your servant,
   for you are like Pharaoh!
19 My lord asked his servants, saying: Do you have a father or
      another brother?
20 And we said to my lord: We have an old father
   and a young child of his old age,
   whose brother is dead,
   so that he alone is left of his mother,
   and his father loves him.
21 And you said to your servants: Bring him down to me, I
      wish to set my eyes upon him.
22 But we said to my lord:
   The lad cannot leave his father,
   were he to leave his father, he would die.
23 But you said to your servants: If your youngest brother does
      not come down with you, you shall not see my face again.

24 Now it was, when we went up to your servant, my father,
    we told him my lord's words,
25 and our father said: Return, buy us some food-rations.
26 But we said: We cannot go down;
    if our youngest brother is with us, then we will go down,
    for we cannot see the man's face if our youngest brother is
    not with us.
27 Now your servant, my father, said to us:
    You yourselves know
    that my wife bore two to me.
28 One went away from me,
    I said: For sure he is torn, torn-to-pieces!
    And I have not seen him again thus far.
29 Now should you take away this one as well from before my
    face,
    should harm befall him, you will bring down my gray hair
    in ill-fortune to Sheol!
30 So now,
    when I come back to your servant, my father, and the lad is
    not with us,
    —with whose life his own life is bound up!—
31 it will be, that when he sees that the lad is no more, he will
    die,
    and your servant will have brought down the gray hair of
    your servant, our father, in grief to Sheol!

---

16 **your servants' crime:** Of selling Yosef?
17 **But he said:** "He" is Yosef.   **this:** Enslaving all of the brothers.
18 **Now Yehuda . . . said . . . :** Yehuda's great speech, masterful in its rhetoric, is chiefly aimed at stirring up sympathy for the father; it contains the
   word "father" fourteen times. Binyamin, whose appearance actually causes
   Yosef great anguish, is hardly treated as a personality at all.   **you are like
   Pharaoh:** Lit. "like you is like Pharaoh."
22 **he would die:** "He" refers to Yaakov, although the Hebrew is somewhat
   ambiguous.
28 **thus far:** A hint that Yosef is still alive, or perhaps a tiny expression of
   hope.
30 **life:** Heb. *nefesh,* also "emotions" or "feelings."
31 **our father:** Is Yehuda unknowingly including Yosef?

32 For your servant pledged himself for the lad to my father,
   saying: If I do not bring him back to you, I will be
      culpable-for-sin against my father all the days (of my life).
33 So now,
   pray let your servant stay instead of the lad, as servant to
      my lord,
   but let the lad go up with his brothers!
34 For how can I go up to my father, when the lad is not with
      me?
   Then would I see the ill-fortune that would come upon my
      father!

45:1 Yosef could no longer restrain himself in the presence of all
      who were stationed around him,
   he called out:
   Have everyone leave me!
   So no one stood (in attendance upon) him when Yosef made
      himself known to his brothers.
2 He put forth his voice in weeping:
   the Egyptians heard, Pharaoh's household heard.
3 Then Yosef said to his brothers:
   I am Yosef. Is my father still alive?
   But his brothers were not able to answer him,
   for they were confounded in his presence.
4 Yosef said to his brothers:
   Pray come close to me!
   They came close.
   He said:
   I am Yosef your brother, whom you sold into Egypt.
5 But now, do not be pained,
   and do not let (anger) rage in your eyes that you sold me
      here!
   For it was to save life that God sent me on before you.
6 For it is two years now that the famine has been in the
      midst of the land,
   and there are still another five years in which there shall be
      no plowing or harvest.
7 So God sent me on before you

to make you a remnant on earth,
to keep you alive as a great body-of-survivors.
8 So now,
it was not you that sent me here, but God!
He has made me Father to Pharaoh and lord of all his
household and ruler over all the land of Egypt.
9 Make haste, go up to my father and say to him:
Thus says your son, Yosef:
God has made me lord of all Egypt;
come down to me, do not remain!
10 You shall stay in the region of Goshen, you shall be near
me,
you and your sons and the sons of your sons,
your sheep, your oxen, and all that is yours.
11 I will sustain you there,
for there are still five years of famine left
—lest you be as disinherited, you and your household and
all that is yours.
12 Here, your eyes see, as well as my brother Binyamin's eyes,
that it is my mouth that speaks to you!
13 So tell my father of all the weight I carry in Egypt, and of
all that you have seen,
and make haste, bring my father down here!

Reconciliation (45): In revealing his true identity at last, Yosef makes two points: first, that it was all part of God's plan; and second, that the family must immediately prepare for migration to Egypt. Thus the personal story is intertwined with the national one, and the text therefore gives limited time and space to psychological details. The motif of God's plan is stressed by the repetition of "God sent me" (vv.5, 7, 8), while the anticipated bounties of settling in Egypt are brought out by the threefold "good-things of Egypt" (vv.18, 20, 23) and by the repeated exhortation to "come" (vv.18, 19).

45:5 (**anger**): At each other, or referring to each individual's feelings of guilt.
11 **as disinherited**: Or "reduced-to-poverty."
13 **all the weight I carry**: I.e., my importance.

14 He flung himself upon his brother Binyamin's neck and
      wept,
   and Binyamin wept upon his neck.
15 Then he kissed all his brothers and wept upon them.
   After this his brothers spoke with him.

16 The news was heard in Pharaoh's household, they said:
   Yosef's brothers have come!
   It was good in Pharaoh's eyes and in the eyes of his
      servants.
17 And Pharaoh said to Yosef:
   Say to your brothers:
   Do this—
   load your animals and go,
   come back to the land of Canaan;
18 fetch your father and your households
   and come to me!
   I will give you the good-things of the land of Egypt,
   so that you will eat of the fat of the land!
19 And you, you have been commanded:
   Do this—
   take you wagons from the land of Egypt for your little ones
      and your wives,
   and carry your father down
   and come!
20 Let not your eyes look-with-regret on your household-
      wares,
   for the good-things of all the land of Egypt—they are yours!
21 The sons of Yisrael did so,
   Yosef gave them wagons in accordance with Pharaoh's
      orders
   and gave them victuals for the journey.
22 To all of them, each man, he gave changes of clothes,
   but to Binyamin he gave three hundred pieces of silver and
      five changes of clothes,
23 and to his father he sent in like manner:
   ten asses, carrying the good-things of Egypt,
   and ten mares, carrying grain and bread,
   and food for his father, for the journey.

24 Then he sent off his brothers, and they went;
   he said to them:
   Do not be upset on the journey!
25 They went up from Egypt and came to the land of Canaan,
   to Yaakov their father,
26 and they told him, saying:
   Yosef is still alive!
   Indeed, he is ruler of all the land of Egypt!
   His heart failed,
   for he did not believe them.

Migration to Egypt (45:16–47:12): Yaakov's descent to Egypt involves three meetings: with God, with Yosef, and with Pharaoh. The first is God's final revelation to Yaakov. God had previously forbidden Yitzhak to go to Egypt during a famine (26:1–2), but his son may now go as part of the divine plan, his people's destiny. The blessing given to Avraham's children (particularly to Yishmael) is repeated in 46:3, and God will be "with" Yaakov (46:4) on this journey as he has been on others.

The meeting between father and long-lost son is brief but powerful, returning as it does to the "face" motif (46:30). Immediately afterward Yosef gives the family advice on how to demonstrate their usefulness to the Egyptians, and one is struck by the precariousness of their situation in even this best of circumstances.

Yaakov's brief audience with Pharaoh is both moving and pathetic. The Patriarch sums up his life in depressing terms, and it becomes clear that long life (he believes his own to be short), in addition to wealth and fertility, is considered a sign of divine favor.

The actual migration is sketched in a few brief strokes. The list of names in 46:8–27 has been constructed on patterned numbers, with a total of seventy.

15 **his brothers spoke with him:** Which they could not do "in peace" in 37:4.
16 **come:** The verb focuses toward Pharaoh's invitation to follow: "Yosef's brothers have come!" (v.16) to "and come to me" (v.18) to "and come!" (v.19).
18 **good-things:** More precisely, "best-things" ("good" has been retained here to indicate a major theme of the story: good and ill).
20 **Let not your eyes look-with-regret:** Possibly "Do not stint."
22 **but to Binyamin he gave:** The original situation (Chapter 37) is set up once more; this time the brothers do not react adversely to the youngest son's being favored.

27 But when they spoke to him all of Yosef's words which he
       had spoken to them,
    and when he saw the wagons that Yosef had sent to carry
       him down,
    their father Yaakov's spirit came to life.
28 Yisrael said:
    Enough!
    Yosef my son is still alive;
    I must go and see him before I die!

46:1 Yisrael traveled with all that was his
      and came to Be'er-Sheva,
      and he slaughtered slaughter-offerings to the God of his
         father Yitzhak.
   2 And God said to Yisrael in visions of the night,
      he said:
      Yaakov! Yaakov!
      He said:
      Here I am.
   3 Now he said:
      I am *El*/God,
      the God of your father.
      Do not be afraid of going down to Egypt,
      for a great nation will I make of you there.
   4 I myself
      will go down with you to Egypt,
      and I myself
      will bring you up, yes, up again.
      And Yosef will lay his hand on your eyes.

   5 Yaakov departed from Be'er-Sheva.
      Yisrael's sons carried Yaakov their father, their little-ones
         and their wives in the wagons that Pharaoh had sent for
         carrying him,
   6 and they took their acquired livestock and their property
         that they had gained in the land of Canaan
      and came to Egypt,
      Yaakov and all his seed with him,

7 his sons and the sons of his sons with him, his daughters
　　and the daughters of his sons;
　　all his seed he brought with him to Egypt.

8 Now these are the names of the Sons of Israel who came to
　　Egypt:
　　Yaakov and his sons:
　　Yaakov's firstborn was Re'uven.
9 Re'uven's sons: Hanokh, Pallu, Hetzron, and Carmi.
10 Shim'on's sons: Yemuel, Yamin, Ohad, Yakhin, and
　　Tzohar, and Sha'ul the son of the Canaanite-woman.
11 Levi's sons: Gershon, Kehat, and Merari.
12 Yehuda's sons: Er, Onan, Shela, Peretz, and Zerah,
　　but Er and Onan had died in the land of Canaan.
　　And Peretz's sons were Hetzron and Hamul.
13 Yissakhar's sons: Tola, Puvva, Yov, and Shimron.
14 Zevulun's sons: Sered, Elon, and Yahl'el.
15 These are the sons of Lea, whom she bore to Yaakov in the
　　country of Aram, and also Dina his daughter;
　　all the persons among his sons and daughters were
　　thirty-three.
16 Gad's sons: Tzifyon and Chaggi, Shuni and Etzbon, Eri,
　　Arodi, and Ar'eli.
17 Asher's sons: Yimna, Yishva, Yishvi, and Beria, and Serah
　　their sister.
　　And Beria's sons: Hever and Malkiel.
18 These are the sons of Zilpa, whom Lavan had given to Lea
　　his daughter,
　　she bore these to Yaakov: sixteen persons.

---

27 **Yosef's words:** In Chapter 37 his words were damaging, but here they are
life-giving.
46:2 **Yaakov! Yaakov!:** Doubled as in 22:11 and other moments of dramatic
revelations in the Bible (e.g., Ex. 3:4).
4 **lay his hand on your eyes:** I.e., be present at your death.
8 **Now these are the names . . . :** This phrase opens the book of Exodus,
making that book a resumption of the Genesis narrative.

19 The sons of Rahel, Yaakov's wife: Yosef and Binyamin.

20 To Yosef there were born in the land of Egypt—whom
Asenat, daughter of Poti Fera, priest of On, bore to him:
Menashe and Efrayim.

21 Binyamin's sons: Bela, Bekher and Ashbel, Gera and
Naaman, Ahi and Rosh, Muppim, Huppim, and Ard.

22 These are the sons of Rahel, who were born to Yaakov,
all the persons were fourteen.

23 Dan's sons: Hushim.

24 Naftali's sons: Yahtze'el, Guni, Yetzer, and Shillem.

25 These are the sons of Bilha, whom Lavan had given to
Rahel his daughter,
she bore these to Yaakov: all the persons were seven.

26 All the persons who came with Yaakov to Egypt, those
going out from his loins, aside from the wives of Yaakov's
sons:
all the persons were sixty-six.

27 Now Yosef's sons, who had been born to him in Egypt: the
persons were two.
(Thus) all the persons of Yaakov's household who came to
Egypt were seventy.

28 Now Yehuda he had sent on ahead of him, to Yosef,
to give directions ahead of him to Goshen.
When they came to the region of Goshen,

29 Yosef had his chariot harnessed and went up to meet Yisrael
his father, to Goshen.
When he caught sight of him
he flung himself upon his neck
and wept upon his neck continually.

30 Yisrael said to Yosef:
Now I can die,
since I have seen your face, that you are still alive!

31 Yosef said to his brothers and to his father's household:
I will go up, so that I may tell Pharaoh and say to him:
My brothers and my father's household, who were in the
land of Canaan, have come to me.

32 The men are shepherds of flocks,

indeed, they have always been livestock men,
and their sheep and their oxen, all that is theirs, they have
   brought along.
33 Now it will be, when Pharaoh has you called and says:
   What is it that you do?
34 Then say: Your servants have always been livestock men,
   from our youth until now, so we, so our fathers—
in order that you may settle in the region of Goshen.
For every shepherd of flocks is an abomination to the
   Egyptians.

47:1 So Yosef came and told Pharaoh, he said:
   My father and my brothers, their sheep and their oxen and
     all that is theirs, have come from the land of Canaan,
   and here, they are in the region of Goshen!
2 Now from the circle of his brothers he had picked out five
   men and had set them in Pharaoh's presence.
3 Pharaoh said to his brothers:
   What is it that you do?
   They said to Pharaoh:
   Your servants are shepherds of flocks, so we, so our fathers.
4 And they said to Pharaoh:
   It is to sojourn in the land that we have come,
   for there is no grazing for the flocks that are your servants',
   for the famine is heavy in the land of Canaan.
   So now,
   pray let your servants settle in the region of Goshen!
5 Pharaoh said to Yosef, saying:
   (So) your father and your brothers have come to you:

-----

27 **seventy:** Once again, the "perfect" number.
33 **What is it that you do:** What is your occupation?
34 **every shepherd . . . is an abomination to the Egyptians:** Speiser under-
stands this as a reference to the Hyksos "shepherd kings," who as foreigners ruled Egypt in the mid-Second Millennium (until they were driven
out).
47:4 **It is to sojourn:** Are they still sensitive to the accusation in 42:12, "For it is
the nakedness of the land that you have come to see"?

6 the land of Egypt is before you;
  in the goodliest-part of the land, settle your father and your
      brothers,
  let them settle in the region of Goshen.
  And if you know that there are able men among them,
  make them chiefs of livestock over what is mine.
7 Yosef brought Yaakov his father and had him stand in
      Pharaoh's presence.
  And Yaakov gave Pharaoh a blessing-of-greeting.
8 Pharaoh said to Yaakov:
  How many are the days and years of your life?
9 Yaakov said to Pharaoh:
  The days and years of my sojourn are thirty and a hundred
      years;
  few and ill-fated have been the days and years of my life,
  they have not attained the days and years of my fathers'
      lives in the days of their sojourn.
10 Yaakov gave Pharaoh a blessing-of-farewell
  and went out from Pharaoh's presence.
11 So Yosef settled his father and his brothers,
  giving them holdings in the land of Egypt,
  in the goodliest-part of the land, in the region of Ra'meses,
  as Pharaoh had commanded.
12 Yosef sustained his father, his brothers, and his father's
      entire household with bread, in proportion to the
      little-ones.

13 But bread there was none in all the land,
  for the famine was exceedingly heavy,
  and the land of Egypt and the land of Canaan were
      exhausted by the famine.
14 Yosef had collected all the silver that was to be found in the
      land of Egypt and in the land of Canaan, from the rations
      that they had bought,
  and Yosef had brought the silver into Pharaoh's house.
15 When the silver in the land of Egypt and in the land of
      Canaan had run out,
  all the Egyptians came to Yosef, saying:
  Come-now, (let us have) bread!

Why should we die in front of you, because the silver is
        gone?
16 Yosef said:
Come-now, (let me have) your livestock, and I will give you
        (bread) for your livestock, since the silver is gone.
17 So they brought their livestock to Yosef, and Yosef gave
        them bread (in exchange) for the horses, the
        sheep-livestock, the oxen-livestock, and the asses;
he got-them-through with bread (in exchange) for all their
        livestock in that year.
18 But when that year had run out, they came back to him in
        the second year and said to him:
We cannot hide from my lord
that if the silver has run out and the animal-stocks are my
        lord's,
nothing remains for my lord except for our bodies and our
        soil!
19 Why should we die before your eyes, so we, so our soil?
Acquire us and our soil for bread,
and we and our soil will become servants to Pharaoh.
Give (us) seed-for-sowing
that we may live and not die,
that the soil may not become desolate!

Yosef the Life-Giver (47:13–26): The events of this section are not at-
tested historically in Egyptian records. Perhaps they have been included
here to confirm Yosef's stature as Rescuer, not only of his family but of
all Egypt as well (see note to 42:2). The description of Yosef's power is
now complete: just as the brothers were ready to "become my lord's
servants" (44:9), so now are the Egyptians (47:25).
    Some have seen the episode as an ironic reversal of what is to come in
Exodus, with the Egyptians' enslavement of the Israelites; if so, this
interlude may have been an amusing one to ancient Israelite audiences.
    The text uses the repetition of the phrase "to/for Pharaoh" to effec-
tively paint the legal transaction.

8 **days and years:** See the note to 25:7.
9 **in the days of:** Others use "during."
17 **got-them-through:** Lit. "led them."

20 So Yosef acquired all the soil of Egypt for Pharaoh
    —for each of the Egyptians sold his field, for the famine
    was strong upon them—
    and the land went over to Pharaoh.
21 As for the people, he transferred them into the cities, from
    one edge of Egypt's border to its other edge.
22 Only the soil of the priests he did not acquire,
    for the priests had a prescribed-allocation from Pharaoh,
      and they ate from their allocation which Pharaoh had
      given them,
    therefore they did not sell their soil.
23 Yosef said to the people:
    Now that I have acquired you and your soil today for
      Pharaoh,
    here, you have seed, sow the soil!
24 But it shall be at the ingatherings, that you shall give a fifth
      to Pharaoh,
    the four other parts being for you
    as seed for the field and for your eating-needs, for those in
      your households, and for feeding your little-ones.
25 They said:
    You have saved our lives!
    May we find favor in my lord's eyes: we will become
      servants to Pharaoh.
26 And Yosef made it a prescribed-law until this day,
      concerning the soil of Egypt: For Pharaoh every fifth
      part!
    Only the soil of the priests, that alone did not go over to
      Pharaoh.

27 Now Yisrael stayed in the land of Egypt, in the region of
      Goshen;
    they obtained holdings in it, bore fruit, and became
      exceedingly many.
28 And Yaakov lived in the land of Egypt for seventeen years.
    And the days of Yaakov, the years of his life, were seven
      years and a hundred and forty years.
29 Now when Yisrael's days drew near to death,

he called his son Yosef and said to him:
Pray, if I have found favor in your eyes,
pray put your hand under my thigh—
deal with me faithfully and truly:
pray do not bury me in Egypt!
30 When I lie down with my fathers,
carry me out of Egypt, and bury me in their burial-site!
He said:
I will do according to your words.
31 But he said:
Swear to me!
So he swore to him.
Then Yisrael bowed, at the head of the bed.

48:1 Now after these events it was
that they said to Yosef:
Here, your father has taken sick!
So he took his two sons with him, Menashe and
Efrayim. . . .
2 When they told Yaakov, saying: Here, your son Yosef is
coming to you,
Yisrael gathered his strength and sat up in the bed.
3 Yaakov said to Yosef:
God Shaddai was seen by me
in Luz, in the land of Canaan;
he blessed me

Yosef's Sons Blessed (48): Yaakov, near to death, blesses his grandsons
(Rahel's!) in moving terms, bringing full circle many of the motifs of his
life. Elder and younger sons are switched by the blind Patriarch, this
time, though, one who is fully aware of their identities. As in both
literature and life, a dying man sees both past (here) and future (the next
chapter) with great clarity, as in a vision.

21 **transferred them:** Hebrew difficult; some read "enslaved them."
24 **a fifth:** Here is the ubiquitous "five" again.

4 and he said to me:
Here, I will make you bear fruit and will make you many,
and will make you into a host of peoples;
I will give this land to your seed after you, as a holding for
   the ages!
5 So now,
your two sons who were born to you in the land of Egypt
before I came to you in Egypt,
they are mine,
Efrayim and Menashe,
like Re'uven and Shim'on, let them be mine!
6 But your begotten sons, whom you will beget after them,
let them be yours;
by their brothers' names let them be called, respecting their
   inheritance.
7 While I—
when I came back from that country,
Rahel died on me,
in the land of Canaan,
on the way, with still a stretch of land left to come to Efrat.
There I buried her, on the way to Efrat—that is now
   Bet-Lehem.
8 When Yisrael saw Yosef's sons, he said:
Who are these?
9 Yosef said to his father:
They are my sons, whom God has given me here.
He said:
Pray take them over to me, that I may give-them-blessing.
10 Now Yisrael's eyes were heavy with age, he was not able to
   see.
He brought them close to him,
and he kissed them and embraced them.
11 Yisrael said to Yosef:
I never expected to see your face again,
and here, God has let me see your seed as well!
12 Yosef took them from between his knees
and they bowed low, their brows to the ground.
13 Yosef took the two of them,
Efrayim with his right-hand, to Yisrael's left,

and Menashe with his left-hand, to Yisrael's right,
and brought them close to him.

14 But Yisrael stretched out his right-hand and put it on the
head of Efrayim—yet he was the younger!—
and his left-hand on the head of Menashe;
he crossed his arms, although Menashe was the firstborn.

15 Then he blessed Yosef and said:
The God
in whose presence my fathers walked,
Avraham and Yitzhak,
the God
who has tended me
ever since I was (born), until this day—

16 the messenger
who has redeemed me from all ill-fortune,
may he bless the lads!
May my name continue to be called through them
and the name of my fathers, Avraham and Yitzhak!
May they teem-like-fish to (become) many in the midst of
the land!

17 Now when Yosef saw that his father had put his right hand
on Efrayim's head,
it sat ill in his eyes,
and he laid hold of his father's hand, to turn it from
Efrayim's head to Menashe's head.

18 Yosef said to his father:
Not so, father, indeed, this one is the firstborn, place your
hand on his head!

48:5 **they are mine:** As it were, adopted. **Efrayim and Menashe:** Note how
Yaakov reverses the order of birth; see verses 14, 17–19.

7 **Rahel died on me:** The memory is still painful to Yaakov, even after many
years.

11 **your face:** The final and most powerful occurrence of the term.

15 **tended:** Or "shepherded."

16 **redeemed me from all ill-fortune:** Despite his words in 47:9, perhaps
Yaakov achieves a measure of peace in the end. **my name continue to be
called through them:** My line continue through them. **teem-like-fish:**
Others use "become teeming (multitudes)."

19 But his father refused and said:
I know, my son, I know—
he too will be a people, he too will be great,
yet his younger brother will be greater than he, and his seed
    will become a full measure of nations!
20 So he blessed them on that day,
saying:
By you shall Israel give-blessings, saying:
God make you like Efrayim and Menashe!
Thus he made Efrayim go before Menashe.
21 Then Yisrael said to Yosef:
Here, I am dying,
but God will be with you,
he will have you return to the land of your fathers.
22 And I, I give you
one portion over and above your brothers,
which I took away from the Amorite,
with my sword, with my bow.

49:1 Now Yaakov called his sons and said:
Gather round, that I may tell you
what will befall you in the aftertime of days.
2   Come together and hearken, sons of Yaakov,
         hearken to Yisrael your father.

3   Re'uven,
         my firstborn, you,
         my might, first-fruit of my vigor!
         Surpassing in loftiness, surpassing in force!
4   Headlong like water—surpass no more!
         For when you mounted your father's bed,
         then you defiled it—he mounted the couch!

5   Shim'on and Levi,
         such brothers,
         wronging weapons are their ties-of-kinship!
6   To their council may my being never come,
         in their assembly may my person never unite!
         For in their anger they kill men,
         in their self-will they maim bulls.

7   Cursed be their anger, that it is so fierce!
       Their fury, that it is so harsh!
       I will split them up in Yaakov,
       I will scatter them in Yisrael.

8   Yehuda,
       you—your brothers will praise you,
       your hand on the neck of your enemies!
       Your father's sons will bow down to you.
9   A lion's whelp, Yehuda—
       from torn-prey, my son, you have gone up!
       He squats, he crouches,
       like the lion, like the king-of-beasts,
       who dares rouse him up?

Yaakov's Testament and Death (49): In this ancient piece of poetry, Yaakov addresses his sons, not as they are, but as they will be. There is little
resemblance, for instance, between the Binyamin as the beloved and
protected youngest son of the Yosef story and the preying wolf of verse
27, but the Benjaminites were later to be known for their military skills.
Scholars have therefore seen the entire poem as a retrojection of Israel as
it came to be on the days of the Patriarchs.

As in the fuller Yosef narrative, the first three sons are quickly dis-
qualified from active leadership, paving the way for the rise of Yehuda
(the tribe from which sprang David and the royal house of Israel). Despite this, Yosef still receives the richest blessing.

The chapter is textually among the most difficult in the Torah. Many
passages are simply obscure, leaving the translator to make at best edu-
cated guesses.

19 **I know:** Though blind, Yaakov knows exactly what he is doing, unlike his
   father in Chapter 27.
22 **one portion over and above:** Hebrew unclear. We do not know to what
   event Yaakov is referring in this entire verse.   **took away:** Others use "will
   take," "must take."
49:4 **when you mounted . . . :** Alluding to 35:21–22.
   5 **ties-of-kinship:** Hebrew obscure. Others use "weapons," "swords" (B-R
   uses "mattocks").
   6 **in their anger they kill men:** See 34:25–26.
   8 **Yehuda . . . enemies:** Heb. *yehuda/ atta yodukha ahikha/ yadekha al oref
   oyevekha.*
   9 **lion:** Eventually the symbol of the (Judahite) monarchy.

10   The scepter shall not depart from Yehuda,
        nor the staff-of-command from between his legs,
        until they bring him tribute,
        —the obedience of peoples is his.
11   He ties up his foal to a vine,
        his young colt to a crimson tendril;
        he washes his raiment in wine,
        his mantle in the blood of grapes;
12   his eyes, darker than wine,
        his teeth, whiter than milk.

13   Zevulun,
        on the shore of the sea he dwells;
        he is a haven-shore for boats,
        his flank upon Tzidon.

14   Yissakhar,
        a bone-strong ass,
        crouching among the fire-places.
15   When he saw how good the resting-place was,
        and how pleasant was the land,
        he bent his shoulder to bearing
        and so became a laboring serf.

16   Dan,
        his people will mete-out-judgment,
        (to all) of Israel's branches together.
17   May Dan be a snake on the wayside,
        a horned-viper on the path,
        who bites the horse's heels
        so that his rider tumbles backward.

18   I wait-in-hope for your salvation, O YHWH!

19   Gad,
        goading robber-band will goad him,
        yet he will goad at their heel.

20   Asher,
        his nourishment is rich,

he gives forth king's dainties.

21   Naftali,
        a hind let loose,
        . he who gives forth lovely fawns.

22   Young wild-ass,
        Yosef,
        young wild-ass along a spring,
        donkeys along a wall.
23   Bitterly they shot at him,
        the archers assailed him,
24   yet firm remained his bow,
        and agile stayed his arms and hands—
        by means of the hands of Yaakov's Champion,
        up there,
        the Shepherd, the Stone of Yisrael.
25   By your father's God—
        may he help you,
        and Shaddai,
        may he give-you-blessing:
        Blessings of the heavens, from above,
        blessings of Ocean crouching below,
        blessings of breasts and womb!

---

10 **until they bring . . .** : Hebrew difficult; others use "until Shiloh comes."
   The phrase is an old and unsolved problem for interpreter and translator
   alike.
11 **colt:** Of an ass.
15 **laboring serf:** The Hebrew *mas 'oved* denotes forced labor.
16 **mete-out-judgment:** Others use "will endure."
18 **I wait-in-hope . . .** : Either a deathbed cry or possibly the cry of a falling
   rider (see the preceding line) (Ehrlich).
19 **goad:** Lit. "attack"; a play on "Gad" (Heb. *gad gedud yegudennu*).
24 **arms and hands:** Lit. "arms of his hands."
25 **Shaddai:** Once again connected to fertility (note the content of the following lines). **give-you-blessing:** Just as Yaakov had blessed Yosef's sons, so
   Yosef is the only one of the twelve brothers to whom Yaakov applies the
   term.

26   May the blessings of your father transcend
        the blessings of mountains eternal,
        the bounds of hills without age.
        May they fall upon the head of Yosef,
        on the crown of the one-set-apart among his brothers.

27   Binyamin,
        a wolf that tears-to-pieces!
        In the morning he devours prey,
        and then, in the evening, divides up the spoil.

28 All these are the tribes of Israel, twelve,
    and this is what their father spoke to them;
    he blessed them,
    according to what belonged to each as blessing, he blessed
        them.
29 And he charged them, saying to them:
    I am now about to be gathered to my kinspeople;
    bury me by my fathers,
    in the cave that is in the field of Efron the Hittite,
30 at the cave that is in the field of Makhpela, that faces
        Mamre, in the land of Canaan.
    —Avraham had acquired that field from Efron the Hittite,
        as a burial holding.
31 There they buried Avraham and Sara his wife,
    there they buried Yitzhak and Rivka his wife,
    there I buried Lea—
32 an acquisition, the field and the cave that is in it, from the
        Sons of Het.

33 When Yaakov had finished charging his sons,
    he gathered up his feet onto the bed and breathed-his-last,
    and was gathered to his kinspeople.

50:1 Yosef flung himself on his father's face,
      he wept over him and kissed him.
   2 Then Yosef charged his servants, the physicians, to embalm
          his father,
      and the physicians embalmed Yisrael.

3 A full forty days were required for him,
  for thus are fulfilled the days of embalming.
  And the Egyptians wept for him for seventy days.
4 Now when the days of weeping for him had passed,
  Yosef spoke to Pharaoh's household, saying:
  Pray, if I have found favor in your eyes,
  pray speak in the ears of Pharaoh, saying:
5 My father had me swear, saying:
  Here, I am dying—
  in my burial-site which I dug for myself in the land of
    Canaan,
  there you are to bury me!
  So now,
  pray let me go up, bury my father, and return.
6 Pharaoh said:
  Go up and bury your father, as he had you swear.
7 So Yosef went up to bury his father;
  and with him went up all of Pharaoh's servants,
  the elders of his household and all the elders of the land of
    Egypt,

Yaakov's Burial (50:1–14): The funeral of Yaakov seems to presage the Exodus from Egypt—here with Pharaoh's permission and a large royal escort (including "chariots and horsemen," who in several generations will pursue Yaakov's descendants into the sea).

Interestingly, the *Iliad* also ends with an elaborate burial scene. The contrast is instructive: the Homeric epic celebrates the deeds and mourns the lost youth of a hero (Hector); Genesis reflects Yosef's standing at court and the desire to bury Yaakov in the land of Canaan, in the family plot. Note too that Genesis has two more scenes, tending to lessen the impact of this impressive funeral sequence.

26 **mountains:** Reading *hararei* for the traditional Hebrew *horei*, "parents" on the basis of Hab. 3:6.
28 **tribes:** Heb. *shevatim*, "staffs," which symbolized the tribes.
31 **Lea:** Not called "my wife." Again the old feelings remain vivid.
33 **breathed-his-last:** Omitted are the "old and abundant in days" that were applied to his father and grandfather.

8 all of Yosef's household,
  his brothers and his father's household.
  Only their little-ones, their sheep, and their oxen did they
     leave behind in the region of Goshen.
9 And along with him went up chariots as well, and horsemen
     as well—
  the company was an exceedingly heavy one.
10 They came as far as Goren Ha-Atad/Bramble
     Threshing-Floor, which is across the Jordan,
   and there they took up lament, an exceedingly great and
     heavy lament,
   and he held mourning for his father, for seven days.
11 Now when the settled-folk of the land, the Canaanites, saw
     the mourning at Bramble Threshing-Floor,
   they said:
   This is such a heavy mourning/*evel* for Egypt!
   Therefore its name was called: Meadow/*avel* of Egypt,
   which is across the Jordan.
12 So his sons did thus for him, as he had charged them:
13 his sons carried him back to the land of Canaan
   and buried him in the cave in the field of Makhpela.
   —Avraham had acquired that field as a burial holding from
     Efron the Hittite, (the field) facing Mamre.
14 Then Yosef returned to Egypt,
   he and his brothers and all who had gone up with him to
     bury his father,
   after he had buried his father.

15 When Yosef's brothers saw that their father was dead, they
     said:
   What if Yosef holds a grudge against us
   and repays, yes, repays us for all the ill that we caused him!
16 So they charged Yosef, saying:
   Your father left-this-charge before his death, saying:
17 Say thus to Yosef:
   Ah, pray forgive your brothers' offense and their sin, that
     they caused you ill!
   Now, pray forgive the offense of the servants of your
     father's God!
   Yosef wept as they spoke to him.

18 And his brothers themselves came, they flung themselves
   down before him and said:
   Here we are, servants to you!
19 But Yosef said to them:
   Do not be afraid! For am I in place of God?
20 Now you, you planned ill against me,
   (but) God planned-it-over for good,
   in order to do (as is) this very day—
   to keep many people alive.
21 So now, do not be afraid!
   I myself will sustain you and your little-ones!
   And he comforted them and spoke to their hearts.

22 So Yosef stayed in Egypt, he and his father's household.
   Yosef lived a hundred and ten years;

The End of the Matter (50:15–26): Drawing out the tension inherent in
the Patriarchs' family relationships to the very end, the text repeats an
earlier situation in Yaakov's life—his brother's feelings of "grudge" and
threats to kill him—in the guise of his sons' fears toward Yosef. Here,
however, there can be no question of personal vengeance, since Yosef
sees the brothers' betrayal of him as but part of a larger purpose. In his
words of verse 20, "God planned-it-over for good . . . to keep many
people alive," the text resolves two of the great hanging issues that have
persisted throughout Genesis: sibling hatred and the threat to genera-
tional continuity.

Left hanging, of course, is the issue of the promised land, since the
narrative concludes "in Egypt," but these final chapters lead to the
assurance that God will "take account" (vv.24–25) of the Sons of Israel,
as they are soon to be termed.

50:9 **heavy:** Three times through verse 11. The root *kbd* connotes "honor,"
   "importance," "weight," and is central here perhaps to emphasize the
   respect shown to Yaakov.
13 **the cave in the field of Makhpela:** Despite God's continual promise of the
   land throughout the book, this is practically all that the Patriarchs possess
   at the end of Genesis.
16 **left-this-charge:** Or "commanded."
22 **a hundred and ten years:** The ideal Egyptian life span.

23 Yosef saw from Efrayim sons of the third generation,
and also the sons of Makhir son of Menashe were born on
    Yosef's knees.
24 Yosef said to his brothers:
I am dying,
but God will take account, yes, account of you,
he will bring you up from this land
to the land about which he swore
to Avraham, to Yitzhak, and to Yaakov.
25 Yosef had the Sons of Israel swear, saying:
When God takes account, yes, account of you,
bring my bones up from here!
26 And Yosef died, a hundred and ten years old.
They embalmed him and they put him in a coffin
in Egypt.

נשלם ספר בראשית
ברוך המחיה והממותת

23 **born on Yosef's knees:** Considered his own; see 30:3.
24 **brothers:** Presumably meant in the sense of "family."
25 **Sons of Israel:** They are no longer merely the sons of one man but are now
on their way to becoming a people.

SUGGESTIONS
FOR FURTHER READING

This list cites selected works in English only. It is intended to supplement *In the Beginning* with reference to the text of Genesis, ancient Near Eastern background, and a literary approach to the Bible. Included also is material referred to in the Commentary and Notes under authors' names in parentheses.

Ackerman, James S. "Joseph, Judah and Jacob." In Kenneth R. R. Gros Louis and James S. Ackerman, eds., *More Literary Interpretations of Biblical Narratives* (Nashville, 1982).

Alter, Robert. *The Art of Biblical Narrative* (New York, 1981).

Andersen, Frances. *The Sentence in Biblical Hebrew* (The Hague, 1974).

Auerbach, Erich. *Mimesis* (New York, 1957).

Buber, Martin. *Good and Evil* (New York, 1952).

———. *On the Bible* (New York, 1968).

Cassuto, Umberto. *A Commentary on the Book of Genesis. Part One: From Adam to Noah* (Jerusalem, 1972); *Part Two: From Noah to Abraham* (Jerusalem, 1974).

Culley, Robert. *Studies in the Structure of Hebrew Narrative* (Philadelphia, 1976).

———, ed. "Oral Tradition and Old Testament Studies." *Semeia* 5 (1976).

Davidson, Robert. *Genesis 1–11 (Cambridge Bible Commentary)* (Cambridge, 1979).

———. *Genesis 12–50 (Cambridge Bible Commentary)* (Cambridge, 1979).

De Vaux, Roland. *Ancient Israel* (New York, 1965).

———. *The Early History of Israel* (Philadelphia, 1978).

Driver, S. R. *The Book of Genesis* (New York, 1926).

Fishbane, Michael, *Text and Texture* (New York, 1979).

Fokkelman, J. P. *Narrative Art in Genesis* (Assen and Amsterdam, 1975).

Fox, Everett. "The Bible Needs to Be Read Aloud." *Response* 33 (Spring 1977).

———. "The Samson Cycle in an Oral Setting." *Alcheringa: Ethnopoetics* 4, no. 1 (1978).

Frankfort, Henri. *Before Philosophy* (New York, 1951).

Gaster, Theodor H. *Myth, Legend, and Custom in the Old Testament* (New York, 1969).

Ginzberg, Louis. *The Legends of the Jews* (Philadelphia, 1933).

Glatzer, Nahum N. *Franz Rosenzweig: His Life and Thought* (New York, 1961).

Greenstein, Edward L. "Theories of Modern Bible Translation." *Prooftexts* 3 (1983).

Gros Louis, Kenneth R. R.; Ackerman, James S.; and Warshaw, Thayer S., eds. *Literary Interpretations of Biblical Narratives* (Nashville, 1974).

Gros Louis, Kenneth R. R., and Ackerman, James S. *More Literary Interpretations of Biblical Narratives* (Nashville, 1982).

Interpreter's Dictionary of the Bible (New York, 1962).

Muffs, Yochanan. "Abraham the Noble Warrior: Patriarchal Politics and Laws of War in Ancient Israel." In Geza Vermes and Jacob Neusner, eds. *Essays in Honor of Yigael Yadin, Journal of Jewish Studies* 33, nos. 1–2 (Spring-Autumn, 1982).

Plaut, W. Gunther. *The Torah: A Modern Commentary*. Volume I: *Genesis* (New York, 1974).

Polzin, Robert M. "The Ancestress of Israel in Danger." *Semeia* 3 (1975).

Redford, Donald. *A Study of the Biblical Story of Joseph* (Leiden, 1970).

Rosenberg, Joel. "The Garden Story Forward and Backward: The Non-Narrative Dimension of Gen. 2–3." *Prooftexts* 1, no. 1 (1978).

Sarna, Nahum. *Understanding Genesis* (New York, 1966).

Skinner, John. *Genesis (International Critical Commentary)* (New York, 1910).

Speiser, Ephraim E. *Genesis (The Anchor Bible)* (New York, 1964).

Spiegel, Shalom. *The Last Trial* (New York, 1979).

Tedlock, Dennis. "Toward an Oral Poetics." *New Literary History* 7, no. 3 (Spring 1977).

Vawter, Bruce. *On Genesis: A New Reading* (New York, 1977).

Non-English works also referred to in the Commentary and Notes:

Ehrlich, Arnold. *Mikra Ki-Pheshuto* (New York, 1969).

Jacob, Benno. *Das erste Buch der Tora: Genesis* (Berlin, 1934).

Redak (Rabbi David Kimhi). *Perush Redak al Ha-Torah* (Jerusalem, 1975).